Jean-Paul Sartre

Jean-Paul Sartre

Hated Conscience of His Century

VOLUME I · Protestant or Protester?

John Gerassi

The University of Chicago Press

Chicago and London

John Gerassi is professor of political science at the Graduate Center and Queens College of the City University of New York. From 1956 to 1966, he was a journalist for *Time, Newsweek, The New York Times,* and Inter-Press Service. His many books include *The Great Fear in Latin America, The Boys of Boise, Fidel Castro, The Coming of the New International,* and *The Premature Antifascist.*

The University of Chicago Press, Chicago 60637
The University of Chicago Press, Ltd., London
© 1989 by John Gerassi
All rights reserved. Published 1989
Printed in the United States of America

98 97 96 95 94 93 92 91 90 89   54321

Library of Congress Cataloging in Publication Data

Gerassi, John.
    Jean-Paul Sartre : hated conscience of his century / John Gerassi.
        p.   cm.
    Bibliography: p.
    Includes index.
    Contents: v. 1. Protestant or protester?
    1. Sartre, Jean Paul, 1905–   .   Philosophers—France—
Biography.   3. Authors, French—20th century—Biography.
I. Title.
B2430.S34G47   1989
848'.91409—dc19   88-27945
[B]   CIP

⊗ The paper used in this publication meets the minimum requirements of the American National Standard for Information Sciences—Permanence of Paper for Printed Library Materials, ANSI Z39.48-1984.

Satanée petite saloperie gavée de merde.
God-damn garbage bag full of shit.
—Louis-Ferdinand Céline

L'historie d'une vie, quelle qu'elle soit, est l'histoire d'un échec.
The history of a life, whatever it may be, is the history of a failure.
—Jean-Paul Sartre, *L'Etre et le néant*

Contents

Acknowledgments

To carry out the research on two continents for this biography was extremely costly, involving hundreds of hours of tapes, transcriptions, deciphering old hand-written manuscripts and typing them, digging for documents in France, England, and Germany, recording them, and so forth. The first grant to help me get started came from Carole and Ping Ferry. Shortly thereafter I received a small fellowship from The Institute for Policy Studies, one of whose founders and directors, Marc Raskin, had long been an admirer of Sartre's notion of freedom as social responsibility. Later, as my project took shape and I was able to put together a coherent schedule and plan for my work, I was very fortunate to receive a fellowship from The John J. Simon Guggenheim Memorial Foundation, followed by a grant by The Professional Staff Congress of the City University of New York. Finally, to finish the research and write the final draft during my sabbatical from Queens College of the City University of New York, I was awarded a fellowship by The American Council of Learned Societies. Without these grants and honors, this work could not have been successfully completed. I am deeply grateful to them all.

I also received tremendous encouragement from Simone de Beauvoir and especially Michel Contat, who spent most of his life dedicated to Sartre, the man and his work, and who often went out of his way to help me find the articles, manuscripts, and sources I needed. During the long and often frustrating years of this project, I had the unwavering support of my colleagues at Queens College of the City University of New York and at the University of Hawaii (where a draft was written), from Professors Peter Manicas and Irving Leonard Markovitz, from Alan Berger of the Boston Globe, and Colin Greer of the New World Foundation. My wife read each version of each chapter various times and offered useful concrete criticisms and suggestions, as did (in Paris) Anne-Marie Hertz, a longtime political activist who transcribed all my interviews, and (in Honolulu) Fred Hellinger, who typed a final draft. To all these people and institutions, my heartfelt thanks.

The quotation from Céline on the frontispiece is cited in Albert Paraz, *Le gala des vaches* (p. 284), reprinted in *Nouvelles Littéraires*, 17–24 April 1980, 28.

PART 1   The Setup

Like all writers, I hide myself. But I am also a public man and people
can think what they like about me, even if it is severe.

Jean-Paul Sartre, *Le Monde,* 14 May 1971

There is not the slightest doubt that I have been eager to liberate popular ethics and justice: this is my crime. A popular court would acquit
me. But how can I reasonably think that a member of society's elite
would be able to lower himself—if it can be called lowering himself—
to the level of the oppressed and exploited people and to consider *with
the eyes of the people* the crushing pedestals on which the bourgeois hierarchy sits?

Jean-Paul Sartre, from a lecture delivered in Brussels, 25 Feb. 1972

1   L'Enfant terrible

"*Alors,* Sartre, don't you have any vanity?" I asked him at lunch at the Coupole one day back in 1970.

A few days earlier in London, my editor at Jonathan Cape Publishers had told me that my last manuscript—the life and writings of Camilo Torres, a Colombian priest and oligarch who had become a guerrilla and died in his first battle—was just fine but that no one was going to read it. "Why don't you write a book that'll sell for a change?" he had asked.

We were silent for a moment, obviously thinking of appropriate subjects for my fortune. Then I mumbled something like, "Well, of course, I could do Sartre, but . . ." He cut me off before I could tell him that I didn't want to.

"Nope," he said, "that's out. He doesn't want a biography. He plans to follow up *The Words,* his autobiography. I've often thought of Sartre. I've sent him a whole bunch of would-be biographers. He's turned them all down."

That, as the French say, put *la puce à l'oreille,* the flea in my ear. I made a mental note to ask Sartre about it next time I saw him.

On that Sunday in 1970 then, as was my custom, I arrived at 2:15 at the Coupole, exactly fifteen minutes late, knowing that Jean-Paul Sartre and Simone de Beauvoir would have arrived ahead of me, at 2:10, ten minutes late. Later, after Sartre had been afflicted by a series of strokes, caused mainly by a life too filled with speed,* I would go pick him up at his apartment. But in 1970, he was still active and agile.

As usual, Sartre and "Castor," the "Beaver" as de Beauvoir was called by all her friends and some enemies, were seated in a corner, protected by a knowledgeable maitre d'hotel, in the "fancy" section of this mammoth brasserie. It was not out of snobbishness that they sat there. La Coupole, which was sold in 1987 and will soon be transformed into offices and fast food joints, was for some 60 years an amazing institution in Paris. Always packed by cordon bleu connoisseurs even though the food was only slightly better than average, it was a restaurant mostly for exhibitionists and voyeurs.

---

* Sartre almost always swallowed huge quantities of amphetamines when writing non-fiction.

To be sure, situated as it was on Montparnasse Boulevard just a wink down from where it crossed Boulevard Raspail—in other words, in the heard of supposedly artistic and cultural Paris, some would say in the center of the world—La Coupole was not a place to visit if you were a flaming rightwinger. Or ostentatiously rich, for that matter. Well, no, that's not accurate. Most people who ate on the "fancy" side did tend to be well off even in 1970, but from showbiz or pot deals or bribes, not as in the eighties from crass entrepreneurism. Indeed, few businessmen seemed at ease in the place in the old days, and customers wearing ties were invariably handled by the swift, sharp, shrewd waiters as if they were tourists. In sum, it was a restaurant frequented by painters and sculptors, writers and poets, producers and newsfolk, punks and anarchists, the successful and the starlets, the self-exiled and the self-doomed.

On the "common" (left) side of this gigantic (7,200 square feet) wood-paneled mess-hall some 300 people could be crammed at laminated tables covered with paper rectangles. On the other, "aristocratic," more roomy (right) side, 180 of the elite could avoid eavesdropping on next-table conversations by talking into their spanking-clean white table cloths. But there was a bit more protection from the curious and the rude on this side, and so that's where Sartre and Castor inevitably took refuge in their "mature" age.

Sartre had always said that he preferred to eat with women more than men. "Women don't play the one-upmanship game," he had quipped. Naturally, this had led to all sorts of macho-pig charges by all sorts of well-meaning and not-so-well-meaning feminists. Sartre claimed that he meant it as a compliment to women. "Men," he told me once, "always want to talk ideas with me at lunch or dinner. Even in bars or nightclubs. What a bore. It's like they always want to prove something. Gives me indigestion. I much prefer the company of women. They don't feel they have to prove anything. They say what they want to, not what they think they ought to. They say what they feel. It's honest. Ideas are what you have when you think, and thinking is a solitary endeavor. Thinking is done at home, at a desk, alone."

That's how I discovered that he really did enjoy eating lunch or dinner with me. Either I had no ideas or I felt I couldn't talk about them with a stuffed mouth. In any case, I knew from Castor that she and Sartre liked to listen to my stories—gossip about the nonexistent left in America, the affairs of Ronnie (R. D.) Laing in England, the uniforms of Carlos Fuentes' maids in Mexico, the incredible sexisms of Pablo Neruda in Chile. And since I always assumed that these "important" people caroused with me mainly because they knew that I was a close friend of both Sartre and Castor, I felt it was only fair if I dutifully reported back to them those juicy tales.

Sartre, Castor and I did sometimes talk ideas. However, they tended to dissect immediate situations. In other words, we talked politics. I knew that they trusted me politically, and I was careful to live up to that trust. The International War Crimes Tribunal is an example. Bertrand Russell had repeatedly written to Sartre to ask him to join it, and Sartre had meticulously forgotten to answer. So Russell asked me in the fall of 1966—I was then head of the Russell Peace Foundation in New York—to go convince Sartre in person. I did. For two hours, I listed every "objective" reason I could remember or invent.

"Okay," said Sartre when I finished. "You've done your duty. Now as a friend, tell me, why should I join this ersatz tribunal?"

"This tribunal will not politicize anyone," I answered, contradicting my just-terminated harangue. "Chances are no U.S. newspaper will give it decent coverage (and none did). It will not convince anyone who is not already certain that the U.S. intervention in Vietnam is both illegal and barbaric. But it will help the Vietnamese. It's good for their morale. And they are the victims." Then I added, "And that's why I am going to Hanoi the day after tomorrow."

Sartre smiled. "That's good enough for me," he said, and joined the Tribunal, becoming its president. And he sponsored my Paris press conference when I returned from North Vietnam in February 1967.

How I gained Sartre's confidence is part of his story, or ours, in the pages which follow, but is certainly rooted in his relationship to my parents, my father Fernando and my mother Stépha, who became Gomez and Sarah in Sartre's trilogy *The Roads to Freedom*. Still, while that relationship opened the door to our own, I think that Sartre chose me to write his biography because in his eyes, without sounding too arrogant, I was first of all a doer, a political activist, a philosophy student turned journalist and then "militant" who thought about theory at his desk, alone, and did his writing as a consequence of praxis, as a consequence of analyzing the forces in battle in a world basically dominated by the rich and the rogues, by greed and guile.

In other words, Sartre thought that my spontaneity in politics meant that, like a woman, first I reacted, then I acted, and only then did I try to justify. To most readers trained by bourgeois rationalizers to "think before you act," what I've just said will appear to disparage both me and women. But it would not appear so to Sartre, who—at least toward the end of his life—viewed logic as a tool of the ruling class. "It is always those who have power who say 'calm down, let's talk rationally, let's be sensible,'" he once explained to a couple of my students. "It is always those who have power who insist that being emotional is being weak. In the home, the powerful are the male. That's why the best way for a housewife to argue against her calm, rational 'provider' is to throw the plate of rice in his face." Then, because the two young women I had brought around to his apartment were Americans, he added, "In your country, all your teachers tell you to think carefully and try to be objective, *n'est-ce-pas*? They refuse to admit the possibility that if you are white and rich you will never think—hear me—think, reason, not just feel, but think like a person who is poor and black. They want you to keep looking at a situation from *all sides,* as they say. That's so you say, 'On the one hand, this; on the other, that.' That's so you *do* nothing." Then, after a pause to fortify this point, he concluded: "If you accept to play the game by the rules set up by those who own or control the board, you will always lose."

Of course, Sartre did not always condemn the world's "rationality." On the contrary, he was a confirmed rationalist himself until his World War II captivity, and relied on his precisely honed logical skills all his creative life. But he did come to realize, gradually and tentatively at first, more affirmatively and acutely after 1950, that every state and established group guilty of mass murder uses reason and logic to define its acts as defensive while condemning, with equal logic, those who oppose them as offensive. "With calm, careful reason," he told my students, "the violence of the 'haves' always ends up being 'in the defense of peace,' while the establishment, and especially the established media, will always condemn the emotional self-defense counter-violence of the 'have-nots' as terroristic." Thus did Sartre feel attached to the poor and exploited all over the world who use even the most outlandish and outrageous means to break out of their predicament.

And so did I. Of course, however violently I may have reacted to the hypocrisy of my academic and journalist colleagues, I was still a bourgeois intellectual, and so was Sartre. After all, who else would read us? So our lives were a bundle of contradictions. And that too, was a reason Sartre chose me to write his biography. For all our disagreements, which will become clear in the pages which follow, Sartre liked in me what he thought I liked in him. I was *l'enfant terrible* who would keep alive what he liked most about himself: that no matter how many mistakes he may have made, he had remained all through his mature life if not *l'enfant*, certainly the young *adulte terrible*, who never once betrayed the underdog, the banished, the outcast, the doomed—whom bourgeois society, at best, inevitably ignored. For all his sharp analytical tools, Sartre remained convinced, as I was, that all intellectuals have axes to grind. "No matter how clear are their ideas," he told me once, "you must distrust their motives and judge them, like anyone else, by what they do."

That's why Sartre almost never read reviews or criticisms of his work and rarely spent more than a few minutes glancing over the pronouncements by the so-called theorists of his time, whether they were on the right (Levi-Strauss by Sartre's standards) or on the left (Althusser, Poulantsas)—unless, of course, they had put their bodies on the line, so to speak, like Frantz Fanon or Che Guevara or Amilcar Cabral. Thus, for example, he had never read a word by Herbert Marcuse.

Marcuse once asked me to set up a luncheon with Sartre. Sartre dreaded it. Contrary to popular myth, the two had never met. While Marcuse had carefully read all of Sartre's works and had written about them, Sartre knew about Marcuse only what he had read in daily papers—and what I had told him, which was mostly gossip—political to be sure, but gossip nonetheless. Among other things, I had told him the following story.

In 1967–68, I had been hired by San Francisco State College (now university) as a visiting lecturer in International Relations. The school had the reputation at the time of being extremely liberal, mainly because its president, John Summerskill, marched in anti–Vietnam War demonstrations in the Bay Area. But Summerskill also insisted that San Francisco State be kept "open," that is, all recruiters were allowed free access to students. I decided to honor this "openness" by inviting recruiters from such liberation movements as the Vietnamese FLN, Mozambique's FRELIMO and Angola's MPLA to offset the death-dealers of Dow Chemical (makers of the napalm then being dropped on Vietnamese civilians) or the CIA. No sooner had I issued my invitations than San Francisco State's true liberalism was exposed, and *openness* was redefined to apply only to the establishment.

On 6 December 1967, all the outrages, racisms, and hypocrisies came to a head and San Francisco State was "seized" by a coalition of radical and black separatist students. It was held as "America's first liberated university" until Summerskill gave in to Governor Ronald Reagan's pressure ("Who ever heard of the inmates running their institution?") and summoned the police. Eleven student leaders and I were arrested. In a brilliant example of ageism, I was charged with instigating the whole thing ("inciting civil insurrection," which of course was absurd; the charge was soon dropped to a misdemeanor) and barred from setting foot on the campus, pending my trial. My classes were to be taken over by a substitute.

Not one of my seventy-eight students went to hear the scab. Instead, they swarmed over to the university chapel (officially off campus) where I was continuing my course as a guest of the chaplain, who was on our side. It so happened that on that day Marcuse was to be my guest lecturer. I had been his guest at the University of California at San Diego (La Jolla), and this was to be a return duel.

Marcuse did not approve of our "seizure." To him, universities were sanctuaries for student activists, and radical teachers were not to jeopardize their forums. So he demanded a formal invitation from the chaplain—in writing. I let my students know this, expecting that they would react by carefully reading his appropriate texts so as not to be intimidated by him. I also called the local public TV station (Channel 9) which, sure enough, sent a team to cover the fireworks.

They were glorious. True, the odds weren't very fair: eight of my very best students, today all successful teachers and writers, against poor old Herbert (I stayed out of it). But he loved it. In his thick, Germanic, voluptuous English, his snow-white hair glistening under the bright TV lights, Marcuse parried thrust after thrust and rubbed his hands harder and harder in delight. I honestly thought that he lost. But as the class ended, he turned to me and gloated: "You see, I haff made my point. I haff von my case. Ziss iss der proof. Now zat you are fired and maybe going to jail, you haff lost your magnificent"—and he pointed grandiosely to my students, who had risen to applaud him—"forum."

And so Sartre agreed to have lunch with Marcuse. "But you must come too and save me if things get rough," said Sartre.

"Rough?" I asked.

"I have never read a word Marcuse has written," he explained. "I know you like him. I know he has tried to link Marx and Freud. And I know he supports activist students. But I can't possibly read his books by next week. Besides I don't want to stop my research on Flaubert. So you join us. And if Marcuse gets too philosophical, if he uses the word *reification* just once, interrupt and say something provocative and political. *D'accord?*"

"*D'accord*," I agreed.

The lunch turned out to be quite a joy. It was at the Coupole, of course, and on a Thursday, which meant that the *plat-du-jour* was *cassoulet*, a gory *toulousain* dish made with sausages, pork loin, lard and lots of beans; in other words, a terribly unhealthy stew served in an earthen pot, which the three of us scraped absolutely clean.

As for the conversation, no problem. Marcuse began the serious part by saying that Sartre's *Critique of Dialectical Reason* was caught in an idealistic bind. I was about to interrupt with some assininity, but Sartre beat me to it. He asked a question about Freud's own idealism, which Marcuse fielded handily. Then Sartre asked another. Marcuse had no problem with that one either. Sartre was ready with a third question. And so it went—for two hours. When I helped Marcuse to a cab outside the Coupole, he shook both of my hands with genuine gratitude and said: "I had no idea he knew my work so well." Never had I seen Marcuse so contented.

When I repeated this to Sartre, he exploded in that marvelously childish but baritone laughter of his, that gutteral he he he (pronounced hay hay not hee hee), and then proclaimed as proudly as a child who had just successfully ridden a two-wheeler for the first time, "And I still haven't read a word he wrote."

"But where or how did you learn so much about his theories?" I pressed.

"Ah, Gerassi," he scolded me teasingly, "you didn't notice that all I did was ask questions. Each time he answered, I picked out an apparent flaw in his answer to ask another question. But since the flaw was only apparent, he could answer my question to his great satisfaction. Thus his vanity soared happily."

Ah, yes, vanity. That's how this story started—with Sartre's vanity. I had asked him, there at lunch at the Coupole that Sunday in 1970, if he had any vanity.

"Of course, as much as any other man," he answered, "why?"

"Because, I hear, you keep refusing writers who want to do your biography, scores of writers, I'm told."

"You mean all those little jerks from *Paris Review*?" He had actually said *petits cons,* but judging by the tone of his voice, Sartre really did mean only jerks.

"How can I let a reactionary write my biography?" he went on. "Yes, I know, all those nice established writers on the *Review* pretend to be radicals. But they don't want to get rid of our system, they just want to correct a few malfunctions. They want to preserve—and prosper. I want to destroy. Do you think a so-called democrat can understand an anarchist?"

"But what about the reverse?" I asked. "How can you, an anarchist, understand a reactionary, Flaubert, who hoped that every *communard* would be put against the wall, who feared and hated the poor?"

"No one is born an anarchist: you make yourself one. We're born into bourgeois society, where rules exist to maintain the powerful in their power. The only way to change it is to act against it. But in acting against it, you understand it. A bourgeois who likes bourgeois values, even if only more or less, can never understand the anarchist. But the anarchist has evolved out of bourgeois morality. He understands his past and lives his present. Besides," and Sartre stopped, took a sip of wine, smiled childishly ear-to-ear, and added, "I'm full of contradictions, aren't I? I am a bourgeois writer in the morning and a rebellious maoist of sorts in the afternoon. And in the evening, what, an aristocrat?" Sartre meant that in the morning he wrote his biography of Flaubert. After lunch, he worked mostly with his young militant friends on the anarcho-maoist newspaper *La Cause du Peuple* (*The People's Cause*). In the evening, often, he simply listened to Berg or Webern in Castor's lush, plush apartment.

"Tell me, Gerassi," which is what Sartre always called me when he liked in advance what he expected would be my reaction, "if you were to write my biography, how would you do it? I mean, what would be your guiding principle?"

There it was. Now I had to say something smart. I kept searching for the bon mot. Hours must have passed (probably a whole minute). But Sartre was the last man in the world I should try to impress or con. For all the lies I knew he had said and written in his life, Sartre was the most honest man I had ever met. The last thing anyone should ever want to do is to get into a game of one-upmanship with him or indulge in a little inauthenticity (a heavy word; we'll come back to it). But there I was—not quite panicking, but close.

Castor grinned. Myth has it that it was René Maheu, her first lover, who became head of UNESCO, who dubbed her Castor, "Beaver," because she worked like one. Not true. He called her "beaver" in English because it sounded close to "beauvoir" in French. Those were the days when, as students, they were all enamored with things American—jazz,

Chaplin, Dos Passos, Nick Carter, Buffalo Bill, "Some of These Days" (the song of Sartre's first published novel, *Nausea*). Maheu simply Americanized Beauvoir's name. Then it got translated back into French because, it is true, Castor did work like a beaver.

Now, across from me at our table at the Coupole, she was smiling expectantly, but with sympathy. Sartre, too, was looking at me intently. Or so I thought. After all these years, I still was not sure which eye could see me and which could not. When people are cross-eyed, you can believe that both their eyes are focusing on you with extra verve. But when they are walleyed . . . for a second I recalled Sartre's classmate at La Rochelle, that cute little twelve-year-old girl he often talked about, the one who quipped that Sartre had "one eye that said 'shit' to the other."

That made me recover. I looked down at my *tarte au citron,* then into his mysterious yet expectant stare, and said: "I guess I would try to explain why it took you forty-five years to reach a position that we reached in five."

"*Pas mal,* good," he responded, expecting more.

He was right. There was more. I said it: "And I would try to explain how someone who has never rebelled against his class—because, Sartre, no matter how much you hate the bourgeoisie, you are still a bourgeois through and through—could become a revolutionary."

"*D'accord*!" he shouted, almost jumping up.

"What do you mean, '*d'accord*?' You agree to what?" I asked, half-elated, half-terrified of the answer I knew was coming.

"That you write my biography," he said, as if that was totally self-evident.

"You have to sign an agreement, something legal you know, an exclusive agreement, if you want me to do it . . ." I started.

"Well, let's do it!" he said, clearing the place in front of him. When Sartre decided something, he got to work; that's what he meant when he promulgated that now oft-repeated cliché, "Inspiration comes with pulling your chair to the table." He grabbed the Coupole menu and turned it over, but the wine list was on the back. He flicked his fingers and told the waiter, who appeared instantly, that he wanted some paper. "*Voilà, maître,*" he waiter said two seconds later, handing him a whole pile of sheets.

As confused as I was at the moment, I couldn't help laughing, remembering that General de Gaulle had once addressed a letter to Sartre with the phrase "*Cher Maître*," and that Sartre had replied, "Only café waiters call me *maître*."

Sartre proceeded to write out an exclusive agreement for me to write his biography. And he stuck to it. When Michel Contat, who had worked so hard and so well on his bibliography and other Sartreana, wanted to do a lengthy interview with him at seventy—an interview which Sartre also needed to do because he was broke, and he knew such an interview would be reprinted all over the world—he told Contat to get my permission (which I readily granted). Sartre often went broke, incidentally, because he gave away fortunes to struggling writers, full-time activists, and unpopular causes.

So there it was. Done. I handed that agreement to my agent, he parlayed it into contracts with publishers, and I was hooked—Sartre's official biographer. My God!

That was fifteen years ago.

What a calamity. For fifteen years, people have asked me, "Where the hell is the Sartre?" Friends have nudged me with care, sometimes even sharing my anxieties. Enemies have done so with ridicule, irony, and scorn. Every year my French editor, Robert Gallimard, has written me a polite letter asking me to give him an idea when to expect the manuscript, more or less.

What could I say? A month after I started seriously interviewing Sartre for the supposed definitive biography, we were having lunch at the Coupole when an acquaintance of Sartre's approached our table. "*Alors,*" he asked good-naturedly, "when can we expect the follow-up to *The Words?*" (which had stopped at age twelve).

Sartre introduced me: "This is Tito Gerassi. He's writing it."

The kiss of death! How could I possibly go on? How could I explain that the man I most admired, the philosopher who had most influenced my views, the political writer I had most studied expected me to write the continuation of his *auto*biography? Maybe I could simply write a book called *My Nongodfather Sartre,* that is, my personal relationship to him. But that wasn't the deal. Besides, my own relationship, not the one I had inherited from my parents, had only begun in 1954, when I was writing my master's dissertation in philosophy at Columbia University on the Sartre-Camus dispute.

I still had no passport in 1954, but I was no longer on deportation. My parents and I had come to the United States in 1940 as political refugees from Franco's fascism and Hitler's nazism, but that was unacceptable to U.S. authorities. So my father, who like Gomez had been a general in the Spanish Civil War and was hence deemed a "premature antifascist" by Washington, used his diplomatic passport to get us past Ellis Island. That document said we were diplomats from the Dominican Republic. It had been given to my father by one of his prewar poker-playing chums, a very high-class Trujillo hitman and diplomatic trouble-shooter (and son-in-law) by the name of Porfirio Rubirosa.

In fact, Porfirio had given my father the whole kit and caboodle, that is, the seal, the stamp, and so forth, with the understanding that he could use it to save whom he wanted. And my father did just that: he gave some eight thousand Spanish Republican refugees Dominican passports so they could escape the approaching gestapo. Unfortunately, and to my father's great chagrin, many of them went to Santo Domingo, where they soon discovered that Rafael Trujillo was as bad a butcher as Franco or Hitler; they plotted against him, and most were killed.

But Fernando and Stépha decided to come to the United States. Of course we were not diplomats, and my father *did* want to tell the truth once we were established. He hoped to stay in America on political refugee status, until after the war.

"Don't you dare tell the truth," his new boss, Arthur Goldberg, told him. "It'll only create unnecessary problems. Donovan will straighten everything out—later."

The Donovan in question was General Bill Donovan, the chief of a new paramilitary counterespionage outfit just created by President Roosevelt called the OSS, the Office of Strategic Services. Arthur Goldberg, the CIO's head lawyer and later Supreme Court judge, was Fernando's immediate superior in the OSS.

So my father said nothing—and went off to war. Among other things, he deciphered Franco's code and then was submarined into Spain to set up an underground which would blow up roads and bridges if Franco allowed Hitler's armies to cross Spain when the allies invaded North Africa. Fernando did the job well and got a citation from Big Bill Donovan for "making the African landing possible" (even though Franco did not let Hitler's troops through). Then he got arrested.

In 1945, just after his job at the OSS ended, just after Sartre had come visiting as a French newsman, my father, mother, and I were arrested for illegal entry into the United States and placed on deportation. A twenty-year-long legal battle to stop Fernando's execution (which is what he faced if deported to Spain) ensued. Goldberg refused to help. Donovan said yes, yes, called the CIA, which had taken over OSS files and resources, and then said no, no. And every time a hearing was scheduled, somebody or some bureau got it canceled on the grounds of national security.

It was only in 1964 that we found out what was really going on. Alexander Calder, the mobile maker and sculptor, who was a family friend, told Presidential Assistant Abe Fortas to do something, and he did. He got our files out of the CIA and showed them to Bobby Kennedy.

When the attorney general discovered that my family had been harassed for twenty years by the CIA disguised as Immigration officials in order to try to force my father to work for the agency, or at least to cooperate with it (which Fernando naturally refused), he made my parents legal residents almost on the spot. Then he sent them a letter apologizing "in the name of America."

In the eyes of the CIA, I guess, my father could have been considered a big enough fish to harass. Born in Constantinople in 1899 to a rich Sephardic family which lost all its fortune when Turkey lost the 1914–18 war, Fernando had fled the draft because he did not want to fight a Russian revolutionary army in 1917. He settled in Berlin, where he studied metaphysics with Cassirer, then in Freiburg, where his teacher was Husserl and his classmate Heidegger. They became *privatdozenten* at the same time, went skiing together during their vacations, and presumably would have become phenomenological eggheads together were it not for the fact that Fernando heard Heinrich Wölfflin give one of his brilliant art lectures. So off he went to Munich to study art, came to France to copy Velasquez, went on to his "native" Spain for the first time in 1924 to do the same, became well known enough to be integrated into the Spanish neo-Cubist school and eventually exhibited with his friend Pablo Picasso at the Salon des Sur-Indépendants.

It was on a visit to Paris in the summer of 1925 that he met anew a Ukrainian feminist he had briefly befriended in Berlin in 1923. At that time, a twenty-year-old runaway from a Catholic convent in her native Lvov, Stépha Awdykowicz was living with a would-be Austrian composer by the name of Alban Berg. In 1925, Berg was no longer would-be, and Stépha was either studying literature at the Sorbonne or, according to Simone de Beauvoir's memoirs, trying to persuade her to pick up Hungarian students at the National Library.

Stépha introduced Fernando to Castor. Castor introduced Fernando to Sartre. A four-way lifelong friendship ensued. Castor even brought into their circle her younger sister, Poupette; Fernando became her first art teacher—and her first lover.

Only Sartre seemed to object. Poupette was "deflowered standing up in a closet," Sartre complained to me in 1971.

"Nonsense," Fernando replied when I interviewed him a year later, "there were no closets in French apartments at that time, only armoires. Sartre was just an old-fashioned moralist. He still is!"

The real source of irritation between them had nothing to do with sex. By 1929, Sartre was a French nationalist, almost a French chauvinist. Fernando was an internationalist, politically conscious and politically wise. Although Sartre, and his friends Nizan, Maheu and Guille, hated the pseudoaristrocratic sons who made up the vast majority of the student body of l'Ecole Normale Supérieure, where he had prepared his *agrégation* (the French educational system's toughest competitive exam, roughly equivalent to a U.S. doctorate) he was still the son of a bourgeois, with very bourgeois tastes.

It wasn't that Sartre respected authority or achievement per se. On the contrary, he often argued against Brunschvicg, the established school philosopher, and often denounced the actions of the government, which was run by bourgeois for bourgeois. But Sartre didn't seem to think that either were really very important. After all, *he* would think for himself and *they* would have no real bearing on his life.

Fernando, on the other hand, was a genuine Spanish anarchist, by temperament at least. He scoffed at authority, both personally and politically, and constantly warned that all men suffer the consequences of its arbitrariness. During the Spanish Civil War, he could be brutal with anyone not following the letter of his orders. At the same time, just before the battle of Guadalajara, where he was chief of operations under General Lukacs (who was killed just before it started), he placed under tent-arrest all the political commissars who were not armed and ready to fight, thus violating strict Communist Party orders. He escaped execution only because the battle was a Loyalist victory and because Malraux pled his case directly to Comintern boss Victorio "Luis" Codovilla.

Fernando was intolerant, loud and proud, sure of himself and of his judgments, very angry and very loyal, flamboyant and charismatic. Sartre, in those early days, was cool and collected, equally sure and proud, but careful and calculating. He was not, as I discovered later, very loyal, except to Castor and those who never contradicted him. In other words, Sartre was a French intellectual, that is, a rationalist.

Still, they managed to stay friends. As the prewar years went by, Sartre got deeper and deeper into his variation of phenomenology, which was profoundly apolitical. Fernando painted and agitated. Surviving as an occasional door-to-door salesman of electrical goods or on Stépha's facial massages, he joined his peers in the Artist and Writers Congress, befriended Ilya Ehrenburg, Malraux, Eluard, Alberti, and Neruda, participated in the 1931 revolution which overthrew Spain's King Alfonso, and became relatively well known throughout Europe as a promising member of the Spanish school of neo-Cubists.

During the Spanish Civil War, Fernando became a close friend both of Randolfo Pacciardi, the anti-Communist Socialist head of the Garibaldi Brigade, and of Luigi Longo ("Gallo"), a die-hard member of the Italian Communist party's Central Committee, both of Russian tank commander (and later General) Zhukov, and of such fiery anarchist leaders as Buenaventura Durruti and Frederica Montseny. No wonder the CIA would not let go and harassed him for two decades.

As for me, however, as soon as I turned twenty-one, they separated me from my parents and handed me an expulsion order. So I married (temporarily) a friend of mine and wrote out my particulars on a piece of paper which, duly notarized, was perfectly valid in lieu of a passport as long as visas were stamped on it. I then got both a U.S. reentry and a French entry visa, and headed for Paris—where my life had begun on July 12, 1931.

That July 12 had been a Sunday. Stépha had been in Paris since early spring because Fernando didn't want her to get hurt during the revolution in Spain. Actually, he had dispatched her to Paris to get an abortion, her sixth, but since this time he wasn't around to check up, she lied to him and told him the doctors had said it was too late. So, one might say that I was, or am, an aborted abortion.

In any case, the Spanish revolution had been a huge success, and Fernando, flush with victory, had somewhat adapted to the idea of having a child. He was still convinced that the viciousness of the Versailles Treaty conditions imposed on the German people, who would have to bear the brunt of reparations to Allied capitalists (who had made fortunes during World War I), would lead necessarily to World War II. But he did try to accept my coming in spite of that.

So there he was, sitting on the terrace of La Closerie des Lilas, awaiting my birth with all his friends. La Closerie is at the angle of Montparnasse, Boulevard St. Michel, and the rue Notre Dame des Champs. A block away, across the rue d'Assas at the Clinique Tarnier, Stépha was in labor. Every half hour or so, Fernando would go up to take a look—and return to the Closerie a bit dejected, mumbling "nothing yet." André Breton or Marc Chagall or Joan Miró would say: "Cheer up, have another drink, it can't be long now."

By the time Sartre arrived from Le Havre, where he was to become a regular lycée philosophy teacher, it was early evening, and everyone waiting for my birth seemed drunk—or at least too tipsy to go see how Stépha was doing. She, not one bit superstitious of course, was pushing like hell so I would not be born on a thirteenth. So, as the only sober one in the bunch, Sartre decided he would go up and take a peek.

Lo and behold—I was born! And that's how Sartre became my godfather—or whatever is the atheist equivalent. Since he had been the first nonhospital person to see me alive, Stépha decided to call me Jean-Paul. But Fernando didn't like *un nom à courant d'air* (a name with a draft in the middle), so it became Jean. John in English. In Spanish, Juan, which gets diminished into Juanito—ergo: Tito.

Castor has described the whole incident in *The Prime of Life* much more cooly: "In June, Stépha and Fernando descended on Paris, highly elated because, after a long period of agitation, upheaval and repression, the Republic had finally been established in Spain. Stépha was heavily pregnant and one fine July morning she entered the Tarnier Maternity Hospital in the rue d'Assas. Fernando summoned all his friends to keep him company outside the Closerie des Lilas. Every hour or so he would rush off to the clinic and come back looking despondent. 'Still nothing,' he would mutter. After much reassurance and encouragement he would brighten up. Early that evening Stépha had a boy. Artists, journalists, and writers of every nationality celebrated the happy event far into the night."[1]

Not a bad way for little Tito to start out in this world, eh?

"*Alors, ça c'est le petit Tito?*" (So this is the small Tito), quipped Sartre when I arrived at the Falstaff in November 1954. He had seen me in 1945 and again in 1946 when he had stayed with us for a while in New York, and he had read a couple of my short stories. But then I was still a child. Now I was twenty-three and preparing a master's in philosophy. Surely he would consider me an adult, I thought.

Le Falstaff was a café just off the Boulevard Montparnasse on a street seemingly guarded, even in the mornings, by the oldest prostitutes in

Paris. Rather decrepit today, in those days it featured a bar and some wooden tables and fake stained-glass windows downstairs, and no bar, no stained glass, but plenty of tables upstairs. There, surrounding two or three of them, were a few Sartrean hangers-on and most of "the family": Jacques-Laurent Bost, Claude Lanzmann, Jean Pouillon, and so on—people I would interview later for this biography. Present also was the editorial staff of *L'Observateur,* a left-wing weekly which eventually became *Le Nouvel Observateur*—and is not at all left-wing today. All these folks were having a planning session with Sartre and Castor. Who would answer Mauriac's attack in *Le Figaro*? Who would reply to Guy Mollet's diatribe on Radio Luxembourg? Who would rebuff Aron's ludicrous lecture at the Sorbonne?

Once business was over, Sartre and Castor brought Jacqueline, the friend I had married and who had come with me, into the conversation. Sartre asked her if she too was studying philosophy.

"No, literature," she replied. "Tito tried to make me read some passages from your philosophical works, but I couldn't understand them."

Sartre seemed crushed. How could anyone not understand what he was trying to say, he must have wondered, for during the next hour he tried to explain Sartrean existentialism, calmly, slowly, simply, yet with passion and zeal. Not one of us moved. Even Castor, who must have heard Sartre expound his views a hundred times, remained glued to his lips. It was like witnessing the unfolding of a love affair: Sartre, that little walleyed man became a dashingly handsome cavalier, wooing a twenty-year-old, French-born American coed with such caring words about freedom and responsibility, choice and values, that she totally opened up to him, received him, gave herself to him and his philosophy for life.

But not me. Oh no, I would be tough and hold out. Later, when only Castor, Sartre and I remained to talk about old times, my parents, and the U.S. invasion of Guatemala, Sartre told me that his task was now to try to unite Marxism and existentialism.

"Impossible," I said, as only a brash twenty-three-year-old philosophy student might say.

"Why?" Sartre asked gently.

"You cannot reconcile your notion of the project with Marxian historicity," I pouted pompously.

"Ah yes," he said, nodding, "that is indeed the tough part. I'm working on it."

Years later Castor told me that Sartre had referred to me that evening as a prodigal child. "This little Tito," he had said, using an international cliché, "will slice right through the fat to get to the meat." Unfortunately, Castor told me this just as I was about to start the research on Sartre's biography. She meant well, of course; she just wanted to build up my self-confidence. But she simply put another weight on my raw shoulders.

Still, I did persevere. I know that most of my acquaintances won't believe me, and my publishers certainly didn't—otherwise, they wouldn't have commissioned another biography of Sartre—but I did begin to work diligently, seeking out the "objective" facts of Sartre's life.

First, I reread his literary works. As a novelist, Sartre had never separated fact from fiction, nor did he believe that a writer should. In his trilogy, *The Roads to Freedom,* each of his major characters is based very closely on someone Sartre knew well, often a person who had deeply affected him—and at times, he himself. On the theory that I could identify each of these persons and eventually interview most of them, I decided to use Sartre's novels as biographical data, to describe his way of thinking by showing what he changed, what he stressed, what he deliberately ignored—in sum, what he chose to write about and why.

Then, comparing this information to what Sartre had said about himself, either in *The Words* or in numerous interviews he had granted all his adult life, I prepared dossiers with which to confront him. From November through May of 1970 through 1973, with updates in 1974 and 1975 and again in 1977 and 1979, I did just that. These sessions were not just interviews. They were conversations, sometimes arguments, occasionally even battles. I would begin something like this: "Mathieu is you in *The Age of Reason,* and he claims that he would never let himself be talked into joining the Communist Party by Brunet, who represents your best friend, Paul Nizan. But the fact is that Nizan didn't want you in the party, and indeed, if you read Brunet's words carefully, neither did he; both Brunet and Nizan characterize you, Mathieu-Sartre, as an intellectual narcissist. And . . ."

By that time Sartre had forgotten the tape recorder that we had half hidden under his chair and was raring to go: "*Connerie!*" (more or less, "bullshit"), he would yell. "Nizan was just as much an individualist as I was, but he had an authoritarian personality which made him seek out the disciplined, fascist or communist—remember, he toyed with the right before discovering the left—but only because he wanted to impose his own will, for to want to be led is the same as wanting to lead. . . ." And off we went.

I know it is part of the mythological Sartre that he never got angry. His adopted daughter will swear she never once saw Sartre lose his cool. But Sartre did get very angry, just as often as anyone else. In our sessions he occasionally shouted at me or at those from his past whom I reenacted. He also used to get quite livid at the politicians of his day. He despised de Gaulle and was angry with me for insisting that de Gaulle, at least, was not a lackey of the United States. He hated Guy Mollet, France's number one Socialist leader, whom he considered the greatest traitor in history. Wrote Sartre in *The Ghost of Stalin*: "Mr. Mollet has thrown himself into betrayal; he splashes about in it comfortably. I don't know anyone in history who has betrayed so many people at once."[2] Sartre would surely have said as much about François Mitterrand, who was in the Mollet government when, contrary to its promises, it decided to intensify the war in Algeria. Sartre violently opposed Mitterand when he ran for president in 1973. He ran a ferocious editorial, "Elections: A Trap for Fools," in his magazine, recommending a boycott of the elections precisely because Mitterrand, who had been part of Mollet's war cabinet when it betrayed their Socialist Party platform and promises, was as bad as Mollet.[3] Sartre died before he could witness Miterrand's betrayals in the eighties.

The anger that I remember best, not unnaturally, was the anger directed at me. It was the Friday after the Lod massacre. A group of Japanese anarcho-communists had opened fire at Tel Aviv's Lod airport in solidarity with the Palestinians. Sartre, who had always supported the right of Israel to exist and also the right of the Palestinians to self-determination, showed me an editorial that would soon appear in the extreme leftist journal which he officially "directed," *La Cause du Peuple*. Though he lamented the death of various American nuns who were caught by the Japanese machine guns, he liked the editorial, which saw this act of terrorism as an example of international cooperation among leftists.

La Cause du Peuple was then the mouthpiece of France's *maos,* a fringe leftist group which was both moralist and Stalinist, headed by a fanatic, diminutive warlord then called Pierre Victor (in fact an Egyptian Jew named alternatively Pierre Bloch or Benny Levy). Since Victor was neither French nor legal (his status was regularized later by President Giscard d'Estaing when Sartre appealed to him personally), it was Sartre who was officially the "responsible editor" of the monthly. But while both he and the *maos* claimed to be equal, Sartre was actually used by the group. Not that Sartre would not have lent his name to their paper even without massage; he willingly lent it to any group opposing oppression. But in this case he tried his best to be part of the group, and the group used his sincerity to hedge their illegal activities.

I read the editorial and scoffed. The Lod massacre was not an example of international solidarity but of Palestinian weakness, I said, and counterproductive. I understood and agreed that because of an international conspiracy to deny the Palestinians even a fraction of their ancient homeland, they had to resort to terror. And I even accepted the direction of this terror at those who, like the Palestinians themselves, were defenseless, that is, at any Jew who supported Israel's expansionism. But indiscriminate fire at people who, for all anyone knew, may have been at the forefront of the two-state, one Israel and one Palestine, policy was stupid.

Sartre was furious. How could he possibly work with someone who didn't understand what internationalism was all about, he shouted. Then he punished me. He canceled our interview. The following week he pinned a note to his door saying he had "gone to the dentist. I think."

But three weeks later, as I sat down in his one-room flat at 222 Boulevard Raspail, he handed me a galley of newsprint. It was a dissenting editorial for *La Cause du Peuple* that said more or less what I had said three weeks earlier. I looked up at him questioningly when I finished reading it. Sartre smiled sheepishly and said: "You see, I listened. I admit it took a while to sink in, but you were right, and this will say so—in print."

The trouble was, the more we talked, the more I discovered another Sartre, one he himself tried to hide and which every interview, every biographical essay had more or less concealed from the public: a very vulnerable Sartre, who worried about his place in posterity, who questioned his motives, the efficacy of his actions, the meaningfulness of his relationships. Sartre had often claimed that he never experienced guilt, nor envy, nor, since he was twenty, jealousy. But as we talked during the seventies, it turned out that this may not have been so. My questions triggered his questions. The answers we came up with appear in the pages that follow.

Beginning in 1973, slowly at first, then increasingly dramatically, Sartre's health weakened. His good eye stopped. His walk faltered. His memory faded. Sartre became an object, and all his close ones wanted to possess it. They turned him into a myth, each to suit his or her needs.

Sartre had never been afraid of death. Now he was petrified—not of actually dying, but of not living. He needed eyes, legs, and hands. In sum, he desperately needed help, and those who offered it made him pay for it—by making them rich or famous. They wrote his words as their own. They published interviews which they concocted. They got him to sign his name to their pronouncements, with the intention of taking full credit later for their brilliance in convincing him to see the world in their own light.

In the last two years of his life, Sartre was made to seem to repudiate his total achievements. Out went his dialectic. Out went his revolutionary fervor. Out went his defense of the counterviolence of the violated. He was paraded with old enemies (like Raymond Aron), for whom he had felt nothing but contempt for half a century. He even started searching for his "Jewish roots," according to some of his fake disciples, who had by then convinced France's reactionary left-wing tabloids that they, and only they, spoke for the master. Surrounded by petty Stalinists, Sartre's history was totally rewritten even before he died. To his old "family," to Simone de Beauvoir, to me, it was all one hell of a manipulation.

But was it?

"Tell me, Sartre," I asked him in 1979 during one of his rare moments of lucidity, "is it true that you have renounced the dialectic and found God?"

He exploded in his famous gutteral laughter. "I tell them what they want to hear," he finally answered me, "but don't you print that until they have all published their *new* analyses. Think carefully, Gerassi. Right now, as France turns far right, all these opportunists will go with it. For the foreseeable future, they *are* the future. Castor, Bost, Pouillon, Lanzmann, even Horst, they are the past." He was referring to what has long been known as "the family," friends or former students who had worked with him for decades on his magazine, *Les Temps Modernes* (*Modern Times*).

He went on with amazing perspicacity: "What would happen if Horst [known as André Gorz to left-wing literati] wrote a new book about me? Could anything he said raise eyebrows? His analysis would be fairly correct, I'm certain; his understanding of my philosophy faultless, I'm sure. And so? But think of it! An article or a book which claimed that I had all along been influenced by the Talmud, by the Cabal, by the Koran for that matter, or Loyola's exercises? Eh? A *scandale,* right? Now answer me this. During this coming period, when the vast majority of intellectuals (who, as we have often discussed, are the cheapest commodity on the market) will turn themselves inside out to be apolitical, which means right-wingers; when they will fawn all over the structuralists and so-called poststructuralists as an excuse to be 'detached'; during these coming years, when they will deliberately rediscover the gulags and other Stalin atrocities in order to avoid talking of America's current atrocities; when they will use all their literary power to convince the world that anti-Stalinism is equivalent to pro-Americanism; in short, during the foreseeable future, when socialists will justify exploitation, murder, and nuclear brinksmanship, what will get people to read me? Gorz, who has been faithfully committed to the underprivilged all his life? Or some slick so-called left-wing journalist or philosopher who can claim that Moses was really an American? All I want out of the future, whatever of it there is, is to be read."

As I write this today, I cannot but shake my head at Sartre's amazing insights: a socialist president rules in France today who campaigned on the promise that he would stop testing nuclear weapons on the heads of France's impoverished, colonized South Pacific subjects and then not only carried out more tests than his conservative predecessor, but also massacred those who objected. And the intellectual community in France? For the most part, just as Sartre had predicted, they cheer Mitterrand and explain their pro-Americanism on the grounds that "we are opposed to the gulags," without a mention of America's atrocities in Salvador, South Korea, the Philippines, Grenada, Nicaragua, Puerto Rico, the Virgin Islands, Lebanon, Liberty City, the ghetto of Philadelphia, Vieques, Youngstown, Angola, Kwajalein, Guam, Palau, indeed all of dominated, colonized Micronesia, Indonesia, Timor, Chile, and so on.

But then, what about me? Was I no more than one of those manipulated manipulators? Had Sartre chosen me to write his biography in order to perpetuate another myth? But which one?

In 1967, Sartre had told Michel Contat that "The Pléiade series is a tomb; I don't want to be buried alive." A few years later, Sartre anxiously awaited the first volume of *Sartre* to appear in the Pléiade. Meticulously printed on Chinese silklike paper and bound in pure leather, Pléiade books are reserved for unquestioned classics and often squeeze an author's entire works into one or two volumes. Volume 1 of Sartre, for example, includes all his novels within its 2,174 pages, yet the object is thinner than any Michelin guidebook. "For a long time," Sartre explained to Contat, "Robert Gallimard has seen to it that I get the volumes as they come out, and these are the only books that I stubbornly refuse to lend."[4]

Sartre had very few possessions in his life. In fact, he often gave away any book he had finished to the next person who walked into his apartment. (He must have given me some 400 books over the years.) Yet the Pléiade he guarded assiduously. The collection stood at rigid attention on his shelf, defiantly permanent in a contingent world, material, i.e., objective, symbols of immortality. But who reads Pléiade books? Who owns them? They may be on the shelf of every self-respecting bourgeois home, but does the French executive read Bossuet or Balzac, Michelet or Machiavalli?

Was there another explanation, or rather an additional one, for Sartre's weird alliances after his eyes became permanently shut? He wanted to stay relevant among the young, yes, but only because he wanted them to keep reading him. Did he think that scandal would arouse their interests? "Funny man that Picasso," he once said to me, "did you see how he got all those heirs and heiresses fighting each other? That's one way of getting people to keep talking about you." As long as people kept talking about him, Sartre thought, or hoped, people would keep reading his works.

That's why he was so pleased about *Obliques*. A very prestigious magazine, *Obliques* came out in 1979, a year before Sartre died, as a special double issue completely dedicated to him: forty articles, all more or less on his side, though some did contradict a few of his basic tenets. Mine was one of those, since it tried to show that it was not true that Sartre had never been motivated by guilt. But it was a very unacademic article, based on Sartre's fiction, interviews, and personal relationships, with no reference to secondary works. All the intellectuals I knew criticized it. I therefore expected Sartre to hate it.

The first time I saw Sartre after the magazine appeared, I was even more anxious than the day of my first interview with him. I had gone to his apartment to pick him and Castor up for lunch, and there it was, the magazine, on the table, obviously well thumbed.

"Ah-ha!" I exclaimed to cover up my nervousness, "I see you've read *Obliques* . . . ," knowing of course that Castor would have read it to him.

"Tell me," she asked point-blank, "do you plan to write Sartre's biography the same way you wrote this?"

Was this the moment that would end it all, then and there? Or was I simply going to get the correct line, so history and myth would forevermore coincide? "Yes," I said firmly.

"Good!" snapped Sartre. "You are absolutely wrong, of course. But at least you've made me alive. Those academicians have dissected me as if I was long dead and buried. They may be more correct, but who is going to care, one way or the other?"

That should have encouraged me, and it did, for a while. But then I reread what I had written. It was fake, false, flat. Not that I had deliberately lied. Like everyone else, I had been caught in the churning wheels of the myth, in the endless images of Sartre as the tough, solitary revolutionary who was (then) still working out his last treatise, his ethics.

"The revolutionary," Sartre's best friend had written in 1938, "is the man who has triumphed over solitude."[5] Sartre, it was said by all, including me, was a solitary figure in our alienating world, but he had triumphed over solitude. Had he?

In fact, did not writing his biography appeal to me, at least in part, precisely because Sartre had remained an unreconciled, solitary figure all his life? Like me? Like Mallarmé, Jean Genet, Baudelaire? Wasn't their estrangement what had enticed Sartre into writing *their* biographies?

Flaubert, of course, was quite different: that liberal, who so feared and hated revolutionaries that he hoped the government would execute all *communards,* gave Sartre the opportunity to dissect France's bourgeoisie and its intellectual spokesmen; to demonstrate that when the chips are down, intellectuals inevitably obey their class breeding and betray the needy.

But then, is not the motive of the biographer crucial? Can there be an objective biography at all? Sartre had claimed that the only way to find out what a man is, any man, is to use his progressive-regressive method, that is, to use the man and his works (or actions) to explain the times, and the times to explain the man. He had in fact insisted, in *Search for a Method,* that only through such forward and backward movement could anyone learn anything about anybody. Sartre had indeed used Flaubert to explain the French bourgeoisie, and the Commune and the fear the rich have of the poor to explain Flaubert. But aren't all good biographies researched in precisely this way? And weren't they always? Why does that make them "objective"?

In a lecture to the Young Lawyers' Association of Brussels in 1972, Sartre said, "Every intellectual has what can be called his ideological interests. . . . For the last seventeen years I have been engaged in a work on Flaubert which can be of no interest to the workers, . . . the product of a bourgeois philosopher's reflections over the course of most of his life. . . . The book ties me to bourgeois readers. Through it, I am still bourgeois."[6] Does this not show that, in its fundamental approach and choices of valuable evidence, all biography is autobiographical? And, then, isn't reading also autobiographical, insofar as readers choose what they are reading, choose to continue, and choose with whom to identify according to their own particularities and not some "objective" standard?

When I was first hired as an editor at *Time* magazine in 1956, Henry Luce, that old missionary who owned it, called me in for a pep talk. "We here at *Time* believe that objectivity is neither feasible nor desirable," he had said. "Any questions?" That was one of the few truths I had ever heard from a top *Time* editor. To the outside world, of course, *Time* did pretend to be objective. It still does. So do Anglo-Saxon academics. So do the French socialists, who in fact are just as xenophobic and chauvinistic as the Jewish Defense League, no matter how "objectively" progressive their rhetoric remains.

Such contradictions inevitably accentuated my dilemma. Had Sartre lived out his own contradictions? "I find myself," he had said in 1972, "among those who are struggling against the bourgeois dictatorship. I want to reject my bourgeois situation. There is thus a very special contradiction within me: I am still writing books for the bougeoisie, yet I feel solidarity with the workers who want to overthrow it. Those workers were the ones who frightened the bourgeoisie in 1968 and are the victims of greater repression today. As one of them, I should be punished. Yet as the author of *Flaubert,* I am the *enfant terrible* of the bourgeoisie and should be co-opted."[7]

Because he never tried to hide behind bourgeois objectivity or mechanical Marxists' determinism, Sartre made some bad mistakes, some fantastic mistakes, indeed such outrageous mistakes that there were moments, sometimes even years, when he was co-opted after all. Co-opted by revolutionaries, by fraudulent rebels, by Communists, by individual bourgeois intellectuals in the useless hope of gaining some acceptance in order to render more successful another more meaningful activity. Sartre, for example, always spoke publicly with some respect for the bourgeois apologists Aron and Levi-Strauss, even though in private he considered them extreme mediocrities, the first a lackey of U.S. imperialism, and the latter a self-glorifying, arrogant clerk with "absurd" ideas meant to fool other intellectuals into rejecting political commitment.

Once blind and helpless, Sartre also became co-opted by the young, soothsayers through whom he hoped to extend his work and keep alive his message, which they quickly perverted the minute he died. That message was this fact: Jean-Paul Sartre was the only genuine intellectual of our times who was never co-opted by the bourgeoisie or by any bourgeois government.

That is why he was loved by the fifty thousand who followed his casket. That is why he is hated by the alienating: the magicians, the prophets, the complacent, the tricksters, the intellectual carpetbaggers, the "watch dogs," as his friend Paul Nizan used to say, in other words, all those who believe in public objectivity.

But I believed in it too. Shortly after Sartre died, I went back to France to see Castor. She had had a nervous breakdown and had been hospitalized for a while, but she was okay now, more or less. We had lunch in some café on Denfert Rochereau, near where she lived, and she cried a great deal. She kept talking about Sartre's last days and his heart-rending last words (which she described so eloquently later in *La Cérémonie des adieux*). Then, trying to smile through her tears, she said: "Sartre had wanted to read your biography before he died. So would I."

By then I had written some seven hundred pages of an objective biography, backed up by more than two thousand pages of notes. Once again I sat down and reread them. Once again I felt a fraud. In my way, I too was perpetuating a myth: the great philosopher-novelist-playwright-journalist who made some mistakes but was a great man. Not true. He wasn't a great man for what he wrote but for what he did, for the example he set, for his constant daring, his genuine audacity.

Sartre defined authenticity—and was often inauthentic. He fought for justice—and was often unjust. He—and Simone de Beauvoir—pretended to the world that they had an ideal relationship, one that almost every feminist has publicly envied, one that nearly all biographers have held up as *the* example of a liberated coupling. In fact, however, Sartre's relationship with Castor was far from perfect, while those with other women tended to be disastrous. He felt trapped by them—mostly out of guilt. Sartre hid reality from us just as much as we hide it from each other. In his personal actions, he was, as he said himself in *The Words*, no better but no worse than any of the rest of us.

One of his great qualities is that he never stopped trying. He never gave up. He always kept looking, listening. He was always willing to learn, from anyone. In other words, for all his lust for immortality, he never took himself that seriously. He always remembered that even the specially treated paper of La Pléiade volumes goes up in flames in any bonfire.

So why didn't I say it. Because no one wanted to hear it. Even *Libéra-tion,* today's successful daily, which existed only because Sartre, once its "responsible editor," made it possible with his name and his money, didn't want to hear that kind of a view. A blast from a rightist? No problem. Idiotic critics like Clément Rosset were perfectly free to damn Sartre and his work.[8] An attack from a Lukacsian Communist or Trotskyist? Good, by all means. But an analysis into the contradictions that make a great man a fraud, or a fraud a great man, written by someone who loved him as he was and whom he trusted? Yech! And since my biography was heralded as the official, that is, authorized version, even a petty Robespierre like Serge July, the boss of *Libération,* would not be able to ignore it.

Then, one day in October 1985, I received in the mail from Paris a fat (728-page) opus: Annie Cohen-Solal's biography of Jean-Paul Sartre.[9] I was saved! It was the "perfect" biography, heavily researched and written equally heavily. And was it ever objective! It was so objective that it listed every street in the town where Sartre's father was born and every name of those attending his funeral. Hailed immediately as "a biography as only Anglo-Saxons can do them,"[10] it was published by Gallimard, my editor, in France, and would soon be issued in English by the same house that had contracted me in the United States. What's more, the author, while she did not know Sartre, had interviewed just about anyone who had ever expressed a thought about him (except Michel Contat who had done more work on Sartre than anyone, my parents, and me).*

Cohen's Sartre had been commissioned in 1981. No one had told me, neither my French nor American editors, nor any of the "family" members she and I had interviewed—not even Castor, with whom I had continued corresponding and whom I had seen after Cohen had interviewed her. An immediate best-seller in France, Cohen's *Sartre* would surely be an equal hit in the United States and indeed in the rest of the world. Annie Cohen was a star. *Libération* called her "the world Sartre specialist," and interviewed *her* friends and *her* lover.[11] And I was free.

The pressure on me was gone. I would no longer have to worry about maintaining any myth. I would no longer have to care if Sartre's

---

* Because Contat, to whom I had shown my interviews with Sartre, quoted passages from them in the Pléiade edition of Sartre (with permission), Cohen-Solal was able to requote a few lines in her book.

adopted daughter approved of my study. I would no longer have to resent giving her the last word—as Cohen-Solal had done. Nor would I have to treat Raymond Aron with the respect he never deserved. I was free to write a book no one would have to read and no one would have to apologize for. I was now free to write what was meaningful to *me,* not what would fit some standard that neither Sartre nor I ever believed in.

According to the *New York Times,* "Annie Cohen-Solal has taken Jean-Paul Sartre away from the intellectual left, whose property he has remained since his death."[12] Translation: Cohen-Solal has twisted Sartre back into the mainstream, where incidentally, the so-called intellectual left is solidly planted. As an *enfant* or *adulte terrible,* Sartre, the twentieth century's greatest intellectual and its most unrelenting conscience, is an embarrassment. So would be a biography, no matter how critical, which traced the trajectory of that conscience.

The day after I finished reading Annie Cohen-Solal's "objective" biography of Jean-Paul Sartre, I finally understood why Sartre had chosen me to write his "auto"-biography. I threw away the seven hundred pages and started anew.

No intellectual, no writer, no man is more hated by academics and newsfolk, by eggheads and politicians on both sides of the Atlantic than Jean-Paul Sartre. Nor is this new: Sartre has been hated by them for half a century. But as long as he was alive, his pen easily deflected their gibes. In France, where he could take to the podium or even to the streets if they tried to stifle his counterattacks, the media had no choice but to report his retorts. In England and in the United States, however, Sartre was dependent on the fair play of his critics. He got none. They smeared him, distorted him, and ridiculed him. When all else failed, they tried to silence him altogether—by ignoring him in the United States, by murdering him in France.

At first, after the war, Sartre was turned into a "national asset"; in *What Is Literature?*, he even complained that "it is not pleasant to be treated as a public monument while still alive."[1] But he was soon damned by left and right. In 1946, Britain's censor banned his play *No Exit*. In 1947, Pierre Brisson, editor of the right-wing Paris daily *Le Figaro,* expressed delight that "the cohorts of Maurice Thorez [longtime head of the French Communist Party] insult him and proclaim him to be the writer of the failures, while the warring faction of the right wing talks of exorcizing him, of covering him with sulphur and setting him on fire on the parvis of Notre-Dame, which would be the most charitable way of saving his soul."[2] In 1948, Pope Pius XII put all of Sartre's works on the Index (meaning that any Catholic reading any part of them is automatically excommunicated). That year too, the Soviet government officially objected to a production of his play *Dirty Hands* in Helsinki on the grounds that it was "hostile propaganda against the USSR." The play remained forbidden throughout the Eastern bloc for decades, and when it opened in France, it elicited this judgment from the Communist daily *L'Humanité:* "Hermetical philosopher, nauseated writer, sensationalist dramatist, demagogue of the third force,* such are the stages of Mr. Sartre's career." Georg Lukács, the highly touted Hungarian Marxist philosopher, added: "Existentialism reflects, on the level of ideology, the spiritual and moral chaos of the

---

* Earlier that year, Sartre had helped launch and was principal spokesperson for the Revolutionary Democratic Assembly, which hoped to keep France divorced from the aggressive policies of both Russia and America.

current bourgeois intelligence."[3] Fadeev, head of the Russian Federation of Writers, at the 1948 Wroclaw Peace Conference, summarized Sartre as "a hyena armed with a fountainpen."

But in France by then, the Communists had already condemned him. The most "learned attack" came from Henri Lefebvre, that professional party hatchetman who had smeared his closest friend, the novelist-journalist Paul Nizan, as a police informer because Nizan had refused to soften his anti-Nazi stance when Stalin signed the Russo-German pact. Now, in 1945, Lefebvre went after Sartre, defining him as "the manufacturer of the war machine against Marxism."[4] (No longer a Communist by the sixties, Lefebvre never apologized to Nizan or Sartre, yet is still respected as a great intellectual in France—perhaps precisely because of that.)

In 1945, meanwhile, the French government had thought enough of Sartre's wartime resistance activity to offer him the Legion of Honor; Sartre had refused. Four years later, André Malraux, onetime Communist sympathizer turned Gaullist mouthpiece, denounced Sartre as a collaborator even though he, of all people, knew better.* In April 1949, Catholic writer François Mauriac intimated in print that Sartre was a foreign agent. The very next month, he offered Sartre a seat for "immortals" by having him elected to the most elite forty-member Académie Française; Sartre scoffed at such a chance to "learn equality" among those who spend their waning years bragging about their "superiority." He also turned down an offer to join that other most prestigious bastion of French culture, the Collège de France.[5]

But the worst insults from fellow French intellectuals while Sartre was alive were provoked by his rejection of the Nobel Prize for Literature in 1964. In private correspondence to the Nobel Committee, Sartre had said that he would turn down, with equal intransigence, the Lenin Prize, were it ever offered to him, and on the same public grounds, that the Lenin and Nobel are equally politically motivated. When the Nobel Committee ignored Sartre's warning and awarded him the prize anyway, and Sartre published the correspondence, ex-Communist-surrealist André Breton nevertheless denounced Sartre for being part of "a propaganda operation in favor of the Eastern bloc."[6] But that sally was nothing compared to the onslaught unleashed by the usually mild-mannered Christian philosopher Gabriel Marcel. Said he, presumably

---

*Sartre had tried to entice Malraux into joining his resistance group in 1941, when Malraux was enjoying the good life on the French Riviera. See chapter 10.

with Christian charity: Sartre was an "invetarate denigrator," a "system-
atic blasphemist" with "pernicious and poisonous" views, a "patented
corruptor of youth," the "grave-digger of the West."[7]

By then, Sartre was used to much more formidable attacks. After
Paris-Match had run an editorial entitled "Sartre: A Civil War Machine,"
hundreds of war veterans marched down the Champs Elysées chanting,
"*Fusiller Sartre! fusiller Sartre!*" ("Shoot Sartre!").[8] On 19 July of the
next year, a bomb went off in his apartment at 42 rue Bonaparte (but
did little damage). Six months later, on 7 January 1962, a more powerful bomb, detonated on the wrong floor, destroyed much of the apartment and either obliterated various unpublished manuscripts or gave
the inrushing firemen the opportunity to pilfer them.

Sartre was not home when the bomb exploded. His mother, who
had moved in with him after her husband, Joseph (Sartre's stepfather),
had died, was in the bathroom, where the heavy wooden door protected her. The suspicion about the manuscripts arose when some from
that period turned up at auctions, but Sartre, who was admittedly very
careless about his possessions, never kept track of what he no longer
worked on.

None of these attacks stopped French students from reading Sartre,
and as they did, his reputation and influence grew. In the Anglo-Saxon
world, however, the attacks had their effect. His plays were rarely performed, his novels scarcely read, his philosophy almost totally ignored.
Dominated by logical positivists and empiricists, Anglo-Saxon university philosophy departments have long been reluctant to take seriously
any epistemology or ontology, much less Sartre's, which is based on
phenomenological descriptions of reality. A. J. Ayer, for example, dismissed all of existentialism as "an exercise in the art of misusing the verb
to be."[9] But then Ayer, like his analytical colleagues, limited the task of
philosophy to analyzing the language of propositions and held that it
"must be content to record the facts of scientific procedure."[10] In a Columbia University philosophy class taught by the eminent Ernest Nagel,
I remember spending hours on deciding whether Bertrand Russell's
sentence, "Is the present king of France bald," was a meaningful question (whether the verb *to be* predicated existence). Similarly, both Iris
Murdoch and Mary Warnock belittle Sartre for not playing the game
the way they do, that is, for not using logic as a philosophical method
relying instead on meticulous descriptions of events, states, conditions, and relations. Warnock, who dismissed Sartre as "not an original
thinker," objected to what was a proof for Sartre, namely "a description

so clear and vivid that, when I think of this description and fit it to my own case, I cannot fail to see its application."[11]

What bothered Ayer, Nagel, Russell, Murdoch, Warnock, and others about Sartre's approach—indeed about any approach which began with the "I" situated *in* the world—is that it risked defining truth according to its human relevance, which is precisely how Sartre defined it. In other words, the approach transformed the so-called dichotomy between object and subject into a dialectic in which each had its own being, yet the two were inseparable—exactly what Sartre hoped to show (not prove) through his phenomenological descriptions. For Anglo-Saxons who want to uphold the purity of "objectivity," this method is very dangerous because it may lead to interpreting speeches, events, indeed all of history, according to class interest. The conclusion may well be—and Sartre emphatically thought so—that for all their liberal, even perhaps socialist pronouncements, such intellectuals as Ayer, Warnock, and others are part and parcel of the bourgeois state and their work ultimately defends that state.

But these philosophers were at least respectful. They sometimes even disagreed with each other. Thus, while Ms. Warnock claimed that philosophy "has perhaps always been something of a sideline for Sartre himself," Denis O'Brien, an expert on Hegel and president of Bucknell University, insisted that, on the contrary, "Sartre was fundamentally, uncompromisingly, and incessantly a philosopher."[12] But then, analytic philosophers never did like Hegel very much; during my ten years as an undergraduate and graduate student at Columbia, he never once earned the right to his own course. Still, better rejection at Columbia than praise at Berkeley, where Denis Hollier had this to say about Sartre's trilogy: "The war puts an end to the clinical narratology of the hypnagogic story."[13] (That phrase may have put Professor Hollier's students to sleep, but it sent Professor Alexander Leupin, another high-minded critic at Louisiana State University, into orgasmic ecstasy—and he got Yale to print it in its *French Studies* magazine.[14]

In the United States, Sartre's most efficient assassin was Germaine Brée, an expert on the contemporary literary scene in France. Infatuated with Albert Camus, Brée felt that she therefore had to demolish his main critic, Sartre. So, in a popular text, *Sartre & Camus,* which gained immense influence in academia, she condemned Sartre for dealing with authority "callously," "pompously," "typically." At least Camus, she wrote, never was guilty of making a judgment on the basis "of class." On the other hand, "Sartre's hatred of bourgeois life," she went on, "re-

veals the streak of irrationality that underlies many of his judgements."[15]
(Brée also had to attack Simone de Beauvoir because she had written in
Force of Circumstance: "Camus became a more and more resolute cham-
pion of bourgeois values."[16])

Brée ridiculed Sartre for his supposed fear of psychoanalysis (page
33) but then scoffed at his supposed neuroses when she learned that, on
the contrary, Sartre quite welcomed the idea of analysis (page 114). She
passed off his opposition to General Ridgeway as head of SHAPE as
"trite" because in her view no one could seriously have objected to the
general's war-making in Korea, then tried her best to discredit Conor
Cruise O'Brien for correctly calling Camus a "colonialist under the
skin." Finally, she damned Sartre because he "never to my knowledge
supported any political candidate who had the slightest chance of
winning nor has he ever supported any action taken by the French government"—thus naively handing Sartre the best compliment he ever
received.[17]

The effect of Germaine Brée was somewhat offset, it is true, by such
erudite critics as George Steiner in England, and Arthur Danto and
Robert Dennon Cumming in America. Cumming, for example, tried to
explain why Americans, who want to turn everything, including poverty and exploitation, into a personal, individual problem, are disturbed
by Sartre for whom "nothing is sacred, . . . not even the Freudian theory of the superego."[18]

But such counterattacks could never dislodge Camus from the pin-
nacle of the literary hierarchy in England or America. There, he is admired mostly because he focused on individual despair and individual
hope, never on class conflicts. He disturbed no conscience. On the contrary, he soothed the self-involved and the self-indulgent by general-
izing individual problems (whereas Sartre concretized the universal
problems, forcing each of us to be responsible for all). No wonder,
then, that someone like Bobby Kennedy discovered Camus "in the
months of solitude and grief after his brother's death," reported Jack
Newfield. "By 1968, he had read, and reread, all of Camus's essays, dra-
mas and novels . . . He memorized him, meditated about him, quoted
him, and was changed by him." Bobby Kennedy's favorite passage from
Camus's *Notebooks* (which he underlined): "Living with one's passions
amounts to living with one's sufferings. . . . When a man has learned—
and not on paper—how to remain alone with his suffering, how to
overcome his longing to flee, then he has little left to learn." The passage eloquently reveals Camus as an Algerian *pied-noir* (French colonial

descendant), as a metaphysical sufferer who never understood the human causes of pain—which is why he never supported the Algerian people's struggle for independence.[19]

It got worse after Sartre died. One British "expert," David Caute, who pretends to support the left but in fact spends his time ridiculing all genuine leftists, cast off Sartre as an *incestueux manqué*. ("Too bad Sartre didn't have a sister," he wrote).[20] Then he added that the only reason Sartre chose to write about Flaubert was because the latter "had left behind thirteen volumes of correspondence."[21]

Concealing the fact that Sartre carefully avoided her because, he said, she was "an arrogant imperialist witch," Mary McCarthy told the *New York Times* that Sartre "didn't care for people."[22] That remark elicited this brilliant non sequitur from the "New Philosopher," Marcel Gauchet: "We want the Christian West to be on top."[23] After this, most French reactionary critics felt free to let loose. The best remarks, perhaps, were issued by the writer Olivier Rolin, who decided that "Sartre lacked courage" because he always maintained the unpopular viewpoint,[24] and by Clément Rosset who bewailed the fact that he could never find in Sartre's work "a solid philosophical or clear political position."[25]

Even the editors of *Libération,* the Parisian daily Sartre had kept alive for years with his own money and scores of exclusive interviews and articles, now turned against him. Reinterpreting his end-of-life musings, they decided that Sartre had abandoned the poor and the powerless, the rebel and the revolutionary, to support the French reactionary left, which he had always despised. Or was it that the "*Libé*" editors now wanted to court the powerful and established in order to be more "relevant?"

And wasn't that similar to the contortions performed by *The New York Review of Books* writers? Do they really think that "Sartre was entirely wrong" in his feud with Camus, as one of them affirmed,[26] or do they simply like the fact that Camus never dirtied his hands (by avoiding commitment), thus giving the *Review* its "moral" justification to do likewise? Is it true that "Sartre has not been forgiven for the retrospective embarrassment caused the leftist intelligentsia for his visceral hatred of 'bourgeois' society, an attitude that now seems corrosive of democratic values," as one *New York Times* critic concluded?[27] Or is it that today's "leftist intelligentsia," who inject morality into yuppie avarice, are lusting for bourgeois respectability—and bourgeois honors?

Sartre did hate bourgeois society and did reject its honors—from the Legion to the Nobel (which compelled *Time* magazine to snort stupidly, "reverse snobbery").[28] To his death he insisted that the job—and the excuse—of the intellectual was to criticize the powerful and defend the voiceless. Few famous and no rich ever agreed, then or now. But today, they are not afraid to praise their perks. Thus, in France and in the United States, the new "intellectuals," those servicefolk of the established media, must show that "the ideology" of commitment of their immediate forebears, as the *Times* put it, "is indeed dead and that for them, private life is worthy of literary celebration."[29]

That celebration of private life, decided David Leitch with acute plebian depth in the *London Sunday Times,* is why Sartre had lost touch with the young.[30] He so wrote on the very day that fifty thousand of those young gathered spontaneously to pay their respects the day of his burial. As they marched across Paris, they attracted another fifty thousand more middle-aged mourners—the greatest testimony to the relevance of an intellectual the world has ever seen.

So, why their hatred—and our love? "How is it possible," asked István Mészáros, "for a solitary individual, whose pen is his only weapon, to be as effective as Sartre is—and he is uniquely so—in an age which tends to render the individual completely powerless?" The answer: his "passionate commitment to the concerns of the given world."[31] With Sartre, there were no escapes, no ivory towers, no retreat into false "objectivity." Those of us who had no power knew he fought for us and with us. Those who had knew they could never say, "I can't help it." The job of the intellectual, Sartre said over and over, is to criticize, to oppose, to denounce. And he cheerfully accepted his resulting solitary fate, just as André Chamsom had moaned during the Spanish Civil War that "the duty of the writer is to be tormented."[32] For Sartre, as Hazel Barnes said, "literature is a means; at its best it is a form of praxis."[33]

Sartre offered the intellectual no peace, no self-satisfaction, no contentment, nothing but hard work—and not even the hope of victory. In *The Words* he wrote: "For a long time I took my pen for a sword; I now know we're powerless. No matter. I write and will keep writing."[34]

But he was wrong. He had a lot of power. The proof? All those who hate him. All those who followed him to the cemetery of Montparnasse. All those who love him. Like Françoise Sagan. Listen to her "Love Letter to Jean-Paul Sartre":

"You've written the most intelligent and honest books of your generation, you even wrote the most talented book in French literature—*The Words.* At the same time, you've always thrown yourself doggedly into the struggle to help the weak and the humiliated; you believed in people, in causes, in universals; you made mistakes at times, like everybody else, but (unlike everybody else) you acknowledged them every time. . . . In short, you have loved, written, shared, given all you had to give which was important, while refusing what was offered to you which was of import. You were a man as well as a writer, you never pretended that the talent of the latter justified the weakness of the former. . .

You have been the only man of justice, of honor and of generosity of our epoch."[35]

PART 2

The Bastard

Naturally, bastards betray, what else should they do? I have been two people all my life. . . . I am composed of two halves which do not fit together; each of those halves shrinks in horror from the other.

Jean-Paul Sartre, *The Devil and the Good Lord*

3 The Faker

No sooner could he talk than Jean-Paul Sartre became a fraud. Of course, it wasn't all his fault, at least not at first. Born a boy, he was raised a girl. Fathered by a small, sickly, Catholic technocrat from the heart of France who shunned books and savored oceans, he was molded by a stout, stolid, Protestant intellectual from its German border who played God and seduced students. This terrifying, bearded, atheist deity treated him and his mother as siblings, and convinced him he was a prodigy.

By the time Jean-Paul was three, he had been made, and made himself, into an ersatz orphan: his surrogate father was a self-glorifying myth, his mother was his sister, and his mission in life was predetermined. A genius who couldn't spell, a saint who couldn't tell the truth, Sartre grew up knowing how to fool adults, especially those pretentious idiots who claimed that "out of the mouths of babes . . ." Defined and catalogued as a good, gentle, mature child who was perfectly happy, Sartre was in fact a traitor: a nasty, conniving, narcissistic, little grown-up who was totally miserable.

Sartre's real father can plead not guilty on grounds of extenuating circumstances: he died too soon. That, however, was certainly the fault of his own parents. Sartre's grandfather, Eymard Sartre, a country doctor with grandiose plans, married Marie-Marguerite Chavoix, the daughter of a large landowner, hoping for the good life. But when it turned out that papa Chavoix was broke, Dr. Sartre stopped talking to Marie-Marguerite, and their three children were conceived, born, and reared in angry silence.[1]

Unimpressed by the lush vineyards or the underground truffles that inhabit the rolling hills of his native country of Périgord, the home of some eighteen hundred history-laden chateaux, Marie-Jean-Baptiste-Aymard Sartre, the bitter couple's oldest offspring, doggedly prepared his escape. He studied math, astronomy, mechanics, even architecture, got into the elite state-run Ecole Polytechnique, graduated 27th out of 223, and promptly joined the navy. His imperialistic dream: to sail the seven seas, in command of a French cruiser, which in turn commanded the seven seas.

By 1904, a promising but disillusioned officer of thirty, Jean-Baptiste Sartre was already being ravaged by doubts of the moral value of French colonialism—and by the rigors of Indochinese fevers. But he didn't know it. So, when he met Anne-Marie Schweitzer, the youngest of four children fathered by an Alsatian teacher of German, he quickly married her and made her pregnant.

By the time Jean-Paul-Charles-Aymard Sartre was born (in Paris, on 21 June 1905), his father, Jean-Baptiste, was dying. "Anne Marie nursed him devotedly," Jean-Paul has written.

"She had not known my father well, either before or after marriage, and must have wondered at times why that stranger had chosen to die in her arms. He was taken to a small farm a few miles from [his native town of] Thiviers; his father came to visit him every day in a cart. The sleepless nights and the worry exhausted Anne-Marie; her milk dried; I was put out to nurse not far away and I too applied myself to dying, of enteritis and perhaps of resentment. At the age of twenty, without experience or advice, my mother was torn between two unknown moribund creatures. Her marriage of convenience found its truth in sickness and mourning. . . . Upon the death of my father, Anne Marie and I awoke from a common nightmare. I got better."[2]

Had Sartre been jealous of his mother's care for his father? Had he been pleased by his death? Sartre claims not. Yet "the death of Jean-Baptiste was the big event of my life," he wrote. It "gave me freedom."[3] In 1960, in the midst of composing a few sentences about his father, Sartre jumped out of his hardwood chair, hustled down to the Austerlitz railroad station, and trained to Périgueux, where he hoped to grill his aunt on what her brother had been like. But she had long been dead.[4] Sartre came back and finished the paragraph: "Jean-Baptiste had refused me the pleasure of making his acquaintance. Even now I am surprised at how little I know about him. Yet he loved, he wanted to live, he saw himself dying; that is enough to make a whole man.* But no one in my family was able to make me curious about that man."[5]

"He wanted something," Sartre said of his father, "and he got it, though it killed him. Still, for me, that's a totality. Everything subordinated to a goal, including affections and even, at the same time, death. Of course, that goal didn't interest me."[6] But it justified his existence. Or, at least, it helped Sartre pretend that his father had not been totally useless. In any case, it allowed him to pass him off: "I know him by

---

*A catchy sentence, often quoted by Sartrologists for its "heavy" meaning, which in fact means nothing, especially for a philosopher who insisted that we are defined by what we do. When I confronted Sartre over it (interview no. 2, 20 November 1970), he laughed and then explained that he had to say something which "rounded him off."

hearsay, like the Man in the Iron Mask and the Chevalier d'Eon, and what I do know about him never has anything to do with me. Nobody remembered whether he loved me, whether he took me in his arms, whether he looked at his son with his limpid eyes."[7]

A totality or not, Jean-Baptiste had clearly betrayed Jean-Paul—by dying too soon. "Had my father lived, he would have lain on me at full length and would have crushed me. As luck had it, he died young." Result: "I have no Superego."[8] Translation: Not to have a father is not to have relations of loyalty or of power. "That accounts, beyond a doubt, for my incredible levity. I am not a leader, nor do I aspire to become one. Command, obey, it's all one. The bossiest of men commands in the name of another—his father—and transmits the abstract acts of violence which he puts up with. Never in my life have I given an order without laughing, without making others laugh. It is because I am not consumed by the canker of power: I was not taught obedience."[9]

He didn't need to be taught obedience. "Child of a miracle," as he himself wrote,[10] he was wrought in God's house, and taught to transmit His word. The all-powerful does not need to evaluate his power: he takes it for granted. So does his progeny. Sartre confused leader with commander. Maybe his father never did leave his mark, but his grandfather certainly did. And Sartre himself was indeed quite certainly a leader, as proved by the millions who follow him. Anne-Marie's father did not need to command. But he was certainly obeyed. His voice was the thunder of truth, and both Anne-Marie and her child wallowed in it when it vibrated.

Chrétien-Charles Schweitzer was born between France and Germany, that is, in Alsace, in 1844, and his loyalties suffered the consequences. Tall, formidable, with a flowing beard that turned white while he was still agile, Karl, as he liked to be called by his German friends, or Charles to the French, could easily pass for any of the great intellectuals of his time: Poincaré, Freud, Bakunin. But instead he chose to pass for God.

"One day he entered a church by way of the vestry," Sartre told us in *The Words*. "The priest was threatening the infirm of purpose with the lightning of heaven: 'God is here! He sees you!' Suddenly the faithful perceived beneath the pulpit a tall, bearded old man who was looking at them. They fled." Added Sartre: "The fact is, he slightly overdid the sublime. He was a man of the nineteenth century who took himself for Victor Hugo."[11]

Charles's father, a schoolteacher turned grocer, had wanted him to be a preacher. But Charles had fled and was never mentioned by name again in his father's house. He got a doctorate in German, became a teacher and pioneer of the direct method, and quickly climbed the academic ladder, if not in rank, certainly in motion: he went from Macon to Lyon to Paris. (His brother Auguste, meanwhile, also refused to be religious, but he was forgiven because he made himself rich selling sausages. That left the youngest, Louis, who was so obedient that not only did he become a preacher, but he also coaxed his son, Albert Schweitzer, into following suit. And the Nobel Peace Prize winner remained in his grandfather's shadow: in his memoirs, *Souvenirs de mon enfance,* he dutifully forgot to mention the existence of any other family member except an older sister, whom he apparently coveted.) [12]

While in Macon, Charles met Louise Guillemin, daughter of a Catholic lawyer, married her, then relegated her to her room, where she remained in semidarkness for half a century. Frightened, "she always gave in to him as soon as he started shouting. He fathered four children upon her by surprise: a girl who died in infancy, two boys, and another girl. Out of indifference or respect, he allowed them to be brought up in the Catholic religion. Louise, though a nonbeliever, made believers of them out of disgust with Protestantism. The boys sided with their mother . . . ," so Charles dismissed them from his heart and, later, from his concern. The youngest child, Anne-Marie, mimicked her mother—without alienating her father. "She was taught to be bored, to sit up straight, to sew." [13]

Anne-Marie's marriage to Jean-Baptiste was supposed to let her flourish. His death imprisoned her: she returned to the Schweitzer household. Charles, who had applied for a retirement pension, "went back to teaching without a word of reproach." Anne-Marie tried to "obtain forgiveness; she gave of herself unstintingly, kept house for her parents in Meudon and then in Paris, became nurse, majordomo, companion, servant." She tried to enlist the aid of Louise, but "that aging and cynical woman," as Sartre described her, only became jealous that she was no longer indispensable. [14] She agreed with Charles that Anne-Marie and Jean-Paul, hereafter dubbed "Poulou," were to be treated simply as "the children."

But Charles was facing death. Not that he was sick. His bones creaked a bit, and his walking cane, long merely an affectation, now became an extension of his arm. Yet, he had begun to question the value of his achievements, and decided he could do no more—the first tragic sign. An atheist, a self-vaunted humanist, Charles accepted everything in nature as normal. "Or at least he wanted to," Sartre told me in our first formal interview for this work, in November 1970. "Death and birth are part of the same natural phenomenon. A child and an old man resemble each other. So he saw in me his survival. A great part of his comedy of loving me came from his fear of death. That is, when he pretended to adore me, he was in fact searching for the life in a child to justify the one ebbing in an old man." But, as his booming voice reverberated far beyond the Schweitzer fifth-floor apartment, whose walls were plastered with multifaceted photographs of himself and whose shelves were guarded by his own gold-embossed leather books on teaching methodology, Charles could never appear a mere mortal. Nor could Poulou, coddled and caressed by a living god, doubt that he was sacred.[15]

Although Charles never read novels published after Victor Hugo's death, he certainly knew what great writing was all about, and he talked to Poulou about Culture as if it defined mankind. Pointing to his shelves as the Mount Olympus the boy would have to climb, he gave him his values and perhaps, too, his long-abandoned dream. It was his way of cheating death. Thus Sartre was born into literature long before he could read and was decreed a genius long before he could write. He was raised to believe that nothing that was not on the shelf—those scores, even hundreds of rigid leather pillars firmly at attention, in awe of each other—was to be considered real.

Chances are that Charles did know what was going on in the world, but he never talked about major events. Freud, Bergson, and Husserl, beginning their fifties, were shaking up the rational world with a new subject—the complex and often elusive "I." Lenin and Rosa Luxemburg, on the contrary, reacting to the failed revolution of 1905, were redefining it as a scientific object to be disciplined in organizations or manipulated through spontaneous mass actions; space was being recast as curved and motion as relative. But none of this was ever discussed at the Schweitzer table. Reality was touchable, firm, permanent, unambiguous—bourgeois. So was God. And so was Poulou.[16]

But he had to be nurtured first. Everyday, Charles would sit Poulou on his lap and expand his horizon. He taught him enough history to fashion him into a Francophobe; he showed him enough Rembrandt reproductions to get him to admire the master's art of chiaroscuro; he read to him enough stories from Maupassant to make him realize that others in the world were not perfect, and enough plots from Anatole France to convince him that they could be. But whatever the message, it came from books: "I went from knowledge to its subject. I found more reality in the idea than in the thing because it was given to me first and because it was given as thing. It was in books that I encountered the universe."[17]

At first, all Poulou could do with these books in Charles's study was stare at them. "I did not yet know how to read, [but] I already revered those standing stones: upright or leaning over, close together like bricks on the bookshelves or spaced out nobly in lanes of menhirs. I felt that our family's propriety depended on them." Then he touched them, "secretly to honor my hands." Finally, he snuck one to his room. He turned the pages reverently yet, like Charles, as if nonchalantly looking for the right spot, made believe he found it—and read.[18]

For hours his eyes went from left to right, following those little black marks on the white leaf, repeating the process line after line, page after page. As he read, he told the story, just as Charles did when he recited out loud. When he finished, he told Anne-Marie and Louise that he had read a book. They laughed. "But my darling little Poulou," quipped Anne-Marie, "you don't know how." The women carried the tale to the patriarch. He caressed Poulou's golden locks. "Very good," he bellowed. "My boy will be a great thinker, no doubt about it."[19] The verdict was in.

Only Charles's verdict really mattered. Louise was either afraid or silent. Anne-Marie was merely useful: "That virgin who is under surveillance, who is obedient to everyone, I can see very well that she's there to serve me. I love her, but how can I respect her if no one else does? There are three bedrooms in our home: my grandfather's, my grandmother's, and the 'children's.' The 'children' are we: both alike are minors and both alike are supported. But all consideration is for me. A young girl's bed has been put into *my* room. The girl sleeps alone and awakens chastely."[20]

Does this passage betray Sartre's incestuous fancy? Not willing to let psychiatrists beat him to the answer, Sartre himself wrote in *The Words:* "I thought for a long time of writing a story about two lost children who were discreetly incestuous. Traces of this fantasy can be found in my writings . . . what attracted me about this family bond was not so much the amorous temptation as the taboo against making love: fire and ice, mingled delight and frustration; I liked incest if it remained platonic."[21] That did not stop the psychoanalytic wags from pressing the issue. To some, Sartre's rejection of Freud's concept of the unconscious was nothing more than his repressed Oedipus complex.[22] To others, it stemmed from his fear that any analysis into hidden motives would restrict our lust for absolute freedom.[23]

Sartre never did accept Freud's unconscious. But he never denied the validity of psychoanalytic proddings into a child's past. "It is childhood which sets up unsurpassable prejudices, it is childhood which, in the violence of training and the frenzy of the tamed beast, makes us experience the fact of our belonging to our environment *as a unique event*. Today psychoanalysis alone enables us to study the process by which a child, groping in the dark, is going to attempt to play, without understanding it, the social role which adults impose upon him. Only psychoanalysis will show us whether he stifles in his role, whether he seeks to escape it, or is entirely assimilated into it."[24]

Of course Sartre meant a psychoanalysis whose method puts both analyst and patient "in the soup," taking equal risks, not the master-slave relationship currently in vogue on analytic couches. As for our freedom, it never does exist outside our conditions, ignoring or ignorant of our history. "Freedom," Sartre liked to repeat, "is not what you do gratuitously. It is what you do with what's been done to you."[25]

What was done to Sartre was to deny him his parents—and weld him to bourgeois freedom. Anne-Marie, his older sister, nursed him, fed him, dressed him, amused him, encouraged him—but to no avail. Treated as a child in front of her child, whose room she shared, she remained a servant, dedicated to the prodigy but powerless to develop his glory. "She got up and dressed before I did, undressed and went to bed after I did," Sartre told me. "So, unlike Stendhal or Freud, I never had a carnal vision of my mother." There was only one exception: "One day, she was in a slip, with her skirt on her arms still bare. As she put on her top I saw her underarm hairs and asked 'what's that?' She answered me, 'A sickness, stupid.' That was that."[26] And it was—at least until his school chums aroused his curiosity.*

But Poulou did not really go to school until he was ten. Educated by his grandfather, he remained his mother's young brother, both of them nonpaying guests in Charles's home. Not even his girlish golden curls could Anne-Marie preserve: one day, when Poulou was seven, fed up with looking at "a sissy," Charles decided "to give mother a surprise,"

---

*But the incident remained ingrained in his memory. Wrote Sartre years later in "Intimacy" (*The Wall*, 58): Lulu "thought of her little brother Robert who asked her one day when she had on nothing but her slip, 'Why do you have hair under your arms?' and she answered, "It's a sickness.'" But, added Sartre, "She liked to dress in front of her little brother . . ."

and whisked him off to the barber shop to be shorn.[27] Anne-Marie was crushed. "Be careful! We're not in our home!" she often warned Poulou. They never were. Yet the boy had everything he needed—on permanent loan. The epitome of security is to have everything but own nothing.[28]

But, of course, Poulou did not have a father, since no grandfather can replace his son. "A father is often jealous of his son, he can often be arbitrary, contradictory, too tolerant and too intolerant, and usually careful not to let his son be too isolated."[29] A father "would have weighed me with a certain stable obstinacy. Making his moods my principles, his ignorance my knowledge, his disappointments my pride, his quirks my law, he would have inhabited me."[30] More important, he told me in 1970, "A father, if he's good, makes his son rebel against him."[31]

But Charles, "whom I saw dominate everyone else, had no authority on me, since everything I did was a sign of genius."[32] Forcing Anne-Marie (willingly) and Louise (reluctantly) to go along with him, he decreed not only that Poulou was a prodigy but also that he was good-looking, and Sartre believed it—even after his right eye died in an infection when he was three. Charles "admired in me the admirable fruit of the earth so as to convince himself that all is good, even our shabby end," Sartre wrote, adding: "All children are mirrors of death."[33]

The result was that "I make childish remarks, they are remembered, they are repeated to me. I learn to make others. I make grown-up remarks. I know how to say things 'beyond my years' without meaning to. . . . I admire myself on trust. . . . It was Paradise. Every morning I woke up dazed with joy, astounded at the unheard-of luck of having been born into the most unified family in the finest country in the world."[34]

And the whole lot of it was fake. "Until the age of ten, I remained alone between an old man and two women. My truth, my character, and my name were in the hands of adults. I had learned to see myself through their eyes. . . . I could feel my acts changing into gestures. Playacting robbed me of the world and of human beings. I saw only roles and props. Serving the activities of adults in a spirit of buffoonery, . . . I adapted myself to their intentions." He "suspected the adults of joking." Nevertheless, he went along with it. "One must feign passion in order to feel it," he insisted.[35]

Jean-Paul Sartre feigned all his childhood. To begin with, that's how he learned to read. Faking it over and over again, he finally deciphered—or so he claimed to me—Hector Malot's *Sans Famille* when he was four, and that gave him the tenacity to read *Madame Bovary,* Corneille, Rabelais, Voltaire, Vigny, and Hugo when he was seven— "without understanding anything, of course."[36] But it made Charles gloat and the family boast. No wonder Poulou saw his role as "the main character" in the Schweitzer play. "Though I had lines to speak and was often on stage, I had no scene 'of my own.' . . . I was giving the grown-ups their cues. Charles made much of me in order to cajole his death; Louise found in my liveness a justification for her sulkiness, as Anne-Marie did for her humility."[37]

No matter what he told Charles & Co., Poulou did not like his role. So, he escaped it. He read *Michel Strogoff* and *Pardaillan,* the swashbuckling novel of Michel Zevaco which was then being serialized in *Le Matin*. The former he found "too goody, goody," but Pardaillan who single-handedly defended honor, justice, and pure love against tyrants French and foreign, "was my master. Firmly planted on my spindly legs, I slapped Henry III and Louis XIII dozens of times in imitation of him."[38] Thus did Sartre become an anarchist before he was ten.

Charles, of course, disapproved. But "admiring everything I did, how could he possibly condemn me? So he blamed the women, without telling me a word."[39] Thus unhampered, Poulou expanded his "trashy" vision: he read the adventure stories of Paul d'Ivoi, Jean de la Hire, Arnould Galopin, and then *Rocambole* by Ponson du Terrail, as well as the illustrated stories of Nick Carter, Buffalo Bill, Texas Jack, Sitting Bull, and Morgan the Pirate. Charles "gave me my self-confidence. I used it to discover the world."[40]

But once discovered, it made no sense. Why did his father die so young, his father's father so old? Cohen-Solal claims that Sartre tried "deliberately" to forget his father's family, the Thiviers side; obsessed with rehabilitating his "normal" half because she lusted for mainstream acceptability—for herself as well as for Sartre—Cohen-Solal hoped to turn Sartre into a rebel, and hence not a revolutionary.[41] But the fact is that Sartre couldn't have cared less about Thiviers. When he did try "deliberately" to get interested, it was out of autobiographical duty; and he failed.* Money-grubbing stuffed shirts with typically French

---

*Cohen-Solal claims that Sartre returned to Thiviers when writing *The Words* out of genuine interest rather than mere autobiographical curiosity. Simone de Beauvoir, who gave me a copy of Cohen-Solal's book with all the errors underlined and comments in the margin, assured me that this was not true. There is no doubt, according to Beauvoir, that Cohen-Solal, influenced by the current right-wing attack on Sartre, does write according to a particular political agenda—as of course we all do.

shop-keeper mentality, all the folks from Thiviers, except one, he told me, "bored me silly and I never did get to like truffles."[42] The exception: a cousin, "my fiancée," more or less his age, who died before ending her teens.

"The more life is absurd, the more death is intolerable," Sartre said repeatedly—and to me on tape.[43] To make life fathomable—and the world real—he decided to dominate it. So, at seven, he began to write. "I wrote in imitation, for the sake of the ceremony, in order to act like a grown-up; above all, I wrote because I was Charles Schweitzer's grandson," he claimed in *The Words*.[44] But in 1970, he told me: "I wrote to avoid death. I had no religion, so I wrote. The way I saw it was: first there would be my death, then the assininities I wrote would become my real life. I would be my writings. In other words, surrounded by books, raised by books, I imagined myself more real *in* my books."[45]

At eight, writing meant filling pages in a notebook. It had to be wide enough to stand on a shelf, with the rest of the gods. Called *For a Butterfly,* Sartre's first "novel" was about a scientist, his daughter, and a young explorer sailing up the Amazon in search of a precious butterfly. It was merely a calligraphic rendition of the illustrated serial then running in a quarterly.[46] The second, entitled *The Banana Seller,* was about a tall man with a long beard who did what had to be done—"to save mankind." The seller "was I in the future, that is Charles in the present." The intellectual and the man of action. "Of course, Charles was no man of action. But he loved *Les Misérables* and looked like Victor Hugo; he believed in progress and was afraid to die. And his only claim to immortality—that is to denying the absurd—was on the shelf." Sartre combined it all.[47]

But he did so by copying. "The cold-blooded plagiarism freed me from my remaining misgivings; everything was necessarily true since I invented nothing." Anne-Marie approved: "She would bring visitors into the dining-room so that they could surprise the young creator at his school-desk. I pretended to be too absorbed to be aware of my admirer's presence. They would withdraw on tiptoe, whispering that I was too cute for words, that it was too-too charming. My uncle Emile gave me a little typewriter, which I didn't use."[48]

Charles disapproved. "He took my notebook, leafed through it, scowled, and left the dining-room, furious at finding a repetition of the 'nonsense' of my favorite gazettes."[49] Not to mention the spelling errors. But it was too late. "If one is called a small marvel, a prodigal child all day long, one ends up believing it. I had the self-confidence to go on."[50] Besides, Charles had taught Poulou that the great writer is inevitably a martyr: "Chénier beheaded, Hugo exiled. . . . The writer suffers and produces. Chateaubriand, dead in despair; . . . Racine, banished. That was what literature was all about. I created a whole religion on it. One writes, one is condemned, one suffers; then just before dying—like Hugo—or a bit later comes the hereafter: fortune for some, fame for all such martyrs."[51]

Eventually, Anne-Marie too fell silent, intimidated by Charles. "Not daring to congratulate me and afraid of hurting me, she stopped reading my work so as not to have to talk to me about it."[52] Thus abandoned, little Poulou wrote more and more, copying less and less, to escape the grown-ups, to prove his existence, to create the real: people behaved according to recognizable standards, and if not, the choice was neither arbitrary nor preordained—it was Sartre's. At first, good vanquished evil; heroes won, damsels survived, honor reigned. But then, as the power of creating became creative power, Poulou began to make his own rules. "One against all: that was my rule. Let the source of this grim and grandiose reverie be sought in the bourgeois, puritan individualism of my environment," he wrote in *The Words*. "I experienced all the temptations of power. I was harmless. I became wicked. What prevented me from plucking Daisy's eyes out? Scared to death, I answered: nothing. And pluck them out I did."[53]

Not true. He plucked them only if the plucking was in the reasoning. "There had to be a norm. For example, I was sure then that the world had to have poor people, because the task of the rich was to take care of them, naturally. The rich were made to save the poor. You have to understand, Gerassi," he said with emphasis. "The world I knew was good, because I was loved and I was important."[54] Thus did Sartre learn about his freedom—and his situation. Without ever having heard of Karl Marx, little Poulou discovered the dialectic. "Men make their own history," Marx had written, "but they do not make it just as they please; they do not make it under circumstances chosen by themselves, but under circumstances directly encountered, given and transmitted from the past."[55]

Until 1913, those circumstances favored the child-genius—but not the child. Pampered, heralded, cherished, shown off, Poulou remained alone. "My grandfather didn't give a damn if I had comrades as long as I was brilliant. My mother did. 'This child is too lonely,' she used to say."

"Did you know it?" I asked Sartre.

"I was certainly aware that my real life would not be spent with people whose mission was to admire me. . . . When my mother took me to Luxembourg park, the other kids played together, but not with me. They had their group. They didn't need me. I was on the outside. I needed them, but to be with them, I had to be their equal. You don't play with people to whom you are superior. But I went home, where I was always the best."[56]

He was so much "the best" that when Charles, who had been responsible for Poulou's education, finally relented in 1913 and decided to enroll him in the top-quality Lycée Montaigne, he dismissed the boy's apprehension by asserting, "You will be first in your class, immediately, you'll see."[57] Indeed, Charles even insisted that his gifted little eight-year-old Poulou be admitted into the fourth grade with kids who were ten. But when Jean-Paul flunked miserably his very first dictation, Charles blew his stack, scolded his boy-wonder for the first time—and withdrew him from school. Sartre claimed that "my failure had not affected me: I was a child prodigy who was not a good speller, that was all."[58] But something had cracked. As Jean-Paul was taken in and out of schools, both private and public, or coddled by private tutors whom Charles terrorized, the boy "developed a dislike for ceremonies" where he would be the center of attention. Seeking instead anonymity, he claimed that he "loved crowds," where he would pass unnoticed.[59] Said he in our second interview, "I began to feel disgust at the fraudulent situation at home."[60]

Nevertheless, he continued to play the game. "I still pretended to listen to the voice that trembled with love when it called me a 'gift from heaven,' but I stopped hearing it." He regarded Charles "as a buffoon of my own kind and did not respect him."[61] This justified, or so he thought in 1970, stealing from him: "I took some history books and some of his own grammars and sold them to a used-book dealer on rue Soufflot. I got very little for them, but I got very little as an allowance, just enough so I could purchase the weekly gazettes I read. Anyway, my mother was always with me, and paid for whatever I wanted, so money wasn't my motive. It was a question of asserting myself."[62]

Without admitting these particular thefts, Sartre explained why he did them in *The Words:* "In order for me to feel necessary, someone would have had to express a need for me. My family had been feeding me the illusion for some time; they had told me again and again that I was a gift of heaven; that I had been eagerly awaited, that I was indispensable to my grandfather, to my mother. I no longer believed it, but I did continue to feel that one is born superfluous unless one is brought into the world with the special purpose of fulfilling an expectation. My pride and forlornness were such at the time that I wished I were dead or that I were needed by the whole world."[63]

But he wasn't. "As an only child and without a friend, I did not imagine that my isolation would end."[64] Besides, the whole world was coming apart. In Germany on 4 August 1914, the Socialist SPD party, with 34.8 percent of the electorate (in 1912) and one million members (in 1914), voted for war credits, thus guaranteeing World War I—the first of its great betrayals, which effectively killed the Second International.

Arguing against Rosa Luxemburg's "mass strike" agitational concept on the grounds that Socialism was "a natural necessity" but only if the SPD did not rock the boat (the Erfurt Program), Karl Kautsky and other SPD leaders destroyed all hope for a successful social revolution in Germany, thereby stimulating Lenin's "revolution from above" authoritarianism, which in turn brought about Stalin's absolutism. As for Karl, aka Charles, Schweitzer, he agreed with the SPD. But when war exploded, he was Charles again, proclaiming his French patriotism even in a children's play he wrote basically for Sartre (who flubbed his lines and got miffed for not winning most applause).[65]

So, "the war soon bored me; it upset my life so little that I probably would have forgotten about it, but I took a dislike to it when I realized it was ruining my reading matter. My favorite publications disappeared from the newsstands; Arnould Galopin, Jo Valle, and Jean de la Hire abandoned their familiar heroes, those teenagers, my brothers . . . their authors had betrayed me: they had put heroism within reach of everyone; bravery and the gift of self became everyday virtues. . . ." Poulou may not have liked this democratization of heroism, but, plagiarist to the core, he followed suit. In October 1914, "I began the story of Perrin the soldier; he kidnapped the Kaiser, tied him up and brought him back to our lines; then, in the presence of the assembled regiment, he challenged him to single combat, downed him, and, with his knife at the Kaiser's throat, made him sign an ignominious peace treaty and give Alsace-Lorraine back to us."[66] All the right ingredients to satisfy Charles' Francophile imperialism while pleasing Anne-Marie's lust for a bourgeois-democratic escape.

Poulou escaped first. No longer protectable from the outside world, he got engulfed by it as Charles agreed to let him go—to a regular school. In October 1915, at ten and a quarter years old, Jean-Paul Sartre entered the Lycée Henri IV as a day-pupil—and came in last on his first test. On his report card, his teacher wrote: "Never gives the right answer on his first try. Must learn to think more."[67] But Charles could only grumble; there was no question of yanking Poulou home again. "I stopped getting special treatment," Sartre wrote, "I got used to democracy."[68] So did Charles. And it paid off: by the end of the next year Sartre was deemed "an open spirit—already a small literary baggage with a powerful memory."[69]

But it wasn't schoolwork that changed Sartre's life. It was his chums: the three Malaquin brothers; Max Bercot who loved literature and hoped to write (and died at 18); Bénard, "gentle, amiable, and sensitive," who died that winter; and especially Paul Yves Nizan who had read everything and wanted to be a writer, and who, like Sartre, was walleyed. "Far from wanting to shine, I laughed in chorus with the others, I repeated their catchwords and phrases, I kept quiet, I obeyed, I imitated my neighbors' gestures, I had only one desire: to be integrated."[70] In other words, he said, chuckling, "I became a true democrat. After school, I played football [soccer] in the street, I fought, I dilly-dallied. I had been such a well-mannered little boy . . . I loved it. I didn't give a damn if I was twentieth in class (except for the effect it had on my grandfather), the essential thing was to be considered their equal by my comrades. I didn't want to be a leader, I never wanted to lead. And I never was. I just wanted to be one among many, like the others."[71]

Yet, he did the reverse at home—as a little adult playing the role of a child behaving as an adult. Loving it, and hating it. While running around the Place du Pantheon with his chums, Sartre the child imitated the adult playing the child. Hating it, and loving it. Fooling himself in and out of home, yet aware in both cases, totally free to play the games according to their strict rules. Where did it leave him? "Fake to the marrow of my bones and hoodwinked, I joyfully wrote about our unhappy state. Dogmatic though I was, I doubted everything except that I was the elect of doubt. I built with one hand what I destroyed with the other, and I regarded anxiety as the guarantee of my security; I was happy." To Sartre, it meant simply that "I came to think systematically against myself."[72]

The curse of the bastard? Francis Jeanson, who knew Sartre well and worked with him for years said just that: excluded without being exiled, Sartre was like everyone and unlike anyone, integrated into two unreconcilable halves which hate each other—a bastard.[73] "Nonsense," Sartre almost shouted at me when I suggested it, "you could say I was an orphan, but the notion of bastardness includes violence, hatred, rebellion.

I had none of those. Whatever my illusions, I was at peace or at least at ease. Jeanson invented that notion to explain how I became a revolutionary."[74] Answered Jeanson: Anyone who tries to be both object and subject together is aware that he is also neither; that contradiction, even if silent, is violent.[75]

Sartre was certainly born and raised by two opposing sides which hated each other: French against German, Catholic against Protestant, country bumpkin against city egghead. He survived the confrontations by faking his adhesions and believing those who claimed to believe in him. In the process he learned that his freedom was unlimited—except by life, which was fully determined. In that dialectical morass, he thrived, traitor to all—until he too was betrayed so deeply he calmly, coldly decided to abandon his emotional attachments. Instead of rebelling, he became a rationalist. He learned disdain.

The betrayer was Anne-Marie, Sartre's older sister, his servant. On April 26, 1917, she became his mother—by marrying a businessman. "I broke with her," he told me, "in order not to suffer. She asked me for my permission. I said yes, but what does that mean? She was talking to me nicely, like an adult, so I said yes, like an adult, but it meant nothing, since I knew, by her asking, that it was over."[76]

Actually, it was only a new beginning.

Convinced, more than ever, that all humans are totally free, Jean-Paul Sartre, at the ripe old age of twelve, was doomed by outside forces to be a punk. He claimed he had been gloriously happy until then. Overprotected and underloved by Charles Schweitzer, his surrogate father, little Poulou had instead been lonely and lonesome. Overloved and underdisciplined by Anne-Marie, his mother in sister's clothes, he had been estranged from his contemporaries, friend and foe. Now, suddenly, as his mother remarried, everything changed—for the worse, he said.[1] Actually, it was for the better.

The man who married Anne-Marie was a self-made bourgeois. Son of a railroad worker, Joseph Mancy studied hard and insulted no one in order to get admitted into *Polytechnique*, France's elite school for engineers; but he deemed himself too poor to ask her out when he met Anne-Marie at fellow-polytechnician Georges Schweitzer's home ten years after his graduation. So Anne-Marie married another of Georges' polytechnician friends, Jean-Baptiste Sartre. But by 1917, with Jean-Baptiste long dead, Joseph Mancy had become the director of Delaunay-Belleville factories, and Anne-Marie, who had been frozen out from starting a civil-service career because of her age, felt trapped enough to seek any moderate escape.

Mancy was an ideal such escape. At thirty-four, she gained a forty-three-year-old husband who was well paid and well respected, a home, a maid, lots of social connections, and especially a father for her increasingly taciturn son. "My mother did certainly not marry my stepfather out of love. He was in fact not very lovable. A tall, skinny young man, with a black mustache, rather bumpy skin, a very big nose, pretty eyes, and black hair," Sartre rambled on at sixty-five. "I didn't like him. I don't think he liked me either. He did his duty, that's all, his bourgeois duty. Having risen in the system through his own means, he had become a total bourgeois."[2]

But totally correct. "He would have liked to exert the well-meaning authority of a father on me, but that had to come from me too, at least a bit at the beginning. He didn't want to impose his importance on me or give me orders right off the bat. So it didn't work. We didn't click. He wanted me to focus on math, physics, sciences. I didn't. He tried to coax me, but I hated math then, so I became insolent. Once, during a

56

lesson with him, I was too shrill. My mother was in the kitchen but heard me. She came up to me, quite calmly, and slapped me. I got up with great dignity and went to my room while he scolded her. That was the last time she ever hit me. But it was all over. She had been mine, totally mine. Now forced to choose, she went against me. I had become a stranger. I was no longer in my home."[3]

Not that Joseph Mancy was a nice man. Sent by his company to salvage its shipyards in La Rochelle, a port on the Atlantic used by U.S. forces after 1917, he was authoritarian and rigid, contemptuous of philosophy and of labor, and hated the Russian revolution so much that Sartre became convinced it must be good. He never did tolerate what he considered abnormal behavior or ideas. Later, when Sartre sent him *The Wall*, his book of short stories, Mancy returned it to him with a note starting, "stopped reading after page thirty."[4]

Nor, on the other hand, was Anne-Marie very unpleasant with her son. "She used to think that God was not just because the world was not perfect. She used to tell me stories about the unfortunate children of an unhappy maid she knew, and I would swell up with feelings of pity. Later, when Mancy refused to meet Castor because we were neither married nor engaged, she would sneak to a pastry shop of her choice for a rendezvous with us and never told him. But she didn't like it and officially claimed he was right. She had made her choice, and our relationship was never the same."[5]

Nor was Poulou's life. Transferred to La Rochelle's Lycée for boys (today the Lycée Eugène Fromentin), he was now on his own, neither protected nor idolized, trying to escape from a world he considered hostile at home, trying to fit into a hostile world he liked at school. La Rochelle, as Sartre himself admitted in a short novel he wrote at seventeen, was pleasant enough, "a five-to-six-o'clock town, an autumn twilight town. The old port at sunset is softened by the vivid evening grayness of the final rays, like an old Vernet print touched up by a hazy modern colorist. . . . In the port, dense water, coated white, lies drowsing like the black swamps of oil that automobiles drop on the pavement. The sailboats float silently, supernaturally, back. Pianos play vividly in the dives around the port, and the mixture of these café tunes brings forth one single vague monophonic melody which takes the place of the sea's missing song."[6]

But Sartre "was only slightly moved by this sight: young boys' eyes are blind to the infinite and unbroken variety of landscapes."[7] What interested him instead was literature and friends. The former was his escape at home. The latter was his confrontation at school. The escape included Victor Hugo's *Les Misérables* (for which he retained a special fondness all his life), Claude Farrère's *Les Civilisés* (which aroused in him a healthy hatred for colonialists), and works by Pierre Loti, Anatole France, and Paul Bourget (which bored him). He also continued to write swashbuckling novels and operettas, having taught himself to play the piano by his usual method, mimicry. It was through reading, also, that Sartre began to develop an interest in, if not politics, current events, which led to some acrid though superficial political discussions with Mancy. "My stepfather was a right-winger like everyone in his milieu. I was a democrat, like my grandfather and everyone in his circle." [8]

There were few democrats at school, however. Entering the fourth form, little Poulou found his classmates distant, disdainful—and violent. "It was at La Rochelle that I made my apprenticeship in violence. In a certain way all the boys there had interiorized the violence raging on the exterior, namely the war," Sartre said. [9] Sons of bureaucrats, functionaries, lower cadre, pharmacists or teachers, doctors or dentists, these middle-class kids dominated the Lycées: the children of workers went to technical schools, those of the rich, to private religious schools. "Notwithstanding politicians' rhetoric, the class differentiations were rigid, and we children knew it. So we fought it out in the streets—class war after class," Sartre affirmed that with pride—in 1970. [10]

Bombarded all day by anti-German propaganda—a constant "hit the Boche!" campaign—the schoolkids of La Rochelle, stripped of their disciplining fathers who were off at the front, demanded total allegiance and obedience. "There was one student, the son of the drawing instructor, for example, who threatened his mother with a huge kitchen knife because she had again served him potatoes for lunch." [11] But mostly they fought each other: "the bourgeois against the *les prolos,* and I fought with my class against those we called the *hoods.* It didn't make sense to me, even then. But it never occurred to me to think that the other side was the good side. I just accepted the fact that those in the Lycée fought those in the technical schools, and while I was constantly aware of the contradictions between what my class said and what it did, I did not end up judging the bourgeoisie or siding with the proletariat." [12]

Indeed, what really bugged Poulou was not that his group was contradictory, but that it did not fully accept him. "I wanted to be totally integrated, but I remained an outsider, a Parisian who quickly became the teacher's pet, who wore fancy pants, who claimed to have attended the opera," Sartre told me in our third interview. He said that he tried

his best to bridge the difference. He fought harder outside, indis-
criminately inside. Worse, he decided to harass the teacher, who was
already overly ridiculed by his classmates. Poor Monsieur Loosdreck,
who "wore a beard cut like a truncated pyramid. His naturally red-
brown hair was disagreeably tinged in his beard with a thousand adven-
titious nuances: white, dirty gray, even black or blond. With his big
hooked nose, sharp as an eagle's beak, his blood-red mouth, his yellow-
orange color, and his nearsighted eyes hidden behind a gold-circled
lorgnon," [13] he never did survive the ridicule. He killed himself two
years later.*

Sartre remained an outsider, at least that first year, and finished it
badly. "I did everything possible to fit in. I fought, but much more
often I was beaten. I told stories. I invented episodes. I lied. I was considered a phony, a good-for-nothing. Yet I persevered. I remember once
showing my classmates one of my stories. It began with a phrase I had
copied from some romance or other: 'The hero of this true story . . .'
When they saw that sentence they burst out laughing. 'It's false, your
story, why do you say it's true?' they shouted. After that, whenever I
started to tell a tale they'd interrupt to state that 'this is a true story' and
roll around laughing." [14]

Scorned by his classmates, punished by his teachers, Sartre the outcast became Anne-Marie's despair. She even became hysterical one day
when, having entered a florist for only a brief moment, she came out to
find "me rolling in mud punching and being punched by one of the
prolos from the other gang. Instead of defending me, she scolded me,
not understanding what made me so testy." [15] How could she: the real
cause was her remarriage, "her betrayal," as Sartre repeatedly said. [16] "It
was because of her remarriage that I decided not to continue writing

---

* *Jesus the Owl, Small-Town Schoolteacher,* written after Sartre passed his baccalaureate
exam (1922), was partly published in a magazine edited by his friends (including classmate Paul Nizan) entitled *La Revue sans Titre* (*The Magazine without Title*). Sartre used the
pseudonym Jacques Guillemin (the maiden name of his maternal grandmother) because
he feared that the real-life model for his antihero, one of his professors at La Rochelle,
who was thought to have committed suicide after years of constant heckling by his students (including Sartre), might be recognized. In fact, literary detectives Michel Contat
and Michel Rybalka, who put together the best annotated bibliography of Sartre's writings (see bibliography), were able to document that the professor in question never did
kill himself. After reconstructing the complete novel for forthcoming publication in a
Pléiade edition, Contat and Rybalka were amazed that young Sartre would write such "a
violently satirical novel condemning Sartre's familial milieu, the academic bourgeoisie"
and what he has called elsewhere "the destructive and anarchic individualism" of his
youth. (*Les carnets de la drôle de guerre* [Paris: Gallimard, 1983], 106.)

The Words," he told me, "and that was before you and I agreed on these interviews for a biography. How could I continue? Anne-Marie was still alive. How could I blame her for not caring enough about me, for abandoning me, for choosing a schmuck (*un con*) over me? Yet that was the real reason I was so desperate to fit into that vile Protestant center of La Rochelle, hoping to be liked by somebody, by any one of those grossly vulgar port merchants' sons."[17]

To be liked, 12-year-old Poulou even tried sex. "I didn't know anything at first. But I drew a man once and for some reason I put pubic hair around his sex. Immediately my classmates assumed I was a dirty Parisian, *un dessalé* (a desalted one)."[18] They laughed, but they seemed curious. So Sartre tried to follow through. He asked Anne-Marie what *buggery* meant. She said, "A spanking," but told Mancy, who proceeded to lecture him about not paying attention to the tales of children. "The more he told me to stay clear of such subjects, the more, naturally, they intrigued me. So, through reading, I found out."[19]

And, of course, embellished it. "Every Thursday, more or less secretly, my classmates went down to the beach with their *chicks*—that's what they called them—and fooled around a bit, probably nothing more than some smooching. 'Did I have a chick?' they asked. 'In Paris,' I said. 'What did I do with her?' they pressed. 'I took her to a hotel,' I boasted. Being realists, they laughed. So I asked our maid to write me a letter as if she were my Paris chick, regretting my departure, remembering all we did in a hotel room. She got a kick out of it and even added a few details when my dictation seemed to falter. I showed it to my classmates. But, idiotically, I told one chum, whom I thought was a real comrade, the truth. He told the others. They really put me down then, not because I had lied—they too lied about what they did on the beach—but because I had invented things out of the ordinary. They concluded that I had a twisted spirit."[20]

A real *chick* is what this twisted spirit sought. And he had one in view: the twelve-year-old daughter of a shipchandler, a very pretty blonde who seemed to hang around with some of his classmates but "belonged" to none. He asked about her and was told to speak to her when she was around, on the mall. Her name was Lisette, and she was warned of Poulou's interest. One day, he spotted her leaning on her bike, talking to her chums, under the trees bordering Le Mail, that flower-bedecked promenade which lines the sea. He approached carefully, silently, stood aside for awhile shifting hesitantly from one foot to the other, then took another stride forward. "Finally," he said, and I sensed that the story still pained him a bit, "I entered her circle. She had obviously prepared her reaction. 'Who is this bum with one eye that says shit to the other?' she asked loudly.* I withdrew, as the group burst out laughing. I knew then that I was ugly. I had had such a hint after my grand-father cut my curls and my mother cried. But now I was absolutely certain: I was really ugly."[21]

Sartre's life was changed. For one thing, "my ugliness protected me from becoming precious. The guy who doesn't feel ugly is at best a reformist, because fundamentally, in his life, all is okay." And for another, "I understood that my ugliness was an obstacle to overcome, and it made me more determined when it came to seducing women; that is, I realized that I could not have one-night stands; that if I won them over despite my ugliness it meant a more profound relationship, which in turn meant that such relationships would also be hard to terminate, another important factor in my life. My first real love affair, a few years later, was with a woman, an actress who used to kid me, but without any harshness, about my ugliness. 'So how come you love me?' I asked her. 'You talk good,' she replied. 'What if I were uglier still,' I insisted. 'Then you'd have to talk all night,' she responded. I often did, in the years to come."[22]

At the time, however, little Poulou was crushed. Still, he kept trying to belong. In July, as the weather warmed, his sought-after pals went swimming. Poulou didn't know how. They taunted him. So he decided to learn—by his old method, mimicking. He jumped into "that disgusting water, full of the port's vomit," and did as they did.[23] They laughed, but he learned. Yet it was still not enough for Sartre to buy in.

Buy in he would, he decided—literally.

"Each night, my mother would leave her bag hanging on the knob of a big dresser in the living room. So each night, for weeks, I snuck into the room and took out some francs, a few pieces, sometimes even notes, at a time. I used the money to buy my classmates some cakes, good stuff at a fancy bakery. One night, after my usual theft, my mother decided to tuck me in. It was a cold night, so she took my jacket to put over the blanket—and heard the pieces rattle in my pocket. "I stole it for a joke from Cardinaud," I explained, for some reason naming one of my class-

---

* Sartre told this story somewhat differently to Catherine Chaine, according to Cohen-Solal (p. 83): "Vieux sot, avec ses lunettes et son grand chapeau." (Old dummy with his glasses and his big hat.) Such a remark would never have made young Sartre so profoundly aware of his ugliness—but "vieux con avec un oeil qui dit merde a l'autre" certainly would.

mates I hated most. My mother ordered me to bring him around the next day, so I did, but I made a deal with him: he could keep ten francs if he went along with the lie. Everything went fine except Cardinaud and his pals kept all the forty francs my mother had found. Then Cardinaud bought himself a swanky lighter, which his mother obviously discovered, and he spilled the beans. And I was really caught."[24] Sartre often described this theft as his second great crisis—and second betrayal.

The first, of course, was his mother's remarriage. The second was Charles's betrayal. Despite his claims to the contrary, in *The Words* for example, Sartre remained tightly attached to his grandfather even after their separation. They had even previously corresponded in verse—rhyming iambic pentameters.[25] "I was certain that he would understand why I had stolen the money," Sartre said, "after all he was on my side. He didn't even like Mancy, though he was always very polite with him. Charles was to arrive in La Rochelle a few days later. I was ecstatic. Now I would have a friend, for surely he would understand what my mother did not, that she had brought me into a city where the kids didn't want me, and therefore where I had to pay to have them, that I stole to have a life. Charles would understand that, and defend me. He didn't."[26]

Worse, Charles insulted Poulou when, a day after his arrival, he accidentally dropped a coin which the boy rushed to pick up: "He stopped me with his cane. Then, with probably exaggerated effort, he bent down slowly and seemingly painfully—and I heard, or thought I heard, his bones crack—to pick up the coin himself, saying, 'You have shown that you have no respect for money.'* It didn't take long for me to translate that into a more accurate statement: that I have no respect for the bourgeoisie, whether Mancy's version or Charles's."[27]

In La Rochelle Sartre thus lost his innocence: his mother, his privileged status, his precociousness, his prettiness, his center stage, his grandfather. Alone and lonely, he became a realist. He entered the world, taught himself how to play the piano, how to swim, how to fight—and how to succeed, by himself, against all odds. A terror both in and out of school, Poulou nevertheless finished third form (1918–19)

---

*Cohen-Solal goes along with Sartre's version in *The Words* of his break with his grandfather before the theft (p. 82). But as Sartre readily admitted in his interviews with me (nos. 2 and 3), he would never have been so hurt by Charles's gesture when he dropped the coin, nor would he have referred to Charles's lack of understanding of the theft as a "betrayal," if he had already crossed Charles off in his mind.

first in French and Latin, second in math and Greek. He did as well the next year. He stopped writing juvenile novels and instead began portraying himself in a strange milieu, "writing to reconstruct the world against God, as if behind it there was true freedom, that is, a goal, in other words, a purpose, thus throwing the imaginary against the real, without ever denying it. I understood that the writer, whatever he claims, no matter how unconscious, wants to change the world by giving it meaning. And since such an endeavor pits the writer against the most powerful creature ever invented, namely god, his method must be violent by definition." Then he added, as if lecturing me, "And of course, he must fail."[28]

To Anne-Marie and Joseph Mancy, little Poulou was a disaster, no matter how well he did at school. To his classmates, Sartre was too bright, too quick: "He was ambitious and had an original spirit, with an imaginative exuberance," said one of his classmates decades later; in other words, they resented him.[29] To Sartre, life in La Rochelle was miserable. He assured me that "I never did make a real friend, someone I could confide in completely, trustfully."[30] But he told me in 1970 that it was in La Rochelle that he stopped being a "copycat" and instead "discovered the class struggle."[31]

Anne-Marie decided to send her son back to Paris, where, said Sartre "bourgeois children were well behaved, whereas they were all devils in La Rochelle."[32] He added in our next interview (January 1971), "She wanted to yank me out of that unpleasant milieu which she blamed for my truancy, for my lies and thefts. In truth my hostility at home was mostly caused by her remarriage and her husband's stodgy character. That's what made me desperately seek my own peer group and, not being able to find it, to try to buy one. I never did make real friends. I never kept one. They all disappeared or died. There was one whom I had bribed with cream puffs who became a naval officer and married well; he survived I believe. But none remained the least important for me. What I got out of La Rochelle was my introduction to violence, my understanding of classes, of alienation, of choices, that is, the conditions under which choices are made."[33]

In the fall of 1920, Poulou was sent back to his old Lycée Henri IV, entering the first form as a boarder. His responsible family, known as *correspondants,* were once against his grandparents, Charles and Louise Schweitzer, who were now living on rue Saint-Jacques. But that wasn't all that had changed: it was now Louise, a cynic and a skeptic, whom Sartre really liked. "She hated people who took themselves seriously.

She would always say, '*Mon petit,* don't put yourself forward,' while my grandfather on the contrary always wanted me in front. He suddenly appeared a ridiculous and senile monument. He would sit at his desk rereading his dissertation—his thesis, written fifty years before!—and exclaim that it encouraged him. He was eighty-two or so, while she at seventy-seven, alert as ever, reread and hence impressed me to read Dostoyevski, Tolstoy, Stendhal, so we could discuss them. I spent hours with her. We even discussed the Russian revolution and I was stunned to hear her say that the poor had no choice but to use violence to better their lives." [34]

That, however, did not make young Sartre political. "There was a lot of political talk in the dorms in those days, and some of my classmates were pressing me to join the Young Socialists. But I kept saying no, partly because I had an esthetic contempt for all parties which were structured, that is hierarchic, and partly because I had too much information, as little as that was, about what was going on." [35] What Sartre did know was that it had been Germany's Socialist SPD Minister of the Interior (Noske) who called out the reactionary Frei Korps to murder Rosa Luxemburg (and Karl Liebnecht), that it had been the Socialists led by Otto Bauer who derailed the Austrian revolution, that it had been the Social Democrats who defeated Bela Kun in Hungary. Still influenced by Zevaco and Ponson du Terrail, whom he kept reading on the sly, Sartre was still an apolitical anarchist and very much, so he claimed retroactively, in support of the Kronstadt rebels against Lenin's bureaucratization of the revolution. But none of this made him deeply interested.

Sartre's apolitical stance in 1920 was partly caused by the newspaper he read, *Le Temps,* the leading reactionary daily, which two decades later would collaborate with the Nazis. It was in *Le Temps* that Sartre read about Leon Blum's election as a Socialist deputy (16 November 1919), about union chief Léon Jouhaux's antibusiness diatribes (3 January 1920), about the "red slaughters" in Lithuania, Latvia, Estonia, and the Ukraine (6 January), about repression of subversives in the United States (12 January), about the bloody demonstrations in Berlin (15 January), and that the U.S. troops, which had invaded Siberia and had been beaten by the Red Army, had been withdrawn for "tactical" reasons (20 January). *Le Temps* praised the British government for sending troops into Caucasian Russia (19 January) and for forbidding Ramsey Macdonald to go to Russia "to see for himself" what the revolution was like (30 January). It condemned striking dockers and sailors in Rouen

(1 February), a Socialist demonstration in St. Denis (3 February), a threat of a railroad strike (7 February), and the Socialist Congress of Strasbourg (24 February). From 5 March until 22 May, *Le Temps* ranted and railed against the General Confederation of Works (CGT), which it wanted outlawed, denouncing on its front page "the perpetual state of revolutionary alert" by the CGT (9 May), which is "against the nation" (12 May). When the various strikes were smashed very violently by police and army during 19–23 May, *Le Temps* blamed the violence on the dead workers and demanded that the state train more police (24 May).

Mostly, however, Sartre was disinterested in politics because he had become totally absorbed again in literature. "I hadn't stopped reading in La Rochelle, but no one read very much there. In Paris, if it rained, it meant you could read Verlaine. In La Rochelle it meant you couldn't go to the beach."[36] Now, a Henri IV boarder, influenced by other boarders, Sartre read voraciously not only the classics but a new breed of writers who brought new rays into his sunlight: Giraudoux, Gide, Valery Larbaud, Paul Morand, Jules Romains, and especially Proust, who became an obsession. "I knew Swann and Charlus inside out," he told me proudly, "their every thought, every mood, every desire. I often played at being one of them."[37]

Sartre played at being Swann with his old friend from the sixth form, Paul Nizan, now also a boarder at Henri IV. They were inseparable, so much so that they were later dubbed Nitre and Sarzan. Their comrades also gave them titles: Nizan, son of a strict moralist, was nicknamed PDM, which stood for *préfet des moeurs* (controller of morals), while Sartre, the street fighter from La Rochelle, became S.O., "Satyre Officiel," the leader of the dorm's distractions. "They would never have elected me S.O. if I hadn't known La Rochelle violence," he explained in 1971. "My language, my gestures, even my way of looking at my comrades had a violent touch. It was a perfect fit with that would-be puritan Nizan. We called each other by our mythological equivalents. I was R'ha. He was Bor'hou. Our friendship became solid."[38]

Bunking next to each other at the far end of the dorm, Sartre and Nizan analyzed at night the world they discovered during the day. Preparing together their baccalaureate exams (letters in June 1921, philosophy in June 1922), they excelled at everything they did, from translating Conrad to crossing Paris on foot, from writing flirtatious letters to one of Sartre's cousins (which they both did), to writing short stories they read to each other then promptly destroyed.[39] Though

Sartre did very well in both history and philosophy, he was interested in neither. "History bored me. In those days it was taught by positivists who were never concerned by the whys, only the hows. For example, we all knew that if Damien had been beaten, it was because he had tried to assassinate Louis XV, but no one was interested in finding out just who this Damien was, that is, what did he represent, what led him to the point where he could conceive of his act. Teachers told us that we shouldn't try to find causes because we never would. One event followed another. They would admit that the revolutions of '48 surely influenced each other, but they never analyzed the various economics, the conditions of life, the social relations in order to see what *might* have brought them about. History would not mean anything in France until historians got shaken up by Hegel and Marx, much, much later."[40]

As for philosophy, also taught by positivists or neo-Kantians, that too "was a royal bore."[41] But, influenced by Nizan, Sartre did not pass it off as readily as history. "Nizan was much more curious about the outside world than I was," he said. "I had interiorized all my problems into my so-called novels. He too wanted to write, and was much more gifted than I, but having stayed in Paris during those crucial years (1917–20), he was much more integrated into his times. He felt instinctively, for example, that the bourgeois act of writing is the refusal to live."[42] It was Nizan who made Sartre read Flaubert (and reread *Madame Bovary,* which Sartre now understood, though it disgusted him). And it was Nizan who made him read Bergson, even though they both scoffed at his jingo-patriotism (Bergson had denounced Germany "for its brutality and its cynicism . . . its contempt for all justice and all truth, its regression to a savage state."[43]

Born in Tours the same year as Sartre, Nizan was the son of a railroad engineer who, like Antoine Bloyé, hero of Nizan's autobiographical novel, had managed to cross the line from the proletariat to the bourgeoisie; his father and grandfather had also worked for the railroad but had been common strokers in Britanny. "Like me," Sartre wrote of his friend, "his eyes were out of focus, but in the opposite direction, that is, agreeably so. This divergent squint made my face into a battlefield. His gave him an air of malicious absence even when he was paying close attention to us. He followed the fashions closely, but insolently. At seventeen, he had his trousers made to hug his ankles, so tightly, in fact, that he had trouble getting into them; a little later, they flared into bell-bottomed trousers, to the point of hiding his shoes; then with one blow, they rose to the knee, and, puffing out like skirts, were metamorphosed into golf knickers. He carried a Malacca walking stick, wore a monocle, little round collars, then turned collars. He traded in his steel-rimmed glasses for enormous tortoise-shell ones; and, succumbing to the Anglo-Saxon snobbery then ravaging youth, he called them 'guggles.'"[44]

When Nizan "burned with violent and passive emotion," Sartre wrote in *The Words,* "he didn't yell, but we saw him go white with rage and stammer. What we took for gentleness was only a momentary paralysis. It was not truth that was expressed by his mouth but a kind of cynical and idle objectivity which made us feel uneasy because we were not used to it, and though, of course, he adored his parents just as we adored ours," Sartre lied, "he was the only one who spoke of them ironically." Concluded Sartre: "He was a complete person."[45] Sartre was clearly a bit jealous, and Nizan was certainly more self-doubting than he appeared to Sartre; he was often rude, eccentric, moody, or depressed. In *Antoine Bloyé,* he described himself as "a taciturn adolescent, already enmeshed in the adventures of youth, and who abandoned childhood with a sort of avid exaltation." But together, wrote Sartre, "we would be two supermen."[46]

Remembered Sartre: "One of our friends wanted to partake of our new-found dignity. We had to put him to the test. He had to declare out loud, for example, that he would befoul the French army and the flag; these suggestions didn't have the boldness which we ascribed to them. They were current at the time, and reflected the internationalism and antimilitarism of former prewar attitudes. The candidate fled, nevertheless, and the two supermen remained alone, and ended by forgetting their superhumanity."[47]

But Sartre was being too modest. In March 1919, Prime Minister Georges Clemenceau, supposedly a leftist, who had helped impose viciously vindictive peace terms on Germany at the Peace conference of Versailles, sent a French expeditionary force against the Bolsheviks in the Ukraine (which provoked a naval mutiny, led by the mechanical engineer André Marty, later one of the chiefs of the French Communist party). In the next election, the French electorate moved even more right, chosing the most reactionary assembly (*La Chambre bleu-horizon*) since 1875. At the beginning of 1920, a new prime minister (Alexandre Millerand) formed a government composed only of big businessmen who had profited from the war; they continued to amass huge profits, drastically deflate the franc, repress unions, and finally (under Prime Minister Raymond Poincaré) wage colonial wars in northern Africa and occupy (in 1923) the Ruhr on the excuse that Germany, totally bankrupt, did not pay reparations for a war for which its current government bore no responsibility.

But as much as such events deeply disturbed young Nizan, they didn't stop him from enjoying his freedom. After "philo," which both he and Sartre completed well, they decided to enroll in *hypokhâgne* and *khâgne,* two years which prepared students for the national competitive entrance exam to France's most elite Ecole Normale Supérieure (ENS). "Even before Charles put me in Henri IV, back in sixth form, I had decided to go to l'Ecole Normale," Sartre said. "He was a teacher and had a good life. I could see, even at ten years old, that he was respected and admired, and had plenty of time to write books. I wanted to be a writer, but he kept saying, 'become a teacher, then you can write all you want.' Mancy, of course, wanted me to go to ENS-Science, so I could teach physics or math. I never even considered it. The advantage of this academic route is that if you graduate from Normale, that is, get your *agrégation* [equivalent to a Ph.D.], then you are guaranteed a teaching post by the government. So Nizan and I, while remaining boarders at Henri IV, decided to go to Lycée Louis-le-Grand, which had a better reputation."[48]

Actually only Nizan was then a full boarder. His father having been transferred to Strasbourg, he was free to do as he wished after class as long as he returned to sleep in the dorm. Sartre, however, was only a half-boarder: Mancy (and hence Anne-Marie) having been transferred once again to Paris, insisted that young Poulou sleep at home. But the rest of the time, Nizan and Sartre not only studied hard together, they also played hard. "We walked around Paris, for hours, for days. We discovered flora and fauna, stones, and we were moved to tears when the first neon advertisements were turned on. We thought the world was new because we were new in the world—Paris was our bond, we loved each other through the crowds of the gray city, under the light skies of its springtimes. We walked, we talked, we invented our own language and intellectual slang, such as all students create."[49] Wherever Nizan went, Sartre followed: to movies, museums, country fairs, technical exhibits. Together, they discovered foreigners, invalids, slums, strikers, scabs, prostitutes—and cruel, arbitrary policemen.

To Sartre such discoveries became raw material for his writings. During the summer of 1922, he incorporated some of it in a short story entitled "The Angel of Morbidity"; in a biting, satirical tone, he described the carnal and spiritual desires of a mediocre small-town schoolteacher who is both attracted to and repelled by a young tubercular woman—Sartre's first attack on academia. It was the first of his stories to be published—in *La Revue sans titre* (*The Review without Title*, "journal for the defense of youth," no. 1, 15 January 1923). The magazine died after issue no. 5, but not before publishing that other story by Sartre, "Jesus the Owl," and pieces by René Maheu, who became a friend of Sartre's in 1924 and later UNESCO president, and of course by Nizan, whose best offering was a sardonic story entitled "Lament of the Medical Student Who Dissected His Girl Friend While Smoking Two Packs of Marylands."[50]

For Nizan, however, what he and Sartre discovered in their meanderings through Paris was very upsetting. So much so that during *khâgne* one day, he went and converted himself to Protestantism. Raised by a very strict Catholic mother whom, judging by his autobiographical novel *Antoine Bloyé,* he did not like, Nizan the atheist explained: "I liked their morality." But his mother threatened to cut off his funds, so he stopped his reformation. "He hated his position in the world, at least vis-à-vis his background," Sartre told me. "He was a rebel and wanted to be a revolutionary. For awhile he aimed right: he joined Action Française. But the fascism of its aristocratic führers disgusted him: he turned left."[51] How can a "well-fed young bourgeois be prevented from having confidence in the future?" asked Sartre later. Occasionally, Nizan "felt a grim enthusiasm, but his own exaltation frightened him and aroused his disgust. Suppose it was still another trap, one of those lies which one fabricates to stifle anguish and suffering? His revolt was the only thing in himself that he liked. It proved that he was still resisting, that he wasn't as yet engaged in those rail tracks which lead irresistably to the garage."[52]

The tracks both he and Sartre were on, meanwhile, headed straight for the top. Both finished *hypokhâgne* well, *khâgne* well enough. True, the tension was horrendous; from March to October 1923, the inseparable friends separated. That summer, in a short story, *La semence et le scaphandre* (*The Seed and the Diving Suit*), which remained unpublished until after his death, Sartre explained why. Their friendship "was more tempestuous than passionate. I was hard, jealous, without tolerance or kindness, like a maniacal lover. [Nizan], independent and morose, seeking occasions to cheat on me, periodically invented excuses to run away Sunday or Thursday. He also created friends: he was seized briefly by a passion for an Algerian Jew, then for a Marseillan. He would then avoid me for days. I could not resign myself to it. Then, bored with those new faces, he returned to me. . . . I think he had for me a certain gratitude that I seemed to be the only one who could make him whole-heartedly laugh."[53]

That laughter got them together again for their final effort—the ENS entrance exam. They read all of Conrad, Valéry, Jules Laforgue, Schopenhauer, Nietzsche, Bergson, Alain, Descartes, Kant, Plato, Spinoza, the Stoics, the Epicureans. Sartre could "concentrate on his studies like no one else," classmate Georges Canguilhem claimed. "But we also knew him for his good humor. . . . He loved to fool around and was not at all averse to creating havoc."[54] In August 1924, the day arrived. Out of thousands of examinees, Sartre was number seven. He had been admitted into l'Ecole Normale Supérieure, which Nizan, who also passed, soon dubbed the "allegedly Normal and supposedly Superior School."

Nizan denounced the school as "a laughable and more often tedious entity, presided over by a little old patriot, powerful and hypocritical, who admires the military." He condemned its inmates, presumably including Sartre and himself, as "adolescents who were worn out by years of lycée, corrupted by the humanities, morality, and bourgeois cooking." But Sartre was delighted to be so corrupted: "From the first day, the Ecole Normale was, for many of us, for me, the beginning of independence. Many can say, as I do, that they found four years of happiness there."[55]

The Loser

In his last year at l'Ecole Normale, Jean-Paul Sartre listened to the advice of an older student—and, objectively, made the worst mistake of his life. As it turned out, however, it was, subjectively, the best thing he ever did.

Until then, Sartre had loved l'Ecole Normale. One of France's most prestigious institutions, indeed unique in the whole world, the ENS, hiding behind a wrought-iron grill at 45 rue d'Ulm not far from Paris' ever-well-manicured Luxembourg garden, was not particularly impressive. A square building framing a square interior patio with its inevitable fountain, it was deemed a dump by some of its residents. Said one: "The School's material conditions of life are in total opposition to the most elementary hygienic concern. The dorm is almost never either swept nor even aired out. Dirt accumulates under the beds, impregnates personal belongings, and saturates the air we breathe. . . . One must wash under a tiny faucet in a filthy closet which is also used to clean shoes, store brooms, and pile up garbage . . . the badly-washed dishes, whose bottoms are always black, and the food-encrusted silverware are marvelous vehicles for germs."[1]

To Sartre, however, it was pretty idyllic: Room, board, tuition and books during four years in exchange for a ten-year teaching contract at decent prevailing wages. Each year, l'Ecole admitted twenty-five to study *Lettres* (humanities) and a few more in the sciences. The total student body was almost two hundred; some 60 percent were boarders; all were considered and thought themselves to be the chosen of the chosen. In Sartre's class were Raymond Aron, Albert Bédé, Georges Canguilhem, Daniel Lagache, Paul Nizan, Alfred Péron; the next year included Pierre Guille, Jean Hypolite, René Maheu, Jean Seznec; the one after that, Maurice Merleau-Ponty—all of whom became more or less famous.

"Until l'Ecole, I was a kept man, I was dominated by my father-in-law, a conservative *polytechnicien* who tried to push me into sciences. Now I was free to do what I wanted."[2] And what he wanted, he told Lagache later, was "to be the man who knows the most."[3] But the fact is, Sartre had never been dominated. Indeed, by any standard, he had been a spoiled brat. But he had been greatly influenced, then and ever after, by his grandfather. It was Charles who had imbued him with his protestant work-ethic, Charles who had convinced him to want to teach, Charles who immortalized books and taught him to seek his own immortality by writing them. It was from Charles that Sartre derived his notion of witness, a notion he shared with most of his ENS peers. Under prodding, Sartre did admit to me that both he and Charles felt similarly superior. "We were predestined by our temperaments, we thought, to be witness to the useless agitation of the world."[4]

In Sartre's head, this sense of being chosen was not elitist. "I never believed in talent, and I still don't," he said toward the end of his life. "I never believed that a writer had special privileges. Writing was simply having the patience, the will to write. Anyone could do it, though most are stopped by society from doing it. It's as if society creates people who are lost, who need to be saved. This society is made up of people who are fundamentally equal, but totally lost, and yet among them are some—who?—lucky ones, who have found the way to write to save not just themselves but save us all. Since our damnation was society's fault, and society was bourgeois, I had a profound contempt for the bourgeoisie."[5]

But Charles was also bourgeois, though the kind of bourgeoisie that Sartre held in contempt was Mancy's. "He was an aristocratic bourgeois, actually a middle-level salaried boss, but he revolted me. All his values were wrong. I was against him, against his side, whatever it was, and for the republican radical-socialists of my grandfather, who believed in freedom, in humanism."[6] Perhaps, yet Charles was just as elitist as Mancy. For example, when Sartre one day announced that he was engaged to a cousin he liked somewhat, Charles bellowed, "She's the daughter of a grocer!" And when Poincaré was opposed for the presidency of the republic by a paper manufacturer, it wasn't his political positions which angered Charles, it was his background. "A cigarette-paper merchant as president?!" he shouted, or so Sartre remembered in 1971.[7] Still, "as vague as was my class consciousness then," Sartre insisted, "I could see that the rich bourgeois were rich because they made workers work long and hard for minimal salaries. Their society disgusted me. But I didn't want to destroy it. I wanted to be uninvolved in it, detached, to be what I called in 'esthetic opposition,' that is, to write against it, refuse its terms, denounce its defenders, its rationalizers."[8]

At ENS, Sartre's "esthetic opposition" meant mostly ridicule of both those who had made it and those who were trying. Like one of the *normaliens* in Jules Romains's novel *Les Copains* (*The Buddies*), which he read at the time, Sartre reveled in creating farces, setting up traps, teasing his peers and teachers. "While I was fundamentally a pacifist, I did not shirk from violence to express my disdain for my fellow students who belonged and wanted to belong to the bourgeois system. For example, there was one idiot we called 'The Nietzschean' who used to claim that the suffering of the lower classes helped them develop. So when he came back early in the morning from some fiesta or party, all dolled up in a smoking, we would await him on the roof and drop balloons full of, well, er, water, or worse, on him, and yell, 'Thus pissed Zarathustra!' In fact, we used Nietzsche's 'water' to discomfort lots of idiots, we being a group of six or seven, sometimes as many as a dozen students, most of whom had been trained by Alain."* [9]

Only one of these students really mattered for Sartre during the first two years at ENS: Paul Nizan, his best friend from early lycée days. Sleeping side by side at the end of the long corridorlike dormitory, a curtain separating them from the rest, and sharing a study cubicle where they read and commented on everything imaginable from ancient philosophy to modern astronomy, avant-garde poetry to contemporary jazz, Sartre and Nizan remained inseparable, despite increasingly heavy disputes. For all that they themselves were elitists, chosen to be witnesses, "we hated those who went around saying, 'But there has to be someone to lead.' We accepted our fate, which was to be alone, since our job was to save mankind, but not because we were better; for if we were chosen, it was out of luck, what Nizan and I later called *contingency,* not superiority. I never had any doubts about my calling. Nizan did. Maybe because he was obsessed with death." [10]

Afraid of death, Nizan did not believe in freedom. Certain of his immortality, Sartre believed in nothing else. As the two friends walked through Paris, they talked of women, literature, "shop." Then, inevitably, the hapless fate of some poor worker or desperate bum faced them. To Nizan, the scene represented the lack of choices, man being doomed, and his own death. "Nizan would withdraw," Sartre related in our sixth interview. "He became mysterious, gloomy, distant. We didn't talk politics. I don't think he really translated his terror or his per-

---

*French philosopher and essayist who taught at the Lycée Henri IV, Alain (real name Emile Chartier, 1868–1951) gave impetus to many future intellectual anarchists by stressing the importance of individual conscience and the right of every citizen to resist abuses of power. Philosophically, however, he remained an idealist, influenced by Kant, and politically a radical-socialist, that is, petty bourgeois.

ceptions into the class struggle, not yet, but we were no longer on the same wavelength, even if we then got drunk together or went to the gym and boxed."[11]

They did not get drunk out of frustration. "When we decided to go on a binge, we really did, to the point of rolling on the floor, maybe once every fifteen days or so, but not out of depression. For me, it was to empty or purify myself, to get rid of all that tension from all that work." And work they did.

"There were a couple of professors from the Sorbonne who came to us, but normally we were to go to them. I never went. Except for a guy called Bréhier, who did an excellent course on the Stoics, and a certain Georges Dumas, who delivered his psychology lectures at the Sainte-Anne hospital, most of the teachers were terrible bores. So I stayed at the school and worked in my cubicle, from 8:00 to 1:00, then 4:00 to 9:00, every day, weekends included. I never went to the Sorbonne or to the classes at l'Ecole Normale. The teachers were just plain retrogrades. There had been one guy, dead by then, who had set the tone for philosophical studies in France at the beginning of the century, who had stated categorically that if any student even just mentioned the name Hegel, he would never let him get his *agrégation*. Jules Lachelier was his name. He was a so-called critical idealist, but I would simply call him an ass. Trouble is, he had a great deal of influence, including on Léon Brunschvicg who totally dominated French philosophical thought while I was at l'Ecole. In Brunschvicg's three-volume *Le Progrès de la conscience dans la philosophie occidentale,** which is like three volumes of the history of philosophy, there's not one word on Marx and barely three pages on Hegel in the third volume. The whole curriculum of philosophy was a farce."[12]

Nevertheless, it was philosophy that interested Sartre the most at ENS.

"I got hooked on philosophy through Bergson while still in lycée. Not that he was right. On the contrary, it didn't take me too long to understand that he too believed in talent, special privileges, inspired insights, and all that. But his thrust was crucial for me. He showed that knowledge begins with intuition, that we must 'seize the world,' so to speak. Philosophy explains these intuitions. To communicate them, one had to resort to some other discipline—literature. So I decided to study philosophy and teach philosophy, but not to be a philosopher, that is

---

* *The Progress of Conscience in Occidental Philosophy* was published while Sartre was a student at ENS (1927).

someone who writes works of philosophy. I was going to be a writer in order to communicate the realities that the study of philosophy made me grasp. I was still denying that I would ever write a philosophical work when I met Castor, in 1929, so that when I suddenly decided I wanted to write something on the intentionality of consciousness, she advised me not to. 'You're mad,' she said, 'express your ideas through literature.' She was right, of course, at the time. My first philosophical work* ended up a long paraphrase of Husserl's view of consciousness. I threw it away and wrote instead a short essay on Husserl."[13]

That was later. Meanwhile, Sartre pushed on—by himself. Well, not quite. Nizan too had committed himself to philosophy. "We never talked about that decision, which we made independently of each other. It just happened. He was a materialist. I was still an idealist, I guess. But we read the same books and agreed on most of them. We loved Descartes, Spinoza, the Stoics, Hume somewhat, Kant much more. We found a great deal to discuss in Plato but were bored by Aristotle. Rousseau fascinated us. I don't remember what Nizan thought of Freud, but I dismissed his determinism without fully understanding him. Meanwhile of course, I kept reading novels. Zola didn't interest me. The surrealists did. Stendhal was my favorite; I wanted to be a modern-day Stendhal. But then Nizan and I discovered Kafka, Joyce, Cervantes. And crowds! We loved crowds. We spent whole days inter-mingling with the workers of the suburbs, the professionals near the rue d'Ulm. Our whole life style changed: we now had a necessity to link our reading with the world out there."

The result was what they called a *new naturalism*. What they meant was realism. "In effect, it was nothing more than a way of challenging or contesting all the idealism that had been dumped into our heads, the sort of mystifications philosophers like to spout, like 'A tree is not just a tree,' or something I remember having read at the time, 'Love is much more than just love.' To this nonsense we simply answered, 'Love is love, a cat is a cat.' This is obvious enough, but when you apply it to human relations or endeavors, such simplicity can be quite violent. For example, 'A jerk is a jerk' tends to eliminate his relevance at any level, doesn't it? How about 'God is a word expressing man's desire for expla-nations?' That tends to destroy all the religious, all the mystical crap—except for the ritual, which is man's way of expressing his need for

---

* Not quite. His first philosophical work was an awkward treatise on Descartes, followed by a hefty "L'Image dans la vie psychologique: rôle et nature" for his diploma of *études superieures* (more or less equivalent to a master's degree).

collective togetherness. To say, as we did then, 'I think, therefore I am," was not merely to mouth Descartes' famous rationalistic starting point, it was also to ban all supernatural claptrap from meaningful discourse."[14]

It also helped them eliminate all extenuating circumstances for their teachers' idiocy. Indeed, Sartre dismissed most of them, and the director of ENS, almost from the start. He did it publicly, but with humor. It was the tradition at ENS that every year the students presented a revue in which they kidded teachers, administrators, and each other. In March 1925, Sartre wrote, directed, and starred in a musical skit lampooning ENS director Gustave Lanson, a highly-reputed literary historian who, like sociologist Emile Durkheim, pretended that "objective" scientific research is possible in their discipline only by scrutinizing official documents. Bearded and proudly sporting a Legion of Honor medal, five-foot-two Sartre played a Lanson seduced by wealth, represented by a rich, gaudy, languishing Brazilian femme fatale, Doña Ferentes, played by six-footer Daniel Lagache. Attended by students, faculty, and Lanson himself, as well as ENS graduates Edouard Herriot, then prime minister, and Paul Painlevé, then head of the Chamber of Deputies and future prime minister, the play was risqué but hilarious, and within traditional ENS burlesque standards.

So was the 1926 revue, which won actor Sartre praise in the press.[15] But in 1927, Sartre let loose all his venom at the bourgeois state. With Canguilhem, Péron and other pacifist pals, he attacked France's militarists and the country's jingoistic patriotism with what he himself characterized happily and approvingly, as "repugnant obscenity."[16] To the tune of *La Marseillaise,* for example, one student, decked out as a captain, lamented in rhyme that

> I opted for this career
> When this trade was great and dear
> For one could hope that war was near
> And earn plenty of stripes and cheer.[17]

A chorus then claimed that deputies, senators, and government officials would all rejoice from such a war, and the rich of course get richer.

To most students, parents, and faculty, certainly to the press, and to Lanson himself, who had lost a son in 1914, Sartre's 1927 revue had gone too far. But Sartre was unremorseful. One day a few weeks later, after Lindbergh had successfully crossed the Atlantic, Sartre telephoned Paris newspapers to "inform" them that the aviator would be feted as an

Honorary Student at 9:30 A.M. His calls brought five hundred journalists and thousands of the curious to the rue d'Ulm, where they "saw him" (a student who looked like him) being carried aloft by Sartre and Company. "The public fell for it, and an old man even kissed his hand," Sartre wrote a friend at the time. The scandal, once exposed, pushed Lanson, who in the aftermath of the revue was severely despondent, to resign.[18]

Sartre, Canguilhem, Lagache, and Nizan were considered the school's tough guys. "But," said Sartre, "we weren't, really. We were moralists. We couldn't stand hypocrisy, at school, in the government, out there."[19] They were certainly not political (except perhaps for Nizan, who didn't translate his concern into activity until the end of 1927). "Sartre was not at all interested in politics," Raymond Aron told me in 1973. "In general, he simply considered reality abominable. He wanted a total change, without being a revolutionary. He was a rebel, in the way a writer or a philosopher might be, without being interested enough in politics to even consider revolution. 'What happens if it comes?' I asked him once. He answered, 'I'll work with it, I'll teach.' He was full of good will, naiveté, a moralist, always a moralist."[20] In his *Memoirs* (published ten years later), Aron added: "If he rarely discussed politics at the time, he already hated privileges. Those who defined their own rights based on their competence or leadership positions [he called] 'the scums' (*les salauds*). . . . He imposed himself on me by his inventiveness, by the richness of his intellectual imagination. But his passions and his moralism, often self-serving, limited his vision."[21]

Aron was "much too distinguished to be part of us," Sartre said. "We were verbally violent, brutal, vulgar. Aron not at all. He was Socialist, because his father was Socialist, the kind of Socialist that a rich man can be. He hated crowds, he hated subways because they smelled of the mass. That kind of a Socialist, a Social Democrat. He damned our excesses. But still, he was drawn to us. We talked philosophy or literature. But he was not a boarder and didn't go out with us, or get drunk, or join our buffooneries—or our sexual exploits."[22]

Most of the sexual exploits enjoyed by Sartre during his four years at ENS as a boarder (1924–28) were casual. "There were all sorts of women hanging around us," he recounted, "not whores, but women who enjoyed going out with us, all of our group, and were not necessarily infatuated with just one. Oh, there was the wife of a café owner who preferred Nizan, and a formidable black woman who preferred me. But by and large, we all benefited from this arrangement. Except

Larroutis. He was extremely Catholic and convinced he should be a virgin when he married. It drove him crazy, of course, and he would drink
more than any of us to quash his frustration. He was very funny, and we
liked him a lot. Anyway, these women would sneak past the concièrge
and end up in our cubicles. One day one of us, another day another.
There was no possessiveness, no jealousy."[23]

The exception was "Camille," Simone-Camille Sans, known later pro-
fessionally as Simone Jollivet, a cousin by marriage whom Sartre met at
the Thiviers funeral of another cousin in 1925. Simone de Beauvoir,
who met her a few years later, described her most eloquently in *The
Prime of Life*.

She was a beautiful woman, with vastly long blonde hair, blue eyes, a delicate
complexion, an alluring figure, and perfect wrists and ankles. Her father owned
a pharmacy in Toulouse. She was an only child; but while she was still a baby
her mother had adopted a pretty little gypsy girl called Zina, who afterward
became Camille's follower, accomplice, and even, as Camille was fond of saying,
her slave. . . . [Camille] marveled at the way she contrived to possess both
beauty and intelligence, and at the exceptional level which each attained in her.
She vowed she would attain a destiny quite out of the ordinary. To start with,
she turned to the sphere of sexual intrigue. When a child, she had been patiently
deflowered by a friend of the family; at the age of eighteen she began to frequent fashionable *maisons de rendez-vous*. She would say goodnight to her
mother (of whom she was very fond) with great tenderness, make a pretense of
going to bed, and then slip out with Zina. . . . Camille possessed an acute sense
of the appropriate *mise en scène;* while awaiting a client in the room set apart for
him, she would stand in front of the fireplace stark naked, her long hair combed
out, reading Michelet or, at a later period, Nietzsche. Her cultured mind, her
proud bearing, and the subtle technique she brought to her task knocked town
clerks and lawyers flat: they wept on her pillow from sheer admiration. Some of
them established a more permanent relationship with her, showered her with
presents, and took her on their travels. She dressed very expensively, but chose
her clothes less from the current fashion than from pictures which happened to
catch her fancy: her room resembled a theatrical set for an opera. She threw
parties in the cellar, which she transformed, according to circumstances, into a
Renaissance palace or medieval château.[24]

When Sartre and Camille met at the funeral, he "was rigged out in a
dark suit and wearing one of his stepfather's hats, which came nearly
down to his eyebrows; boredom made his face expressionless, and gave
him an aggressively ugly appearance. Camille was thunderstruck. 'It's
Mirabeau,' she muttered to herself. Her own beauty had taken on a
somewhat crazy quality under its black mourning crepe, and she had no

trouble in arousing his interest. They stayed together for four whole days, at the end of which period, they were hooked back by their worried families. Camille was being courted at the time by the son of a wealthy furnace manufacturer, and had toyed with the idea of marrying him; but she had no more intention of becoming a reputable middle-class housewife than of remaining a tart. Sartre convinced her that he alone could save her from provincial mediocrity."[25]

But to do so, he would have to see her, and she lived in Toulouse. Although the families of Sartre and Aron were the only ones rich enough to cause the ENS to cancel their allowances (the state normally allotted each ENS student one hundred francs per month spending money, a fair sum in those days), Sartre was always broke, since he refused to take Mancy's money. And while he did give private lessons to lycée baccalaureate candidates, he still could afford the journey to Toulouse only every five weeks or so. On one such visit, Sartre noticed in Camille's dressing room four bottles, each identified only by one letter; he meant to ask what the letters represented, then forgot. On a subsequent visit, however, he noticed five such bottles, and the fifth was marked *J-P.* Each contained a different perfume. Sartre blew his stack, demanding Camille immediately discard her other four lovers.

"What? Do you own me?" she fired back. "Am I supposed to sit here and wait for your *occasional* appearances? How dare you expect me to conform to your wishes; do you conform to mine? Are you prepared to abandon l'Ecole Normale? To move to Toulouse? To take me around the world?"

Sartre hesitated. "I paced back and forth in her lush, heavily-scented bedroom thinking over what she had said," he told me, "but not too long, for she was right, of course, and I knew it. I concluded that jealousy *is* possessiveness. *Therefore,* I decided never to be jealous again."[26]

Ah yes, there it was, that famous *donc* (therefore), the most important word in the rationalist's lexicon.

"My relationship with Camille was my first serious affair," said Sartre, "and it was an unhappy one. She was in Toulouse, I in Paris. She was free in her behavior, I was still somewhat straight-laced. She was materially demanding, I was broke. I had to borrow and beg from my comrades, which was very embarrassing. But I was saved by the fact that I never let her demands or the affair itself interfere with my own tasks, with my destiny."[27] Oh, but it did, so much so that he wrote a very pretentious novel about that affair.

Entitled appropriately *Une défaite* (*A Defeat*), of which only one section (*Empédocle*) of some one hundred pages survived, the novel was meant to be a modern-day retelling of the Richard Wagner-Cosima Wagner-Friedrich Nietzsche love triangle. Richard, a famous but aging composer and writer, married to Cosima, a mysterious, youthful femme fatale, hires as a tutor to his children Fréderic, a twenty-three-year-old philosophy student enrolled in "the greatest" of all schools. Fréderic (Sartre) falls in love with Cosima (Camille) but cannot domesticate her to his liking and laments that he "feels predestined to suffer" in life (Sartre's martyr complex). The novel pays homage to Richard, who could easily though coincidentally represent Charles Dullin, one of the period's great theater actors and directors, whom Camille coveted at the time of her affair with Sartre and whom she eventually did seduce, remaining his mistress and star for years thereafter. Overwritten and tedious, *Empédocle* nevertheless was full of self-revelations. It described Sartre as a ferocious games-player, who broke with one mistress, Geneviève, by writing her an obscene letter. He revealed himself incapable of giving—or of accepting. Cold and calculating, Fréderic at one point asks himself if he would marry Cosima were Richard to die: "This manner of considering the question, which may appear naive, was extremely useful. By it he eliminated [Richard] and focused totally on Cosima, isolating her from all that went with her. That was the way to solve the problem, just as mathematicians, dealing with theorems, complicate or simplify the equations on which they work. Thus, to Fréderic, Cosima alone lost all interest. 'I would not marry her,' he thought, 'I would forget her just as I forgot Geneviève.' He understood that Cosima was part of an indissoluble bloc to which his love was addressed. He fused [Richard] and his wife."[28]

A *Defeat* also seemed to predict the defeat of his friendship with Nizan. While he characterized him as "ever present," Sartre described him as "*l'Ancien Ami,*" which in French connotes either an old or a former friend or both. "Their friendship was always a struggle. But at least, back when they were virgins and feeble, their weakness itself and the feeling of their future strength united them against the world which they timidly despised. Love and their half-realization of their ambitions separated them. Each loved elsewhere now, and their battles, their triumphs were no longer on the same ground." From these revelations, Sartre at twenty-two concluded that "no one can accept being impenetrable. That others are impenetrable, who cares. But each wants to be revealed. All men need a witness. Some invent conscience. Others cannot think without telling everyone what they think and try to be transparent. Others still become irrational, imagining gentle and pretty girls looking into their hearts. And all that is God, God spread among men."[29]

A Defeat was not Sartre's only writing while a student at ENS. In addition to the musical comedies which he staged at the school, he also wrote short stories, critical essays, and original philosophical treatises, each of which gave clear hints to where he was heading. Already in the short story about his friendship with Nizan, *La Semence et le scaphandre,* which he dashed off the year before entering ENS, Sartre revealed an amazing understanding of the fickleness of socialist intellectuals. In that story, the director of a new magazine dedicated to publishing youthful dissident views is a self-taught socialist who bewails the fact that "literature is becoming the domain of the careerists, of the businessmen, of the sugardaddies' sons," then sells out to them completely. The man who inspired Sartre to write such a portrayal was in real life Charle(s) Fraval, the editor of *La Revue sans Titre* (*The Magazine without a Title*), where both Sartre and Nizan published early works. In 1931, Fraval was both a pacifist and a Socialist; ten years later he was violently anti-Semite, profascist, and advocated the sacred union of France and Germany.[30]

More important among his ENS works was a long (some three hundred pages) essay on the image, which served later as an outline for his major early philosophical volumes, *Imagination* (1936), *Psychology of the Imagination* (1940), and *Being and Nothingness* (1943). Written in 1927, this essay concluded, long before Sartre was even aware of the views of the German phenomenologists, that "to think, feel, suffer, is to be conscious of our bodies in movement, with an understanding that gives immediate intention and value to these movements." He reached that conclusion by giving a rigidly empirical description of each act of looking at an event, deriving the process from the relationship between the looker and what was being looked at. The process revealed choice: an active decision by the ego. Sartre was thus defining people as beings conscious not only of their actions but of their visions as well: people were responsible for the way they looked at the world. At twenty-two, the young Sartre was already linking choice (freedom) with responsibility.[31]

In September 1926, meanwhile, Paul Nizan left l'Ecole Normale and, as tutor to a rich merchant's son, journeyed to Aden. He returned to ENS a year later, totally transformed. Wrote Sartre: "We regulars of the Ecole Normale were shocked by his departure, but, as Nizan intimidated us, we found a harmless explanation for it: love of travel. When he returned the following year, in the middle of the night, no one expected him. I was alone in my study. The misbehavior of a girl from the provinces [Camille] had plunged me, since the day before, into pained indignation. He came in without knocking. He was pale, grim, a little out of breath. He said to me, 'You don't look very cheerful.' To which I replied, 'Neither do you.' With which we went off drinking, and put the world on trial, delighted that our friendship had resumed. But it was only a misunderstanding. My anger was only a bar of soap, his was real. He gagged on the horror of returning to his cage, and entered it undone. He was looking for help that no one could give him. His words of hate were pure gold, mine was counterfeit." [32]

A rebel and an anarchist, Paul Nizan sought that help first on the extreme right (in a group led by a certain Georges Valois who talked about "thinking clearly" as Norman Podhoretz or Jerry Falwell do today), then on the extreme left: he joined the Communist Party and teamed up with its young philosophers—Henri Lefebvre, Georges Friedmann, Georges Politzer, Norbert Guterman, and Pierre Morhange. Having failed to buy an island on which they hoped to establish a philosophy center, these young committed intellectuals had already twice launched radical magazines (*Philosophies,* March 1924–March 1925, and *L'Esprit,* May 1926–January 1927). Now they were conniving to unleash another (which would be *La Revue Marxiste,* February 1929–September 1929). Hoping to show that Communism was as progressive and positive as the natural sciences, these young writers saw themselves as the heirs of Diderot and the French Encyclopedists, proclaiming, in the words of Politzer, then recognized as the most brilliant of the early French Marxists, that "materialism is no more than the scientific understanding of the universe." [33]

It has been claimed that Sartre never understood Nizan. Certainly, Nizan's main biographies make that claim outright. [34] But the fact is that to this day all such biographies have been based on interviews and interpretations offered by Nizan's wife, Henriette, known as Rirette, and none reveal the extent to which she hated Sartre and Castor. They, in turn, felt acute contempt for their friend's widow and considered her so bourgeois that she clearly belonged to the enemy camp. In 1927, however, Nizan and Sartre were so close that Nizan asked him (and Raymond Aron) to be his witnesses: Nizan had decided to get married.

"He just couldn't stay still," Sartre said about his friend. "He wanted to leave l'Ecole Normale at all costs; it weighed heavily on him. I was having a ball, but he was going through some kind of neuroses. He wanted to reverse his father's trajectory, you know, going from being a bourgeois back to a proletarian. He wanted to be a cameraman or simply a projectionist, some manual job. He considered his father, like Antoine Bloyé, a traitor to the working class. He had met Rirette before he left for Aden. In fact, they were already engaged, claiming to be madly in love. But in our cubicle he had hung up a huge fever chart on which he would register, everyday, the intensity of that love, and it never went very high. Although she was the spoiled daughter of a banker, I liked her a lot then. She was a good comrade. We used to go out together, the three of us, and later, she would join us, Guille, Maheu, Castor, and me. She fitted into our group. Nizan's fever chart went up and up, but it was mostly physical love. Then he went to Aden, just like that, without discussing it with Rirette, a nasty blow for her."[35]

According to the letters he wrote Rirette, Nizan was fully aware of his craziness. He apologized for his moodiness, explained his restlessness as being unable to sit still with himself, warned her he might flee into a monastery one day. But while his letters to her were loving ("You are the best tonic I know"), to his ENS friends he bragged of his various other affairs.[36] He married Rirette on Christmas eve 1927 and that very night was rushed to a hospital with an acute attack of appendicitis, which was "so bad he was out of action for three months, the first month cliniging to a hair separating life from death."[37]

Nizan returned from Aden even more enraged. Now profoundly anticolonial, he hated not only his government and his country's ruling cliques, but his professors as well. Sartre and Nizan had long thought of them as "created by God or nature as old, tiny, wrinkled pedants who understood nothing about life," Sartre said jokingly, stressing the contradiction inherent in someone who believed neither in essences nor God, "but now Nizan looked at their social conditions and their benefits, and concluded that our profs were all running dogs of capitalism."[38] In 1932, Nizan indeed published a whole book about them. Called *The Watchdogs* in French and in its English translations, the original did in fact connote *running dogs*.

Discarding the claim of scholars to be "objective" and "neutral," Nizan understood long before Sartre that not to choose is a choice. Wrote Nizan: "To abstain is to make a choice, to express a preference. It requires making a broad value judgment (though this is rarely spelled out) and taking a definite position." He added, in a remark as aptly true today as it was then: "The philosophers are satisfied. These men, the products of bourgeois democracy, express their gratitude by fashioning whatever myths this democracy may require: they elaborate a democratic philosophy. This regime seems to them the best of all possible worlds. It is extremely difficult for them even to conceive of the possibility that other worlds may exist. . . . The audacity of their philosophy consists in identifying human society—all possible human societies—with bourgeois society, and human reason—all possible forms of human reason—with bourgeois reason. And, one might add, human morality with bourgeois morality."[39]

Convinced that "every bourgeois considers himself one of the elect,"[40] which Sartre took as a personal dig, Nizan scoffed at the bourgeois defense of reason, and hence in passing at Sartre's rationalism. Wrote Nizan: "Because Reason has been invested with quasi-religious character, bourgeois thought can always make a dignified retreat to the safe havens of religious faith. This Reason does not produce a life after death. Moreover, the bourgeois thinker reserves the right to invoke some God to serve as Reason's guarantor."[41] Was Nizan deliberately confusing Sartre's rationalism, which Nizan also shared, with the logic used by the ruling class as a tool to dominate its lower classes? As early as 1926, in a letter to Camille, Sartre had well understood that such a logic is a function of power. "Give up logic!" he had written his beloved. "It never helped anyone. Try to avoid contradictions as much as possible but if you end up with one, don't be afraid; it won't bite. There are so many of them! The five or six great philosophers, which university programs forced me to study this year and who were very acceptable people, thrive in contradictions. It doesn't bother them one bit. . . . Logic is the bread-earner of impotent intellectuals."[42]

But Nizan was not out to get Sartre. His targets were mostly his old teachers. He focused on Brunschvicg, the most important philosopher of his day: "I do not see why M. Brunschvig would ever desert the party of the bourgeosie and rally to the cause of mankind. After all, he is a rather clear-sighted individual and he knows well the price of prosperity. . . . What reasons would M. Brunschvicg have had for even flirting with dangerous ideas? His life has nothing difficult or tragic about it; there were never any agonizing problems to overcome.* . . . It is im-

---

*Indeed, Brunschvicg had written the following in *Bulletin de l'Union pour la Verité*, no. 3 (1929): "I am a taxpayer; and not only am I a taxpayer, I am also a man who likes being protected by patrolmen; I am a man who is obliged to tolerate, if you will, the existence of a secret police force (an organization the existence of which cannot, perhaps, always be frankly acknowledged) to guarantee his security. Nevertheless, I do tolerate its existence, and consequently, not a day passes that I am not guilty of a certain pharisaism,

possible for these bourgeois thinkers to get to the heart of the problem of the common man. They can deal with it only in the most superficial manner. Their knowledge of it is pitifully inadequate, for they obtain their information through hearsay alone. They do not feel its crushing weight or the sense of desperation and the terrible anxiety it engenders. They make no attempt to examine it in depth. They simply accommodate themselves, passively, to the fact that the problem exists—somewhere far away."[44]

But it was not only his teachers whom he attacked. Nizan was angry at the whole liberal education system, to which he referred simply as *Philosophy*. He wrote: "Its mission is to gain universal acceptance for the established order by making it palatable, by conferring upon it a certain nobility, and by furnishing rationalizations for its every aspect." (Were he writing today, he might have said, "by pretending to defend academic freedom, fair employment, civil liberties, and the right to privacy.") Thus, he went on, the system "mystifies the victims of the bourgeois regime, all those who might some day rise up against it," convincing them that imperialism or exploitation "is not an evil in itself. . . . The deviations, atrocities, assassinations, expropriations, insults to native pride . . . in no way detract from the dignity of true colonialism" or the lust for profits. Then, with amazing foresight, Nizan predicted that "it will not be long before the socialists, the latest addition to the ranks of the bourgeois thought-mongers, will be extremely proficient at manipulating these nuances." The reason? "A State cannot rely solely on the timely application of brute force by its judges, soldiers, functionaries, and policemen. It also requires more subtle means of domination."[45]

Concluded Nizan: "The whole parasitic existence of this philosophy is a constant assault upon the lives of those men who, through some accident of birth or fortune, find themselves outside the gates of bourgeoisdom. It is time for us to declare that human needs, that human life itself, is absolutely incompatible with the values, the virtues, the hopes, and the self-serving wisdom of the bourgeoisie. He who serves the

---

for which a man like me might well be reproached. But, actually, it is as if I were clothed in a series of sheaths. There is the sheath of the bourgeois, of the taxpayer, of the professor, of whatever you wish. But there remains something more: the inner me, who is striving to break out of these sheaths." "How do we know since he never succeeds?" asked Nizan, and answered: "Those forces on which he leans so heavily—the patrolmen and the secret police of our philosopher-taxpayer, our philosopher-bourgeois, our philosopher-professor—are the very forces which have tormented men for so long."[43]

bourgeoisie cannot serve mankind." He stated in the last lines of his *The Watchdogs,* "Our most distinguished philosophers are still too ashamed to admit that they have betrayed mankind for the sake of the bourgeoisie. If we betray the bourgeoisie for the sake of mankind, let us not be ashamed to admit that we are traitors."[46]

Nizan's ENS buddies were shocked. Said René Maheu, the future head of UNESCO: "We were taken by complete surprise. I mean, we knew that Nizan was enraged, that he hated all forms of conventional behavior, but he himself was always so elegant. . . . What his ferocious attacks revealed most to me was the depth and authenticity of his anguish. It made me remember that it was Nizan who had made me discover Kafka and Cicero. He was our precursor, our discoverer. He had such natural grace, such apparent intellectual ease, and behind it all, such anguish. But you see, our ambitions were reversed. He came from a bourgeois background and sought to return to his family's proletarian roots. I was very poor. My grandfather, my father had all been provincial workers. My goal in life was never to be like them. My first concern was never to be a proletarian."[47]

Aron too was shocked, although "I really liked *Aden-Arabie,*" Nizan's first book which described not only the brutishness of British colonialism but also the stifling life at l'Ecole Normale.[48] But Sartre was upset by both works. Nizan had written that "we were 'adolescents who were worn out by years of lycée, corrupted by the humanities, morality and bourgeois cooking.' We decided to take this as a joke. We would say: 'Now, really, he didn't spit on the Ecole when he was there. Then, he really had a good time, with all those worn out adolescents.' And remembering all our clever pranks, we recalled that he had participated in them wholeheartedly. Forgetting his moods, his scorn, the great uprooting which carried him to Arabia, we saw in his anger only exaggerated rhetoric. For my part, though, I was foolishly hurt; he had tarnished my memories. Since Nizan had shared my life at the Ecole, he had to have been happy there, or else our friendship must have already been dead at the time. I preferred to salvage the past. I said to myself, 'He is exaggerating.'"[49]

"When I think of it now," Sartre told me in 1971, "I realize that Nizan could have thought that the school stunk all along. We never discussed it. He was always very mysterious about his innermost preoccupations."[50] While Sartre always wrote about his own experiences and described anecdotes of his own life, thus was much more willing to talk about his dreams and desires, Nizan, "more discreet and more of a builder, preferred to remain impersonal. I did not want to save our society; I was perfectly willing to throw bombs at it, or, to be honest, to cheer someone else doing it. That's as far as any of my thoughts about the future actually went. Nizan hated our society as much as I did, but he dreamt of building a new one. I think that he was so terrified of death that he kept looking for god, but his kind of god, one here on earth, namely a just society. Read carefully *Aden-Arabie,* you'll see. Nizan, who did not believe in freedom, thought we could change the world and he wanted to be identified with the new man, to be part of *Him.* Underline and put a capital *H* when you write that, because it's the same kind of *Him* as when they talk of Christ or God Himself."[51]

Whatever their differences, Sartre and Nizan retained their friendship after the latter returned from Aden. While he had been away, Aron had moved into Sartre's cubicle and the two had worked hard to get ready for their great final exam—the *agrégation*. Sartre even attended a few classes. According to Aron, it was in Brunschvicg's class that Sartre, answering the question, "Was Nietzsche a philosopher?" presented his ideas on contingency.[52] But already in 1926, Sartre had written Camille: "The weather here is the kind you like: rain and wind. Perfect to write on Contingency."[53] What Sartre proceeded to explain to her, in a letter which was lost, is that there are two kinds of facts or conditions in the world: those that are unavoidable, like gravity, the rotation of the earth, parents, a digestive system, all of which are necessary for our existence, and those that are the result of luck or accident, like the bomb falling on this house rather than that one, or tripping on a run for the bus causing one to miss it and then meeting the love of one's life on the next one; events which, from the subject's point of view, are totally the result of chance—contingency. Without the necessary events of our lives there can be no freedom, said Sartre, for the word would have no meaning if we could be both tall and blue-eyed and small and blind, if we could fly in the heavens and swim in the deep simultaneously. Freedom demands choices, and the act of choosing is meaningful only if it is made in context, that is, within parameters, limits, conditions. Freedom is possible and necessary only because we live in concrete situations.

But what kind of meaning can life have if most of what happens to us is contingent—accidental, arbitrary, unforeseeable? Is life therefore devoid of meaning, "absurd" as later "existentialists" would be accused of claiming? In 1928, Sartre seem to think so. He wrote:

It is a paradox of the human mind that Man, whose business it is to create the necessary conditions, cannot raise himself above a certain level of existence, like those fortune-tellers who can tell the other people's fortunes but not their own. . . . It's not that Man does not think of himself as a *being*. On the contrary, he devotes all his energies to becoming one. Whence derive our ideas of Good and Evil, ideas of men working to improve Man. But these concepts are useless. Useless, too, is the determinism which oddly enough attempts to create a synthesis of existence and being. We are as free as you like, but helpless. . . . For the rest, the will to power, action, and life are only useless ideologies. There is no such thing as the will to power. Everything is too weak: all things carry the seeds of their own death . . .[54]

One day in 1928, contingency struck Sartre in the face—hard. By pure accident, he had run into the student who had been first in the competitive exam the year before. "'Be careful,' he told me, 'what they like is originality. You gotta interest them.' What I failed to take into account, though, was that this guy was totally banal, so that what was the epitome of originality for him would have been no more than a re-hash, perhaps in his own language, of what the examining professors thought themselves. But I fell for it. I gave them my ideas, not theirs. And boy, did they let me have it. My grades were among the very worst."[55] Aron was first; Emmanuel Mounier, who would become France's best-known Catholic philosopher, was second. Sartre was number fifty. It is said that Aron danced a jig atop of his hat in joyful ecstasy, not just because he was first, but because Sartre had failed.[56] To me he said simply: "Sartre didn't play the game."[57] Simone de Beauvoir, who had not yet met but knew all about Jean-Paul Sartre, was stunned. She was a student at the Sorbonne and was also studying for *l'agréga-tion*, a year behind Sartre. "I had heard all sorts of stories about him, mostly that he was a terror but absolutely brilliant. From everything I heard about him, I just could not believe that he had flunked."[58]

But Sartre could. "I knew I had written one of the best exam papers ever presented for *l'agrégation*," he told me. "It was the best lesson I ever got. It made me realize how totally immoral and rotten was the bourgeois system. Not that these 'learned' clerks were deliberately vindictive. Not at all. Besides, the papers are numbered in such a way that the graders have no idea whose exam was written by whom. No, what I mean is that when you play the game long enough—and you have to if you want to make it to the top, and only that top gets to judge *agreg* students—your soul, your whole being becomes so imbued with bourgeois values that you can no longer recognize originality or have any tolerance for ideas not your own."[59] During the Third Republic, Vincent Descombes explained in 1979, "the State invested university philosophy with a mission: to teach its students the legitimacy of the new republican institutions. Two doctrines were offered for this task: the sociological positivism of Durkheim and the neo-Kantian rationalism (. . . later incarnated by Brunschvicg). . . . [Today, in France's Fifth Republic, the two candidates are the structuralism of Levi-Strauss, Lacan, and even Foucault and the neo-liberalism of Raymond Aron. In both cases, more or less] it is the latter which finally won."[60] Said Sartre in 1974: "I never forgot that lesson, which is just as true today as it was then, even if I ignored it occasionally."[61]

He did not ignore it for his second try at *l'agrégation*. Moving out of l'Ecole Normale, where he never set foot again, Sartre rented a room at the Cité Universitaire (university student hall) and went back to writing. He wrote *Epiméthée,* a play about Greek gods fighting over human fates with poets, writers and artists; *Er l'Arménien,* a story which tried to explain his views on contingency; with Nizan, he helped edit the translation of Karl Jaspers's *General Psychopathology;* and he began *The Legend of Truth,* a three-part philosophical allegory which tried to show that science, the product of collective efforts, establishes commerce and democracy, while philosophy, the result of solitary meanderings, discovers truths but imposes tyranny. But mostly he studied for his exams. With Aron gone, his collaborators were now Nizan, who had lost a year because of his travels and illness, and René Maheu and Pierre Guille who had been a year behind.

Simone de Beauvoir explained what they were like in the four-hour interview film, *Sartre,* a documentary made by Alexandre Astruc and Michel Contat.

They came to very few lectures because they despised *sorbonnards* and the courses offered at the Sorbonne, and so among us *sorbonnards* we talked of them as terrible men, who had contempt for things and hence no soul. Sartre was considered the worst because, it was said, he was a womanizer, a drunk, and very nasty. They all looked very different. Nizan was always a dandy, with golf pants, very chic. Maheu very bourgeois. He was well married, and dressed with perfect bourgeois elegance. And Sartre was not dressed at all. He'd show up with open shirts, more or less clean, with more or less slippers, as if he were inside l'Ecole Normale still. We looked upon him with a kind of terror. No one dared talk to him, and they did not address us a single word. But I met Maheu at the National Library and through him Sartre, of whom he spoke with total admiration. 'He never stops thinking, he thinks all the time, he's extraordinary,' which of course intrigued me a great deal, and it was Maheu who brought me to the Cité Universitaire to prepare the exam. That's how I started becoming intimate with them."[62]

"She appealed to me," Sartre told me. "I wanted to meet her, but Maheu was in love with her, and very jealous. He kept her for himself. When we were together, he would not even nod to her in fear of then being forced to introduce her. And she was in love with Maheu; in fact, he was her first lover, so she wasn't in a particular hurry to meet us."[63] This is not quite what Castor writes in her memoirs. She found Maheu

amusing. I was very conscious of the charm of his mocking voice, and of the ironical twist he gave to his mouth. Weary of gazing upon the gray mass of students, I found his pink face with its baby-blue eyes very refreshing; his blond hair seemed as tough and springy as grass. . . . We used to talk chiefly about the little world we both belonged to: our friends, our professors, the competition. . . . He made my head swim with his anecdotes, with unexpected juxtapositions. He could handle everything—bombast and dry wit, lyricism and cynicism, naïveté and insolence—with such happy ease that nothing he said ever seemed banal. But the most irrestible thing about him was his laugh. [Still,] I was dismayed by the triviality of his ambitions, by his respect for certain conventions, and sometimes by his aestheticism; I would tell myself that if we had both been free, I should never have wanted to link my life with his; I saw love as a total engagement: therefore I was not in love with him.[64]

Ah, yes, that rationalist *therefore* again.

After they had taken the written section of the *agrégation* exam, the result of which they would not learn for weeks, Sartre invited Castor to join him and his friends to prepare for the orals.

I was feeling a bit scared when I entered Sartre's room; there were books all over the place, cigarette butts in all the corners, and the air was thick with tobacco smoke. Sartre greeted me in a worldly manner; he was smoking a pipe. Nizan, who said nothing, had a cigarette stuck in the corner of his one-sided smile and was quizzing me through his thick lenses, with an air of thinking more than he cared to say. All day long, petrified with fear, I commented on the 'metaphysical treatise' [of Leibnitz]. . . . I came back each day, and soon I began to thaw out. Leibnitz was boring, so we decided that we knew enough about him. Sartre took it upon himself to expound Rousseau's *Social Contract*, on which he had very decided opinions. To tell the truth, it was always he who knew most about all the authors and all the aspects of our syllabus: we merely listened to him talk. I sometimes attempted to argue with him; I would rack my brains to find objection to his views. "She's a sly puss!" Herbaud [Maheu] would laugh, while Nizan would scrutinize his fingernails with an air of great concentration; but Sartre always succeeded in turning the tables on me. It was impossible to feel put out by him: he used to do his utmost to help us benefit from his knowledge. "He's a marvelous trainer of intellects," I noted. I was staggered by his generosity, for the sessions didn't teach him anything, and he would give of himself for hours without counting the cost.[65]

Sartre, Castor, and Nizan passed the written exam; Maheu failed. He would try again the next year, and succeed. But the intimacy he had nurtured so adroitly with Castor was over: she had to go on that year, with Sartre, who proclaimed, "From now on, I'm going to take you under my wing."[66] Said Maheu, shortly before he died, "Sartre was incredibly generous, and a genius. Nizan had grace, anguish, courage, and torment. But Castor . . . what a heart! She was so authentic, so courageously rebellious, so genuine, and as generous as Sartre. And she was so distinctly attractive, her own genre and her own style, no woman has ever been like her. I consider myself incredibly privileged and honored to have known her as well as I did. But they had to continue. We had lived in a kind of cloister, collective lives which put reality in parentheses. And then our monastic lives ended."[67]

Life changed for Aron, too. "I think that our relationship changed the day Sartre met Simone de Beauvoir. There was a time when he was pleased to use me as a sounding board for his ideas; then there was that meeting, which resulted in that, suddenly, I no longer interested him as an interlocutor."[68] To me he added, "She really helped him as no one else would, making him rewrite again and again work she thought was unsatisfactory. She was his most severe critic, but always on his side."[69] And Castor herself said, "Sartre corresponded exactly to the dream companion I had longed for since I was fifteen: he was the double in whom I found all my burning aspirations raised to the pitch of incandescence. I should always be able to share everything with him. When I left at the beginning of August, I knew that he would never go out of my life again."[70]

The exam was over. Out of seventy-six who took it, only thirteen passed (among them Nizan, Guille, Hyppolite). Sartre was first, Simone de Beauvoir a very close second (the three-member jury had not been unanimous: two had voted for Sartre, one for Beauvoir). Sartre had played the game—and won. But, as he was to ask so often later in life, does not the winner lose? For him at least, the reverse had certainly been true: by losing in 1928 he had won in 1929. He had met Simone de Beauvoir.

PART 3   The Loner

Our business in this world is not to succeed, but to continue to fail, in good spirits.

Robert Louis Stevenson, *Ethical Studies*

And though he greatly failed, more greatly dared.

Ovid, *Metamorphoses* (the epitaph of Phaeton)

On October 25, 1929, it could well have appeared that the West was beginning its final collapse—but Jean-Paul Sartre and Simone de Beauvoir couldn't have cared less. True, the Wall Street crash did not affect France at first: the banks which failed, the factories which closed, the executives who killed themselves were all American, too far away to concern lovers on their way to stardom.

Yet France, too, had long shown vivid signs of dangerous decay. In 1928, though statistically in full boom, the economy had flourished only because of increasing speculation, inequality, and repression. A vicious campaign had been launched against Socialist leader Léon Blum, and massive police violence had been unleashed against those who protested the execution of Sacco and Vanzetti.[1] Then, on October 11, 1929, the modestly liberal government of Aristide Briand fell, bringing to power a brilliant autocrat named André Tardieu whose primary ambition was to get rid of Parliament. He and his successor, ally Pierre Laval, dominated French politics until 1932 and, using the police to smash dissent, did nothing to confront the deepening depression. Indeed, the progovernment reactionary daily *Le Temps* did not even bother to mention that world financial crisis; its main concern, instead, was to get the government to enact draconian measures to crush unions and purge universities of left-wing professors.[2]

None of this seemed to affect Sartre. His interests, Castor admitted, were limited to "life and *his* ideas; those of others bored him."[3] At best, he and Castor focused on each other. "The self-evident obviousness of our respective vocations seemed to us to guarantee their eventual fulfillment," Castor wrote in the second volume of her memoirs. "There were no scruples, no feelings of respect or loyal affection that would stop us from making up our own minds by the pure light of reason—and of our own desires. We were unaware of any cloudiness or confusion in our mental processes; we believed ourselves to consist of pure reason and pure will. This conviction was fortified by the eagerness with which we staked our all on the future." Convinced that they were masters of their fates, Castor insisted that "we had no external limitations, no overriding authority, no imposed pattern of existence. We created our own links with the world, and freedom was the very essence of our existence." It was only much later that she understood that "Our indifference to money was a luxury we could afford only because we had enough of it to avoid real poverty and the need for hard or unpleasant work. Our open-mindedness was bound up with a cultural background and the sort of activities accessible only to people of our social class. It was our conditioning as young petit bourgeois intellectuals that led us to believe ourselves free of all conditioning whatsoever."[4]

Yet, starting in November, Sartre's freedom was to be severely restricted: like all French males, he faced eighteen months of military service (but served fifteen). Thanks to Aron, however, it wasn't going to be too bad: drafted the year before and now a sergeant-instructor in meteorology, Aron arranged for Sartre and their friend, Pierre Guille, drafted with Sartre, to slip into his own particular nook.

Son of a Protestant peasant, aggressively modest, secretive, sarcastic, and totally unambitious, Pierre Guille was interested in good literature, good conversations, and good food. "It seemed to him quite sufficient to sample, intelligently, what the world had to offer, and to make one-self a pleasant niche in it."[5] Sartre and Guille spent hours together, discussing gestures, the tone of voices, appearances, anything esoterically out of the ordinary; once in the army and forced to listen to Aron's lectures on weather instruments, they enjoyed irritating him by tossing paper darts at him during his classes. From that play-pen at Fort Saint-Cyr, not far from Paris, Sartre was transferred to Saint-Symphorien, near Tours, in January 1930. His chief was a civilian who let the military contingent decide its schedule as the soldiers wished, and Sartre and Company duly arranged to be off a week per month in addition to regular passes and leave. Sartre was thus rarely separated from Castor, who said, "Paris remained the center of our life together."[6]

Yet Sartre claimed to be unhappy. From Saint-Symphorien he wrote Castor: "Think that the details of my life are so minutely regulated that I know without a doubt that in eight times 24 hours, at 6:15 pm, I will pick up the radio receiver, which will begin with the same numbers, after having accomplished the same feats. This could all be mechanical, but I know that the same thoughts will come back, along with the same hope and despair and all those schizophrenic constructions to which, I have come to realize, I have been giving more and more credit. I am sinking deeper into a feeling of total sequestration."[7]

For a draftee, however, Sartre was amazingly free. He read voraciously and wrote frenetically. He even concocted some poems, he admitted to me somewhat reluctantly. One of them, called "The Tree," describing the pointless proliferation of nature, symbolized contingency; that symbol would be vastly expanded later in *Nausea*. But his principal achievement was finishing the first two sections of *The Legend of Truth*. Part One, "The Legend of the Certain," defined truth as "a by-product of commerce," which meant democracy, the basic characteristic of which was that citizens viewed themselves as interchangeable, and hence viewed the world similarly. The result: science, and therefore "vigorous thought." After that came "The Legend of the Probable," a more "distinguished type of thought, obsessed with form and connections, idealistic and soft, ideas of the elite—ideology." All elites hate "democratic thought," Sartre wrote. They consider it crass, vulgar, plebian. Instead they "hammer out so-called general ideas for their own special use, ideas which at best possess only an uncertain degree of probability." This aristocratic thought leads to the truth of the philosopher—and of the dictator.[8]

Part Three, "The Legend of the Solitary Man," was never completed; representing Sartre himself, it was meant to reveal the journey needed to go beyond the certain and probable to discover what Sartre would later call the *concrete universal*, the product of a dialectical thought which establishes universal truths (in each situation) that constantly change (as situations change). Sartre concluded that the privilege of grasping living, concrete reality belonged only to the writer, to the artist, to the solitary man dedicated to saving himself through his lonely, isolated, painful task of saving mankind. While *The Legend of Truth* represented what Nizan continued to denounce—the bourgeois intellectual's arrogant conviction of being chosen—he liked it enough to try to get it published by Gallimard, France's premier publishing house where his friend André Malraux was a reader.[9] When Malraux turned it down, Nizan got the first part into *Bifur*, a journal he helped put out, and identified Sartre as a "Young philosopher. Is at work on a volume of destructive philosophy."[10]

Nizan was then also doing his military service, but in Paris, and Sartre, Castor, Rirette, and Nizan still managed to spend agreeable moments together. "We never had discussions with Nizan," Castor reported, "he refused to approach serious subjects directly. Instead he would tell a series of carefully selected anecdotes, and refrain from drawing any conclusion from them: he preferred to bite his nails and mutter dire prophecies and sibylline threats. As a result, our differences were passed over in silence. On the other hand, like many Communist intellectuals of this period, Nizan was not so much a revolutionary as a rebel, which meant that over a whole range of topics he privately agreed

with us—though in some instances this agreement rested on miscon-
ceptions which we left undisturbed. Between us we tore the bourgeoisie to shreds, tooth and nail. In the case of Sartre and myself, such
hostility remained individualistic, ergo bourgeois." She added: "We
sympathized in principle with the workers because they were free of any
bourgeois blemish; the crude simplicity of their needs and the constant
struggle they kept up against physical odds meant that they faced the
human situation in its true colors. Accordingly while we shared Nizan's
hopes for a revolution of the proletariat, it was only the negative aspect
of such a revolution that concerned us. In the Soviet Union the great
blaze of the October Revolution had long since flickered out, and, as
Sartre said, by and large what was emerging there was a 'technological
culture.' We should not, we decided, feel at all at ease in a socialist
world. In every society the artist or writer remains an outsider, and one
which proclaimed with such dogmatic fervor its intention of 'integrat-
ing' him struck us as being about the most unfavorable environment he
could have." [11]

Self-centered and self-indulgent, self-aggrandizing yet self-satisfied,
Sartre, at twenty-five, saw himself both as a Protestant witness and as a
protesting outsider, a totally free critic in a world where most are condemned to be poor. He thrived from the bourgeois society he hated.
He lusted for honors from a system he wanted to explode. Like most
spoiled bourgeois elitists, he wanted to have his cake and eat it too, and
he could become downright nasty if he couldn't. Once, in 1926, for
example, when Camille canceled an engagement with him, Sartre fired
off a letter calling her "selfish, frivolous and a coward to boot," then
reminded her of his own crucial importance: "Who made you what you
are, who tries to stop you from selling out to the bourgeois, from being
an esthete or a whore? Who develops your intelligence? Me alone." [12]
Nor was his superiority limited to women. "He distrusted Aron's logic,
Herbaud's [Maheu's] aesthetic theories, and Nizan's Marxism," wrote
Castor. [13] And even with Castor herself, whom he quickly learned to
consider his equal, he imposed his values as if they were absolute and
hence unchallengeable. Fortunately for their relationship, Castor up-
held most of those values herself.

"Sartre was not inclined to be monogamous by nature," wrote Castor. "What we have," he told her, "is an *essential* love; but it is a good
idea for us also to experience *contingent* love affairs." [14] To me he put it
this way: "We both knew that our relationship was *necessary* and, therefore, would not be affected by any *contingent* affairs." [15] By and large, it

was true: during their lives, the couple Sartre-Castor survived the crises, tantrums, and jealousies caused by the amorous meanderings of each. But it is not true that such sideline incidents had no affect on the main game. When Sartre continued to see Camille after he and Castor had become lovers, for example, she began to worry that "despite our understanding and intimacy, Sartre had a higher regard for her than he did for me. Perhaps she was in fact a more estimable character. I should not have been so worked up about her had I not been a prey to the pangs of jealousy." [16]

Later, when Castor was teaching at a Rouen lycée and she, Sartre, and one of her students, Olga, developed a trio relationship, Sartre revealed himself "demanding, possessive, extremely jealous." Castor, who described the history of that threesome in her first novel, *L'Invitée* (*She Came to Stay*), told me: "Sartre (Pierre in the novel) was already jealous of me (Françoise) whenever my closeness with Olga (Xavière) excluded him, but when Zuorro moved into the picture, he went really wild." [17] Marc Zuorro, whom Castor called Marco in her memoirs and Sartre named Daniel in *Les chemins de la liberté* (*The Roads to Freedom*), was "a quite extraordinarily handsome person: his swarthy, amber-tinted complexion, together with that face and those burning eyes, called to mind both a Greek statue and some of El Greco's portraits." Homosexual by preference, bisexual by habit, Zuorro considered Castor and Sartre, whom he had befriended at the Cité Universitaire, as "a typical bunch of 'Frenchies,' and sometimes the mere sight of us was enough to send him off in a gale of laughter. Despite this he affected to treat his friends with the greatest consideration: we refused to be taken in by this gambit, but we agreed that he did it all most gracefully." [18]

Flighty, irresponsible, a pathological liar who later collaborated with the Germans, Zuorro had nothing in common with the "necessary" couple. When I asked Sartre why he continued to court his friendship, he answered only that Zuorro was "amusing." When I pressed the issue, he quipped "I guess, as my novels show, I've always been intrigued by homosexuals." When I suggested "fascinated," he laughed: "Who knows? There can be a camaraderie among boarders, or soldiers, or prisoners which, since they consider each other equal, can never be duplicated in normal society." [19]

In her memoirs, Castor explained their fascination with Zuorro as being "amused by his love of intrigue, his indiscretions, and his scandalmongering. He assumed a pose of unbending moral purity. He had had an affair with a girl from Sèvres [Olga], but very soon he put the relationship on a purely platonic footing."[20] Nevertheless, when Zuorro seduced Olga, probably out of spite,[21] Sartre went stark raving mad. "He was extremely jealous, he was irrational." But, reacted Castor in 1973, when I said that today he would be dubbed a terrible male chauvinist, "Still, you must remember that with me his rapport was always one of strict equality. He never tried to oppress or dominate me. On the contrary he always tried to help me, encourage me to do what I wanted to do, not what he thought I ought to. With other women, yes, he was always an emotional imperialist, although, later, as his affairs became more complicated, he did become less demanding."[22]

Partly because of Marc and Olga's meaningless one-nighter, the threesome broke up. That was just fine with Castor, who had become jealous of both Sartre and Olga. Known as "the Little Russian," although she was half Ukrainian and half French, Olga was spoiled and spirited, indeed testy and tempestuous, the cranky, irascible, childlike blonde whom Sartre used as the model for Ivich in his novel, *The Age of Reason*.* In her own novel, Castor (as Françoise) got to the point of hating her:

Françoise felt painfully at the mercy of that passionate, touchy soul. She seemed to exist only through Xavière's capricious feelings for her. It was as if a voodoo sorceress had taken possession of her through the medium of a waxen image and was subjecting her to the most horrible tortures. At that moment, Françoise was an untouchable, a wasted and shriveled up soul. She had to wait for a smile from Xavière before she could hope to regain some self-respect. . . . It was true agony to feel that her happiness and even her intrinsic being was dependent to such an extent on this strange, rebellious spirit.[23]

So much so, that Françoise eventually escaped this anguish in the only way she could, murdering Xavière.

In reality, however, not only did Sartre and Castor keep their "contract," they also remained close friends with Olga. That contract, to begin with a "two-year lease" while Sartre was in army, required that they live apart, abroad if possible, "then rejoin one another," Castor wrote. "We would never become strangers to one another, and neither would appeal for the other's help in vain; nothing would prevail against this alliance of ours. But it must not be allowed to degenerate into mere duty or habit; we had at all costs to preserve it from decay of this sort. I

---

* Olga's younger sister, Wanda Kosakiewicz, told me (Interview, Paris, 23 March 1973) "I'm mostly Ivich, not Olga. Ivich has my character." But Sartre, Castor, and Olga have always insisted that Ivich was patterned on Olga, not Wanda.

agreed."[24] She could do so primarily because she was secure: "Sartre and I were very lucky, but also our backgrounds were very particular, every exceptional," she told me in 1975. They had "similar motivations. To both of us, literature had replaced religion. . . . Both our childhoods were very solid, very secure. This meant that neither of us had to prove something to ourselves or the other. We were sure of ourselves. It was as if everything had been preordained from the beginning."[25]

That does not tell it all. Both Sartre and Castor were secure, true, because they had been raised in solid bourgeois homes where their success was assumed. Yet Sartre had been severely traumatized by two "betrayals," and Castor had been harangued all her adolescence by her reactionary father to get married to someone not too intelligent. Neither Sartre nor Castor, true, had ever met someone of the opposite sex whom they respected more. Yet neither considered love or happiness to be primary objectives in life; both were adventurous, curious and ferociously independent. What's more, both of them, but especially Sartre, wanted to try everything that expanded their vision, from sex to drugs, from different travels to diverse friendships. But these desires were mostly conceived, rarely experienced, at least up to then. Sartre claimed not to fear death, because his writing would guarantee him immortality. Castor was almost as obsessed by death as was Nizan, but she could forget its inevitability by focusing her energy—and her writing—on the present. Preordained to be what they became, they were intellectuals—cool and calm, rational and reasonable.

And smug, precisely because they were so secure. "Sartre was only three years older than I was—an equal," she wrote, "and together we set forth to explore the world. My trust in him was so complete that he supplied me with the sort of absolute, unfailing security that I had once had from my parents, or from God. When I threw myself into a world of freedom, I found an unbroken sky above my head."[26] In other words, so secure were they in each other that they could pass off most of each other's amorous flings as no more threatening than eating lunch with an old friend. Most ordinary people, doubting themselves as well as their gods, fear losing their mates to rivals more pretty, more potent, more powerful. Sexual infidelity can therefore easily destroy complacent security. But for Sartre and Castor, that security was virtually mental, rarely tactile. Only a rival more intelligent, better educated, and surer of success could threaten it. Significantly, Sartre and Castor spent the rest of their lives surrounded by students and disciples, by people (with some crucial exceptions) who were neither equals nor colleagues. When, in 1929, Castor could say, "that autumn my past lay dormant; I belonged wholly to the present," it was only because she was absolutely certain of her future.[27]

She had gained that certainty before meeting Sartre. Rooted in her whole upbringing, it sprang forth after she placed second in the 1927 general philosophy exam (equivalent, more or less, to a master's; first had been the proletarian Catholic philosopher Simone Weil). ENS student Maurice Merleau-Ponty, concealed behind the name Jean Pradelle in Castor's memoirs, was third and, "pretending to be vexed at being beaten by a couple of girls, said he wanted to meet me. . . . Brought up, like myself, in a pious home, and now an unbeliever, he had been branded by Christian morality. At the Ecole Normale he was classed among the Holy Willies. He disapproved of his fellow students' [among them, Sartre] coarse manners, their indecent songs, rude jokes, brutality, debauchery, and cynical dissipations." He was, she added, "like me, an intellectual: but he had remained perfectly adapted to his class and its way of life, and accepted bourgeois society with an open heart." All of Merleau's rationalizations were flawed. "After I demolished them one after the other" and "he finally gave in on every point," Castor asked herself, "Do men marry women like me?" Merleau was interested but obviously scared. Concluded Castor: "I'm so sure that the one who would really be all to me, who would understand the whole of me, and be fundamentally the brother and the equal of myself, simply doesn't exist."[28]

Castor's premonition that she "was destined to a life of loneliness,"[29] was also due to her fear of spontaneity. That fear was confronted for the first time during the summer of 1927, when Castor, invited to the home of her best friend, Zaza, met Stépha Awdicovicz, a twenty-four-year-old Ukrainian student hired by Zaza's mother as governess. Stépha was such a bundle of spontaneous actions and reactions that Zaza's mother was "sure she's no lady." But Castor loved her: "She had pretty blonde hair, blue eyes that were both languishing and gay, a broad, full mouth, and a quite exceptional attractiveness which I then hadn't the nerve to call by its right name: sex appeal. Her gauzy dress revealed a pair of deliciously rounded shoulders;* in the evenings, she would sit down at the piano and sing Ukrainian love songs with a coquetry that enchanted Zaza and me, but which scandalized everybody else. At bedtime, I was startled to see her putting on a pair of pajamas instead of a nightdress. She opened up her heart to me at once. Her father had a

---

* Euphemism, in those days, for breasts.

large candy factory at Lwów; while studying at the university, she had taken part in the struggle for Ukrainian independence and had spent a few days in prison.* She had left home to complete her studies, first in Berlin, where she had spent two or three years, then in Paris; she was attending lectures at the Sorbonne."[30]

Stépha taught Castor how to dress, dance and drink. She would never hesitate to walk into a bar alone, tease any appealing young man, and tell him off if he got too fresh. At the library,

with her roving eye and ready smile, she was too attractive to men and they too much interested in her for her to be able to get much work done. She would have barely taken her place beside me when she would put her coat over her shoulders and go outside to have a chat with one of her boyfriends: the teacher studying German, the Prussian student, the Romanian doctor. . . . She had a bright blue room in a hotel in the rue Saint-Sulpice; she had hung reproductions of Cézanne, Renoir, and El Greco on the walls, together with some drawings by a Spanish friend who wanted to be a painter. I liked being with her. I loved the soft feel of her fur collar, her little toques, her dresses, her scent, her warbling voice, her loving gestures. My relationships with my other friends— Zaza, [Merleau . . .]—had always been extremely formal. But Stépha would take my arm in the street; in the cinema she would hold hands with me; she would kiss me on the slightest provocation.[31]

And that's how I got into the picture—eventually—for Stépha became my mother. Her Spanish friend was to be my father. "His name was Fernando. He was a descendant of one of those Jewish families that had been driven out of Spain by the Inquisition four centuries ago; he had been born in Constantinople and had studied in Berlin. Prematurely bald, with a round face and skull, he would talk with romantic intensity about his 'daimon,' but he was capable of irony and I liked him very much. Stépha admired him because, though he hadn't a sou, he managed somehow to go on painting, and she shared all his ideas: they were unshakeably internationalist, pacifist, and even, in a Utopian sense, revolutionary. The only reason she hesitated to marry him was that she wanted to keep her freedom."[32]

Two years later, Castor introduced Stépha and Fernando to Sartre and the four of them became very close. "Everybody was in love with

---

*Wrong: Stépha's father, a poet and rector of the university, had died of the flu when she was eighteen. She had rebelled against Polish domination earlier, as a high school student, and was sent to a convent, from where she escaped to Berlin in 1921 when her father died. Her mother did own a candy factory, which was seized by the Germans in 1941 and nationalized by the Russians in 1944.

Stépha," Sartre remembered in 1971. "I especially recall that Ilya Ehrenburg was absolutely, passionately, madly in love with her. I was very,
very fond of her myself, but I was never a romantic, nor was Castor, so
that for us the kind of love that bourgeois romantics like to imagine was
impossible, the kind where you are willing and able to abandon everything for the love of your life, *coûte que coûte,* no matter what the cost.
Castor and I always felt that our writing was primordial. And that's
what attracted me so much to Fernando. He affected me then more
than any other man alive. He was an intellectual, like me. He was a
painter, I a writer. He had the same point of view, the same basic vision
of life. To him, painting was more important than anything else. And
then, just like that," he said, clicking his fingers, "Fernando went off to
fight. This really upset me. We had both always wanted revolution, but
then suddenly, here was an intellectual like me, saying in effect, intellectuals must do what they preach." [33]

When that happened, in 1936, it was simply the epitome of what
Sartre had felt all along—that Fernando could jump into the world totally spontaneously, yet with meaningful purpose, whenever events so
demanded. It was that spontaneity which, in fact, had so appealed to
Sartre, Stépha's spontaneity which so enthralled Castor, Olga's spontaneity which so attracted them both. Rationalists to the core, Sartre
and Castor were rarely capable of acting, and then only after long, reasonable consideration. That is why Sartre rarely enjoyed sex. He always
preferred to talk, to play, to seduce, rather than to have sex. His explanation: "If both partners have a commitment to life that is enduring,
like to writing, then when sex is over, their relationship deepens." [34]

Rationalists cannot be spontaneous. Without spontaneity there can
be no passion. Did Sartre regret it? One day in 1973, I arrived late for
lunch at La Palette, a restaurant less crowded than La Coupole a little
higher on Montparnasse. I came alone. Sartre had expected me to show
up with "la petite," the young woman I had been living with. He was
fond of her and asked why she hadn't come. I told him that we were
breaking up. He asked for details. As I answered, my eyes blurred and
soon a tear or two ran down my cheeks. Since his one eye was still per-
ceptive, he felt my chagrin, yet interrupted me to say "I envy you. In all
my adult life I have never shed a tear for a woman. I wish I had, I wish I
still could. I envy you."

At first I was tempted to interpret his comment philosophically: had
not his hero Roquentin in *Nausea,* seeing Lucie "suffering with a fren-
zied generosity" reacted by saying, "I envy her . . . she is lucky. I have

been much too calm." Or again, when Roquentin, intimidated by a doctor, says: "There's a lucky man: as soon as you perceive him, you can tell he must have suffered, that he is someone who has lived."[35] Was Sartre being only literary? I asked him about his relationships to the women I knew had deeply affected him, about an actress who had committed suicide, about a magnificent mulatta he had befriended in America, finally about Castor herself. "I was always free, Castor was free, we were always free to pursue any desire that we felt was important to us," he answered calmly. "To have such freedom, we had to suppress or overcome any possessiveness, any tendency to be jealous. In other words, passion. To be free, you cannot be passionate."[36]

Perhaps. But over the years many incidents easily provoked passionate responses by Sartre and Castor. The most dramatic at the time involved Zaza. Kept in tight rein by her fanatic Catholic mother, Zaza was constantly shifted about to stop her from developing friendships with intellectuals. Rebelling then retreating, affirming her individuality then acceding to parental authority, Zaza became weaker and weaker. Her mother wanted her daughters married to strict, moral businessmen—who, of course, happened to be rich. Merleau-Ponty, whom Castor had introduced to her friend, was indeed such a moralist and fairly well off to boot. But he was not rich enough for Zaza's mother's ambitions. Nor was he a businessman. So she asked Merleau to stay away. To Castor's dismay, Merleau did. The result: Zaza became "gravely ill; she had a high temperature and frightful pains in the head . . . if her temperature did not come down, there was no hope for her. . . . The fever did not abate." The doctors had no certain answer. It could have been meningitis or encephalitis. To Castor it was bourgeois conformism: "We had fought together against the revolting fate that had lain ahead of us, and for a long time I believed that I had paid for my own freedom with her death."[37]

But for a long time, too, she could not forgive Merleau-Ponty. "True, we didn't like him very much," Sartre told me, "I always thought he was too haughty, too arrogant. But we shared some philosophical positions and, during the war and early postwar periods, we had similar political positions. So we worked together. But, influenced by what I knew of his disgusting cowardice towards Zaza, I remained aloof. It wasn't until much later, just before his death, I think, that one of Zaza's sisters told us the whole story: when Zaza told her mother that she wanted to marry Merleau, the mother wrote him that she had hired someone to check up on his family and knew that he was not the son of Merleau-

Ponty, that his mother had been unfaithful with a certain François, an engineer from Tours who was his real father, and that if he persisted trying to see Zaza, it would all be made public."[38] Stuff that passions—and novels—are made of.

For years after Zaza's death, Simone de Beauvoir did try to write a novel about her. But it just didn't come out. At Sartre's suggestion, she then decided to write about what was happening to her, not to friends no matter how close. Sartre took his own suggestion, and started developing a novel about the trajectory of a bourgeois obsessed with understanding his human condition in the very place where he worked, slept, ate, daydreamed, and got drunk. For Sartre, after 1 March 1931, the day after he had been discharged "with honor and fidelity"[39] from the army, that place would be Le Havre. Assigned to the lycée there for the third quarter of the 1930–31 school year to replace a philosophy professor struck down by a nervous depression, Sartre decided to write a "factum" on contingency. "Arriving in Le Havre," he told me, "with various little writings behind me, I said to myself, 'It is time now to start the real thing.'"[40] Years later, that turned out to be *Nausea*—what most critics to this day believe was Sartre's best novel.

"Because I called Le Havre *Bouville* (Mudville), most people assumed I hated it," said Sartre. "Not so. It's terribly ugly today, but that's because it was totally rebuilt after having been destroyed during the war. The Havre which I knew was very pretty, with quaint old houses, an appealing port full of clubs and bars catering to sailors from all over the world, lots of green parks, wide avenues, cafés, cinemas, and a lot of atmosphere."[41] In *Nausea*, most of the names of streets or cafés are changed, but just enough "to let the reader have the pleasure of believing he can recognize them."[42] In the novel as well as in real life, the old, rich merchant and shipowning families still live on the cliffs overlooking the city, the nouveaux riches along or around the boulevard Maritime, and the port is still the best equipped in France. "Yes, I liked it," said Sartre, "but the center of my life was always in Paris."[43]

Sartre remained at his Havre lycée four academic years (1931–33 and 1934–36). "A professor's life is not so hard," Sartre recalled; "he has Thursdays, Saturdays and Sundays off, and lots of free time the other days. I had my books. I'd go to cafés, to read or write. I enjoyed my courses. And my students. Whenever I was not off to Paris, or writing, I would hang out with some of them. We boxed, and believe me, they would hit me as hard as they could. We talked. We even went to a brothel together once, but I was too drunk to be a consumer there."[44]

Indeed, so close was he with some of them that they remained friends ever after. The closest was Jacques-Laurent Bost, son of the lycée's Protestant chaplain who, wrote Castor, had "a dazzling smile and a most princely ease of bearing. . . . He possessed the casual grace of youth, so casual that it bordered on insolence, coupled with a certain narcissistic fragility." She added: "At some time during the past few years we had amused ourselves by inventing a character called Little Noddle, to whom we made frequent references." Since "we loathed the whole idea of *la vie intérieure* [an interior life], and Little Noddle was totally devoid of any such thing, . . . a modest, peaceable, but obstinate fellow, who, far from taking a pride in thinking for himself, always said and did the accepted thing, Jacques Bost—whom we called Little Bost to distinguish him from his [older, known playwright] brother Pierre—struck us as being the very embodiment of Little Noddle." In other words, she wrote, "he had no ambitions, . . . did not possess an original mind [but] was quick-witted and droll."[45]

When I interviewed Le Petit Bost in 1973 I was struck by how un-*petit,* how enormous he was. Always shy, he was reticent about himself and his work. At that time he was managing editor of what was then the only politically relevant left-wing weekly, *Le Nouvel Observateur,* but was not happy with its pedantry—nor with his boss, editor-publisher Jean Daniel, an arrogant, conceited tyrant. He did tell me that his wife, Olga Kosakiewicz, Castor's student whom he had met through Sartre, had cancer.* And he did point out that the legacy of General de Gaulle had brought France, under Prime Minister Pompidou and especially the very repressive Interior Minister Marcellin, to the edge of fascism. Yet none of this seemed to provoke a reaction from him. He seemed crushed, defeated. But he was certainly willing to talk about Sartre, whom he admired as much then as when he had been his student in Le Havre.

He was not a prof like the others. He did deliver formal lectures, as was the custom then, but it became quite clear very quickly that one could interrupt him at anytime to ask questions or make statements. Everyone called him *Le père Sartre* precisely because they trusted him, they liked him, they admired him like a father. He was small, ugly, friendly. Some of us boxed with him, and he would fight hard but explode with genuine, good-natured laughter if we knocked him down. He was very generous with his time, helping whoever asked, to prepare them for their exams. Me, for example, since I had flunked the baccalaureate the

---

* She died a few years later.

year before. And all that help—two, three hours a week for me alone—he made appear as perfectly normal, even though that was a period when he considered time very precious, since he was working on *Nausea*. And it wasn't all work either: we went for walks, got drunk, went to the movies. He was so sure of himself, yet so open. To this day, I swear, I think he felt he could learn from us like we from him.[46]

Albert Palle, another of his students, added: "He was extraordinarily pleasant, simple, surprisingly funny. He took a lot of things seriously, but never his own status as a professor, nor the fact that we were merely students."[47] Jean Pouillon, another former student who, like Bost, also became a member of "the family," got to know him as a graduate student. "In those days, before the philosophy *agrégation,* candidates were expected to attend the lectures of some professor or other who would, supposedly, introduce them to the task of teaching. It was called a *pedagogical stage,* and you could not take the *agrég* exam without a favorable report from that 'stage' professor. I asked for Sartre and got him, but it was not very pedagogical. On the first day, Sartre simply said, 'Okay, come to class if you want. Your report is done and is favorable. All you have to do is, here, correct these papers.' But his course was so fascinating, and he was so out of the ordinary, that I went just the same, and we started talking. We became friends."[48]

At least one of Sartre's former students disagreed. Born in Le Havre of American parents, his Georgian father being a cotton broker and importer, Troupe Matthews thought that Sartre was very ordinary. "He was a typical neo-Kantian, who enjoyed hearing himself pontificate, and was quite terrifying," he told me recently.

It's true that he wasn't very formal, that he did walk into class wearing a leather jacket and no tie, that he boxed with some students and got drunk with them. But Sartre was very elitist, and the students he hung out with all had special talents or skills or advantages. He was not open to all his students, just the chosen few, and, if I remember correctly, they tended to be Protestant as well, not because he was pro-Protestant himself but because he hated the Catholics' notion that any idiot could gain grace. Sartre believed in the Protestant ethic: those who work hard deserve to be recompensed. Yet with me, he bent quite easily. I was a terrible student, but I had lots of jazz records, especially blues. Sartre loved the blues. I lent him some, I gave him some, and he passed me.* Nevertheless, I was scared of him, and so were most of my classmates, even though I remained friendly enough with him to be part of his large coterie, if not the inner. Still, I met Simone de Beauvoir in Le Havre, and later, since my

---

* Sartre never flunked any student according to Bost, Pouillon, Castor, and himself.

folks brought me home before the war, he introduced me to Dolores * and to your parents in New York after the war. But in 1931, Sartre terrified me.[49]

That was the year that I was born—and that my parents, Stépha and Fernando, perhaps because of it, got married. It was very hot in Madrid in July 1931, so Stépha and child stayed in Paris, while Fernando went back to work. "He had been forced to take a job there which he much disliked, selling radio sets," reported Castor; nevertheless he told her and Sartre that if they decided to vacation in Spain, he would find the time to show them around without "the tourists' ambiguous status."[50] He put them up, took them to the Prado Museum, showed them the "deep, gloomy cafés" where the revolution was plotted,[51] and forced them to sit through a *corrida,* which they thought they would hate but learned to love: "Each fresh fight was a work of art, and gradually, I came to discern what qualities gave it meaning and, sometimes, beauty. There was much I still missed, but both Sartre and I had definitely become fans."[52] He also took them to see Madrid's famous underground nightlife, from illegal drinking posts full of gamblers, smugglers, and thieves to Flamenco caves where "they had goatskin bottles full of a heavy, resin-scented wine, and the waiters shouted the menu aloud."[53]

"But what impressed me the most," Sartre told me, "was that through it all, his job, his politics, his incredibly time-consuming tour-guiding, Fernando painted. That was very important for me. Here was somebody who was first and foremost a painter. That was his *raison d'être,* just as writing was for me. And, like me, he had accepted a job, because of his responsibilities, which he chose. Fernando was the guy who said, 'I have a family; I must support them,' and did and still painted, whenever he could, during siesta time, at his office between clients, instead of lunch or dinner if he had no business or guests. And then, he also was political. You can see why Mathieu, in the *Age of Reason,* is as influenced by Gomez as I was by Fernando. It took time for it all to jell, but I think that's the origin of my revolutionary thought."[54]

Perhaps. But meanwhile, Sartre was willing to play the bourgeois game. Castor had been offered a job in a lycée in Marseilles, more than six hundred miles from Le Havre. Sartre's reaction was to say, "If we got married, we would have the advantages of a double post, and in the long run such a formality would not seriously affect our way of life."[55] But Castor felt differently: "I didn't feel like it very much, and I knew that he felt like it even less, since to be a professor, under a censor, was

---

* Sartre's most important American lover, to whom he dedicated one of his major works.

bad enough, but on top of that, to be married. . . . And since there was
no question of having children—not that I didn't toy with the idea at
eighteen or nineteen, when I contemplated a bourgeois marriage. I
didn't reject the idea a priori, but with the life I expected to lead, having
to earn my living and write, there would be no place for children."[56] So
off to Marseilles went Castor—and she loved it "at first sight."[57]

Sartre rarely kept the letters he received. Castor usually held on to
hers assiduously. In 1983, she published many of them, including one
date 9 October 1931 that Sartre had sent her from Le Havre. In it he
described his daily routine: early morning coffee at the Terminus café,
reading, classes, walking, private lessons to some shmuck (*un con* in the
original though Castor left out that word), staring at a tree "with little
green stems" (the formidable chestnut made famous by *Nausea*) and re-
flecting on Contingency, lunch of haddock and a 1913 calvados, more
reading (*Turgeniev* by Maurois), and finally letter-writing in which fi-
nances were discussed (Sartre insisted he could get by on his salary).[58]
The rather typical schedule of a rather typical provincial professor, "that
dull, boring aspect of existence, as you described later in *Nausea*," Castor told Sartre.[59] Yet she in Marseilles and he in Le Havre—Guille in
Reims and Zuorro in Amiens—led privileged lives, and they fully enjoyed them.

Not so their old friend, Paul Nizan. Teaching at Bourg-en-Bresse,
five hours southeast of Paris, he had thrown himself into the local
battles, organizing the unemployed, running for local electoral offices,
agitating among his students and colleagues, and writing at the same
time. "Why did you not admire Nizan as much as my father?" I asked
Sartre in 1971. After all, Nizan was a writer who worked, who politicized, who did as much as Fernando in those days. Answered Sartre:
"I don't know. Perhaps because Nizan was rich, through his wife. I
didn't like his wife at all. Fernando and Stépha were penniless. Perhaps
because Fernando was a moralist, like me. No, I think it was because
Nizan was an agitator first, a writer second. He was already convinced
that to save himself he had to save the world, but he had the full support
of a powerful party, at that time anyway. He was a terribly solitary figure, but he wasn't alone. Fernando and I, we were alone. Nizan's writing was at the service of mankind. Fernando's painting, my writing, was
against the world."[60]

Seen through Sartre's French eyes, the world seemed to be getting
better by the end of that 1931–32 academic year. The fascist government of Pierre Laval had fallen on 10 February, and though the dis-
armament conference at Geneva had failed and violence had spread

throughout France (leading to the assassination of Paul Doumer on 6 May), the moderate left had won the elections of 8 May. But the so-called radicals quickly torpedoed all hopes for progress by voting against restrictions on arms commerce, against the forty-hour week, and against the nationalization of insurance companies. That summer, while Adolf Hitler became an official candidate for Germany's chancellorship, Sartre and Castor went off to Spain with Guille and a mutual friend. They were in Seville when General Sanjurjo unleashed his unsuccessful "amusing" coup, which "delighted us."[61]

More delightful, though, had been the news that Castor had been appointed to the Lycée Jeanne d'Arc in Rouen, "an hour's journey from Le Havre, and an hour and a half from Paris. The first thing I did on arrival," she wrote in her memoirs, "was to get myself a commutation ticket. During the four years I taught there, the town center, as far as I was concerned, always remained the station."[62] The second thing she did was to go find a fellow teacher at the lycée, a tempestuous Trotskyist named Colette Audry, recommended by Nizan. "It was in the Fall of 1932," remembered Audry in 1973,

when this young woman approached me in the faculty lounge and said, "Paul Nizan spoke to me of you." She knew that I was very political and was recruiting teachers into the CGTU, a union federation accused of being full of anarcho-syndicalists and Trotskyists, and she seemed willing to join, but that was only to please me, not out of conviction. I met Sartre with her soon thereafter, and we got into lots of political arguments. He used to call me *"La" Communiste* ("The" Communist), even though he understood full well that the Communist Party opposed us. His main argument then was simply this: workers can only escape their condition by joining the CP, but we intellectuals have other means, so why commit ourselves to political sides? . . . What he really meant, of course, was that we intellectuals had no reason to change our conditions. I would say that he was a left-winger who was neither a revolutionary nor a rebel.[63]

Castor's explanation was this:

Sartre was vaguely tempted to join the Communist Party. His ideas, aims, and temperament all militated against such a step; but though he had just as great a liking for independence as I did, his sense of responsibility was far greater. On this particular occasion we decided—our decisions were always provisional—that if you belonged to the proletariat, you had to be a Communist, but that though the proletarian struggle was of concern to us, it was even so not *our* struggle; all that could be asked of us was that we should always speak out on its behalf in any argument. We had our own tasks to fulfill, and they were not compatible with joining the Party. What we never considered was the possibility of joining a Communist splinter group. We had the very highest opinion of Trotsky, and the idea of "permanent revolution" suited our anarchist tendencies far better than that of constructing a socialist regime inside one single country. But both in the Trotskyite party and the various other dissident groups, we encountered the same ideological dogmatism as we did in the Communist Party proper; the only difference was that we had no faith in their effectiveness.[64]

To which Sartre himself said, "I did not believe myself committed by my past, so I was free. Individual freedom meant perpetual detachment. A writer, I insisted, must keep his independence. But I was also very moralistic. In that Rouen café incident, what happened was that a very badly dressed worker walked in and the owner immediately ushered him out. I reacted on the spot by saying to Castor 'I should join the CP.' But that was not a political statement. It was a moral reaction to the café owner's action. I was simply expressing my hatred of his class, the bourgeoisie. In any case, I just said it. I didn't do it."[65]

Indeed Sartre didn't do anything about his moral outrage. In January 1933, textile workers all over the North went on strike, and Hitler came to power in Germany, the French left took to the streets. Sartre stayed in his café. In March, Hitler gained a majority in the Reichstag while in France, in April, miners and agricultural workers struck, demanding decent wages. France's Croix de Feu young fascists poured into the plazas to beat up the pickets. The left called for help; Sartre wrote the first draft of the history of his bourgeois soul which was to become *Nausea*. "All the same," Castor insisted, "we did not regard ourselves as wholly uninvolved. We aimed to make an active personal contribution through our discussions, our teaching, and our books: such a contribution would be critical rather than constructive, but at this particular period in France we felt that criticism had a most important role to fulfill."[66]

To prepare for that role, Sartre and Castor read "everything that came out," from Breton's *Immaculate Conception* to Silone's *Fontamara*, from Moravia's *Time of Indifference* to Marcel Aymé's *The Green Mare*. They liked Malraux' intentions in *Man's Fate* but not the result. In *Fifty Grand* and *The Sun Also Rises*, they felt Hemingway managed "to endow physical objects with extraordinary reality, just because he never separated them from the action in which his heroes were involved."[67] Two other novels greatly affected them (and strongly influenced Sartre): Céline's *Journey to the End of the Night*, and Dos Passos's *The 42nd Parallel*, which had just appeared in translation. Céline "attacked war, colonialism, the cult of mediocrity, platitudes, and society generally in a style and tone which we found enchanting," wrote Castor, without catching its antidemocratic elitism. As for Dos Passos, "he had worked out a bifocal perspective for the presentation of his main characters, which meant that they would be, at one and the same time, drawn as detailed individuals *and* as purely social phenomena."[68] Five years later, Sartre would write: "We are neither robots nor possessed; we are worse: free. All together *outside* or all together *inside*. Dos Passos' human being is a hybrid, internal-external. We are with him, in him, we live with his vacillating individual consciousness and, all of a sudden, it gives way, weakens, dilutes itself into the collective consciousness. [The world of Dos Passos] is contradictory. But that's why it is beautiful: beauty is a veiled contradiction. I hold Dos Passos as the greatest writer of our time."[69]

In 1933 Sartre also discovered Hegel and the German phenomenologists. In the film *Sartre*, he claimed he never heard of the latter and ignored the former until 1933. The fact is, he had had long discussions about both with Fernando, who had been Heidegger's classmate in Husserl's class. "I remember that one day in 1929, Sartre told me he wanted to describe, philosophically, a stone as a stone in the world, instead of loading it with links to spiritual or metaphysical entries," Fernando told me. "I explained to him that Husserl was doing just that but that to understand him, Sartre would first have to read Hegel's *The Phenomenology of Mind*. He did, because we went on to discuss it, and to talk about Husserl."[70] Both Sartre and Castor insisted, however, that it was Aron, who had spent the 1932–33 academic year at the French Institute in Berlin, who first got Sartre excited about Husserl.[71] In any case, Aron did get Sartre to buy Emmanuel Lévinas's *The Theory of Intuition in Husserl's Phenomenology*. Sartre was so anxious that he started leafing through the volume as he walked along. "His heart missed a beat when he found references to contingency: had someone cut the ground from under his feet then? As he read on, he reassured himself that this was not so. Contingency seemed not to play any very important part in Husserl's system,"[72] at least according to Lévinas's "very superficial book."[73] Sartre wanted to know more. He asked Aron to help him succeed him at the French Institute in Berlin and made arrangements for Aron to fill in for him at his Le Havre lycée.

But first, it was vacation time. For all his moralism, Sartre did not hesitate to profit from the largesse of fascism. Mussolini had decided to stage a massive Fascist Exhibition during the summer of 1933; to woo foreign tourists, he had cut train fares by 70 percent. "We took advan-

tage of this without scruple," Castor admitted. They visited Pisa, Flor-
ence, Venice, and Rome. To get their benefits they duly attended the
Fascist Exhibition, where the "pistols and cudgels of the 'Fascist martyrs' were on display."[74] Sartre claimed he couldn't stand the country
because of all the Black Shirts. But shortly after returning to France, he
joyfully packed his bags and went off to Berlin, home of the Storm
Troopers—and the Brown Shirts.

For all his stated contempt for the bourgeoisie, the shopkeepers and
capitalists, the bureaucrats and censors, the fascists and Nazis, Sartre
was still the little faker who used adults to forge for himself his own
road to salvation. Blessed and chosen, he believed in the power of his
thoughts and the meaning of his endeavor. He was still very much the
typical bourgeois intellectual, the "watchdog," who had long to go
before understanding that, as his tormented companion Paul Nizan put
it, "Nobody can be saved nowadays by private thoughts or private
passions."[75]

"It was in Berlin in 1933–34 that I first took a position, that I committed myself in print for the first time," Sartre told me proudly in 1971. He did not mean politically. "Influenced by Husserl, I wrote *The Transcendence of the Ego,* in which I attacked Husserl." [1]

The phenomenology, or reflexive study of consciousness, of Edmund Husserl had appealed to Sartre—and to Aron and Fernando before him—for its strict descriptions of immediate experiences and how they are internally digested by the mind, or presented to consciousness. Husserl had shown that consciousness was always consciousness *of* an object, that it had no content in itself, that it was a movement in the world, that it was "intentional." As Sartre wrote later: "It is not in some retreat that we discover ourselves: it is on the road, in the city, in the center of a crowd, thing among things, man among men." [2]

But Husserl had then gone on to claim that a transcendental ego "stood behind" consciousness because he wanted to study the object as separate from the I seeing or knowing it, as he put it, he wanted to "bracket" off the world so as to study the "pure phenomenon." In *The Transcendence of the Ego,* his first philosophical essay, Sartre denied such transcendence. Consciousness of objects is always an activity happening to a particular person in the world, he said. "The ego is neither formally nor materially *in* consciousness: it is outside, *in the world*. It is a being of the world, like the ego of another." [3] So, with no transcendental ego or contents to confuse consciousness—and, most crucially, with the dichotomy of subject-object now firmly grounded in the empirically observable—phenomenology could concern itself with human activity in concrete situations, with existing, and hence, as we shall see, become an existentialism.

Sartre's concrete situation in Berlin was a large room with an antique desk, table, and chairs on the first floor of the once luxurious villa owned originally by a General von Kluck. Facing a Swedish church on a residential street in Berlin's Wilmersdorf sector, the villa was still charming but now somewhat austere, conducive to maintaining the seriousness of France's cultural tradition. From the balcony of his room, overlooking the villa's meticulously manicured garden, Sartre could contemplate a tree "which had nothing in common with my old friend in Le Havre, but it helped keep the memory of that chestnut alive." [4] He

could also flirt with one Marie Ville, the wife of a stiff, passionless phi-
lology teacher. Attractive, graceful, seemingly ever-lost in her private
fog, yet capable of that spontaneous naive exuberance Sartre admired so
much, Marie quickly responded to Sartre, and they discovered much of
Berlin together.

What they discovered were high-brow theatres and cinemas, low-
brow beer halls, homosexual clubs, transvestites, female wrestlers, ex-
plicit sex acts, and loud, unabashed drinking bouts. When Castor
arrived in Berlin for a visit in February 1934, she was little disturbed by
this fun-loving couple. She met "Marie Girard," as she called her in *The
Prime of Life,* "and liked her; there was no feeling of jealousy on my
part. Yet this was the first time since we had known one another that
Sartre had taken a serious interest in another woman; and jealousy is far
from being an emotion of which I am incapable, or which I underrate.
But this affair neither took me by surprise nor upset any notions I had
formed concerning our joint lives."[5]

In his *War Diaries* six years later, Sartre explained it thus: "I'm not so
sure I didn't seek out women's company, at one time, in order to get rid
of the burden of my ugliness. By looking at them, speaking to them,
and exerting to bring an animated, joyful look to their faces, I'd lose
myself in them and forget myself. . . . In order to seduce, I counted on
my power of speech alone. I can still recall the trouble in which I found
myself in Berlin. I'd set off determined to experience the love of German women, but I soon realized I didn't know enough German to con-
verse. Stripped of my weapon, I was left feeling quite idiotic and dared
attempt nothing—I had to fall back on a French woman."[6]

To me, Sartre repeatedly admitted that sexual relations bored him
but were inevitable. "Most of the time we have no choice," he said, for
example. "To be close to a woman demands that a love relationship be
established, and most women find love incomplete without sex."[7] Yet
he constantly pursued attractive women. Partly, as he said, success made
him forget his ugliness. Partly, however, it was because he simply did
not like men or their social concerns. Wrote he: "I prefer to talk to a
woman about the tiniest things than about philosophy to Aron. It's because those are the tiny things which exist for me; and any woman, even
the stupidest, talks about them as I like to talk about them myself: I *get
on* with women. I like their way of talking, and of saying or seeing
things; I like this way of thinking; I like the subjects they think about."[8]

It seems to me that what Sartre meant at the time—but did not dare
express—was that he simply did not like to talk about social concerns.

Or think about them. Those "tiny things" he happily discussed entailed no responsibility—like the clubs he favored, while ignoring the Nuremberg Congress and the November plebiscite which guaranteed Nazi hegemony for years to come, the anti-Semitism and book burnings, Goebbels' incendiary speeches and Brown Shirts beating Jews in public squares. Nor were Sartre's blinders limited to German streets, out of some misguided respect for his visiting status. Indeed, he was not interested in what was happening in Paris either. There, on 6 February 1934, after weeks of right-wing agitation along both banks of the Seine River, all fascist groups converged on the Chamber of Deputies to overthrow the Republic, causing fifteen deaths and two thousand wounded. They failed mainly because they were not united in one insurrectional party, as had been the case in Germany and Italy; still, the moderate government resigned and was supplanted by conservatives, which scared the left into uniting, eventually, into the Popular Front. That union, however, was never based on common commitments, only on fear of the enemy. Nor were its main leaders willing to use that fear to weld tough, antifascist popular forces. The Socialists, for example, were more determined to weed "Bolsheviks" out of their party than capitulationists. Léon Blum, their leader, did pretend to be a Marxist, but he never accepted Marx's antichauvinism and internationalism and "proved unable to advance beyond generalities about the failure of capitalism," as George Lichtheim rightly said. "By the time the issue came to a head politically, in 1933–36, the enemy was at the gates, and democratic socialism was under attack as never before."[9]

Sartre did not leave Germany before the events of early summer, 1934: starting with "the night of the long knives," 30 June–1 July, Hitler unleashed his S.S. to wipe out his fascist rivals, executing Roehm and scores of his Brown Shirts, to become uncontested dictator. Nevertheless, Sartre and Castor visited Hamburg, which "remained, first and foremost, a great port."[10] Though they did not enjoy the stifling atmosphere of Potsdam or Dresden, and in Munich "found it hard to stomach vast Bavarians who displayed their great hairy thighs while wolfing sausages," and in Nuremberg were shocked at the "thousands of swastikas" which revealed "a whole people hypnotized," neither Sartre nor Castor were yet overly worried that Nazism would soon affect them. On a boat going up the Elbe River, a German veteran of 1914–1918 told Sartre, "If there's another war, we shall not be defeated this time. We shall retrieve our home." Sartre replied, "We all ought to want peace." Said the German, "Honor comes first. First we must retrieve our honor." (I heard veterans of the Vietnam war say exactly the same thing to justify America's massive invasion of tiny Grenada.) But even after the assassination of Austria's Dollfus, reported Castor, "We were so imbued with the characteristic optimism of the period that, for us, the true condition of the world *had* to be peace."[11]

Optimism or egocentrism? Like any other petit bourgeois intellectuals, Sartre and Castor had a fundamental need to matter, to be relevant, to believe that their work made sense, that their lives were not absurd. Like any other intellectuals, they found it extremely difficult to accept the contingency of their individual deaths. But unlike the thinkers of all time who have spent centuries creating (or "discovering," if you wish) explanations, Sartre and Castor rejected all such artifices—god, hereafters, external souls, self-evident causes, perfect purposes, not to mention ideas-in-themselves, hidden universals, reincarnations, transmigrations, transubstantiations, and every other kind of karma imaginable. Realists to the core, they faced their contingency with dogged determination—and refused to shun the very real possibility that their lives, all our lives, were indeed absurd.

Sartre described that absurdity and faced his contingency in *Nausea,* whose second, key draft he composed in Berlin. Written in diary form, it is the story of Antoine Roquentin's discovery that "things are entirely what they appear to be—and behind them . . . there is nothing."[12] Sartre himself summarized his novel thus:

After lengthy travels, Antoine Roquentin has settled in Bouville among ferociously good people. He lives near the railway station in a hotel for traveling salesmen and is writing a thesis in history about an eighteenth-century adventurer, M. de Rollebon. . . . In the evening, Roquentin goes and sits at a table in the Railwaymen's Café and listens to a record—always the same one—'Some of These Days.' And sometimes he goes upstairs with the woman who runs the place. Anny, the woman he loves, left four years ago. She always wanted there to be "perfect moments," and she constantly exhausted herself in minute and vain attempts to reconstruct the world around herself. She and Roquentin broke up. Now Roquentin is losing his past drop by drop; every day he sinks more deeply into a strange and suspicious present. His life itself no longer makes any sense; he thought he had had great adventures; but there aren't any adventures, there are only "stories." . . .

It is then that his real adventure—an insinuating, softly horrible metamorphosis of all his sensations—begins; it is Nausea, it grabs you from behind and then you drift in a tepid sea of time. Is it Roquentin who has changed? Is it the world? Walls, gardens, cafes are abruptly overcome by nausea. . . . Roquentin

Calder

Jean-Paul Sartre by Alexander Calder.
Courtesy of Mr. and Mrs. Klaus G. Perls.

Sartre with his philosophy class,
Lycée Pasteur (Neuilly), 1937–38.
Jean Kanapa is second to his right.
Private collection.

Gerassi family on the beach at Nice in 1937,
during Fernando's leave from the Madrid front.
Private collection.

Sartre and Simone de Beauvoir at
Juan-les-Pins in 1939, just before the war.
Private collection.

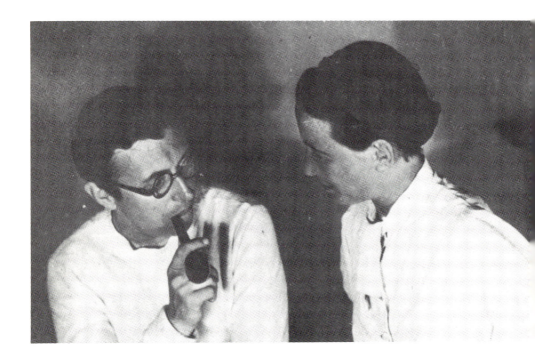

Sartre in 1939. Private collection.

Olga Dominique (Olga Kosakiewicz) in Sartre's *Les Mouches (The Flies)*, Théâtre
Vieux Colombier. Photo © Lipnitzki-Viollet.

Cast of Picasso's wartime play *Le Désir attrapé par la queue* (Desire caught by the tail). First row from left: Sartre, Albert Camus, who directed, and Michel Leiris; back row center: Pablo Picasso with Zette Leiris to his right, and Simone de Beauvoir to his left. Reproduced by permission of Gilberte Brassai.

Sartre at the Café Flore in 1945. Reproduced by permission of Gilberte Brassai.

wanders the streets, voluminous and unjustifiable. And then, on the first day of spring, he grasps the meaning of his adventure: Nausea is Existence revealing itself—and Existence is not pleasant to see. Roquentin still clings to a feeble hope: Anny has written to him; he is going to see her again. But Anny has become a sedentary woman, fat and desperate. She has given up her perfect moments just as Roquentin has given up his adventures. She too, in her own way, has discovered Existence. The two of them have nothing more to say to one another. Roquentin goes back to his solitude at the depths of this enormous Nature which is oozing suffocation on the town and which he senses will soon be rent by cataclysmic upheavals. What is to be done? Call to other men for help? But the other men are good people: they tip their hats to one another without knowing they exist. He is going to leave Bouville; he goes to the Railwaymen's Café to listen one last time to "Some of These Days," and while the record is playing, he catches sight of a chance, a slim chance of accepting himself.[13]

That chance was to stop floundering in the past, to abandon writing the dead history of the Marquis de Rollebon for a living novel, "something that could never happen, an adventure. It would have to be beautiful and hard as steel and make people ashamed of their existence."[14] In *The Words,* Sartre explained: "At the age of thirty, I executed the master-stroke of writing in *Nausea*—quite sincerely, believe me—about the bitter, unjustified existence of my fellowmen and of exonerating my own. I *was* Roquentin; I used him to show, without complacency, the texture of my life."[15] That texture, as Roquentin says, is "a comedy! All these people sitting there, looking serious, eating. . . . Each of them has his little personal difficulty which keeps him from noticing that he exists; there isn't one of them who believes himself indispensable to something or someone. . . . Here we sit, all of us, eating and drinking to preserve our precious existence and really there is nothing, nothing, absolutely no reason for existing." In a world where existence is everywhere, "limited only by existence," Roquentin, each of us, can only feel "de trop," superfluous. That feeling is nausea: it "is not inside me; I feel it *out there* in the wall, in the suspenders, everywhere around me. It makes one with the café, I am the one within it." Nausea is being conscious of the absurdity of life and, through it, that "I am free. . . . Alone and free."[16]

"The implication, of course, is that Roquentin is saved," Sartre told me. "Not so. Oh, there was a possibility that one could be saved through action, but certainly not through writing a novel. And I think I already knew that."[17] He certainly did by 1964 when he told an interviewer

"Weighed against a dying child, *Nausea* doesn't count,"[18] raising the question, What does literature mean in a hungry world? At the time, however, it remained possible that Sartre did continue to believe that he could be saved by writing, and his old friend Paul Nizan condemned him for it. Reviewing *La Nauséa* in the Communist daily *Ce Soir,* Nizan characterized it as obsessed with "absolute solitude" and chastized him for being "entirely unconcerned with moral problems."[19]

"Let's put that period in perspective," Sartre defended himself in 1971. "First of all, despite all the efforts by my grandfather to teach me German, I did not speak it well at all, and reading it was an effort. Second, no one at the French Institute really believed that these Nazis were going to last. After the night of the long knives, I understood that something brutal had taken place, but there was no one in the streets, and no one knew anything for sure. We were dependent on the French left, and it did not seem very apprehensive. Aron, who was still a socialist then, told me that Hitler and his horde could not possibly last another year. And then, true, I still believed in the special status of the writer. My job may have been to denounce fascism, but in my writing, at my desk. And that, if you read *Nausea* carefully, you'll see that I did, within of course the context of the time, and of my political consciousness, which was petit bourgeois, individualistic, and democratic."[20]

Within that context, there's no doubt that *Nausea,* as Genevieve Idt pointed out, was addressed to other petit bourgeois intellectuals tempted to betray their commitment and become Nizan's watchdogs.[21] The word *worker* appeared only once, and strikes were nothing more than obstacles that kept the rich from becoming richer; the only social conflict mentioned was the one pitting the old shipowning families against the new speculators; as for what was happening in the world, Roquentin's only awareness of it was: "I am alone, but I march like a regiment descending on a city. At this very moment there are ships on the sea resounding with music; lights are turned on in all the cities of Europe; Communists and Nazis shooting it out in the streets of Berlin, unemployed pounding the pavements of New York, women at their dressing-tables in a warm room putting mascara on their eye-lashes."[22]

But, Sartre insisted ex post facto, "I described the ruling class, and the potential rebels, the marginals, crushed by that class. That is the beginning of political awareness."[23] Surrounded by the portraits of Bouville's founding fathers, Roquentin, upon visiting the local museum, did indeed see in the eyes and posture of one of them a "faultless man" who "had used his right to live. The slightest doubt had never crossed those magnificent grey eyes. . . . He had always done his duty, all his duty, his duty as son, husband, father, leader. . . . I was in the center of the room, the cynosure of all these grave eyes. I was neither father nor grandfather, nor even a husband. I did not have a vote, I hardly paid any taxes: I could not boast of being a tax-payer, an elector, nor even of having the humble right to honour which twenty years of obedience confers on an employee. My existence began to worry me seriously. Was I not a simple spectre? 'Hey!' I suddenly told myself, '*I am the soldier!*'" [24]

Roquentin had discovered that the objective world (nausea) cannot exist without subjective thought, that solitude is a bourgeois complex, that life begins on the other side of despair. Staring at those portraits in the Mudville museum, Roquentin, for a moment, became the opposite of Sartre—a rebel. While Sartre still lived with one eye on history and his future biographer (for example, he wrote his letters, even to Castor, with the view that "they would be published after my death"),[25] Roquentin understood, as Iris Murdoch put it, that "as language may solidify and kill our thoughts, so our values may be solidified if we do not subject them to a continual process of breaking down and rebuilding." [26] He knew, even if Sartre said so only much later, that those who think they can win are the *salauds,* the scum, those powerful bourgeois whom our society heralds, indeed all those who justify their existences by giving themselves public tasks. They are the enemy, Roquentin told himself, and they did not interest Sartre except as such. It was the "soldiers," those petit bourgeois running dogs who respectfully visit the museums of the world's Mudvilles, those collaborationists who are ever ready to accept the ideology of the dominant class, of the enemy, that Sartre really hoped to change. He wanted to change himself. But in *Nausea,* he merely condemned them.

And thus condemned himself. For, no sooner had he returned to his Mudville, Le Havre, and settled back into the hotel for traveling salesmen near the railway station, than he behaved as the soldier who refuses to deal with his nausea, as a *salaud* who thought he could win. He taught philosophy without rocking the boat: no Hegel and no politics. He did not like his colleagues but avoided confronting them. He did not want to discipline students but kept them in line just the same. Sometimes he even used verbal terror: he would walk into the classroom "with a nauseated expression," remembered Le Petit Bost, and "chew his nails and, every now and then, stare at the class, and then, after a silence of forty-five seconds, would say: 'On all these faces, not a hint of intelligence!'"[27]

Commuting between Le Havre, Paris, and Rouen, where Castor was teaching, Sartre enjoyed his train rides by reading mystery novels one after the other.[28] In Paris, he saw my parents a lot and occasionally Camille and her paramour, the director Charles Dullin, with whom he was rapidly becoming very close.[29] In Rouen, while keeping up his trio relationship with Castor and Olga, he also became intimate with Colette Audry, and the three of them (Castor, Audry and Sartre) spent hours talking, walking, arguing together. Wrote Audry, "Never has conversation made me so happy. . . . We would meet almost every week on the train to Paris; once, I went with Castor to Le Havre, often we lunched together in a small bar-restaurant. . . . They knew Rouen better than I, who had preceded them there by two years. . . . They offered me the spectacle of a true relationship, so rare, so difficult, between two people who loved each other. . . . I consider meeting them one of the greatest accidents of my life."[30]

In Le Havre, meanwhile, Sartre wrote, as usual. He had set aside *Nausea* temporarily to determine what images were. Commissioned by a former professor to produce a work for an encyclopedic series, Sartre, still greatly influenced by Husserl, turned out a massive phenomenological study of *The Image*. The publisher kept only the first part (issued under the title *L'Imagination* in 1936), in which Sartre reviewed and discarded past descriptions and concluded that the image, distinguished by its intention, "is an act and not a thing. The image is consciousness *of* something,"[31] thus condemning all previous thinkers on the subject for having confused essence with existence—an absolutely key distinction for all of Sartre's subsequent philosophy. Even Mary Warnock, the much-touted but much-biased English philosophical critic who kept trying to find fault with Sartre, admitted the importance of this Sartrean conclusion. Under Sartre, she wrote, "imagination has been *re*defined. All the definitions which made it a kind of thinking, or a kind of peering at mental entities, have been rejected. It has been redefined as the mode of consciousness of an object, whether an existent or non-existent object, which entails the bringing into fleeting existence of an appearance which fades at once into nothingness . . . Man's ability to imagine things, which, of course, was never in doubt, is now shown to be connected, in its essence, with his ability to choose."[32] Would this be contradicted by a person hallucinating who does not know whether he or she is imagining or perceiving? Sartre said no, because the object hallucinated would not relate "properly" to the rest of perceptual existence. And this he knew from experience.

Indeed, in February 1935, Sartre's old classmate and friend Daniel Lagache, now a doctor, had suggested that in order to be better equipped to pry into imagination, Sartre should let himself be injected with mescaline. Lagache warned him that "it would be a mildly disagreeable experience, although not in the least dangerous," Castor said. "The worst that could happen was that Sartre might 'behave rather oddly' for a few hours afterward." In fact, Sartre "freaked out." Umbrellas became vultures, shoes turned into skeletons, "and faces acquired monstrous characteristics, while behind him, just past the corner of his eye, swarmed crabs and polyps and grimacing Things." Nor did such apparitions disappear; days, weeks later, "houses had leering faces, all eyes and jaws, and he couldn't help looking at every clockface he passed, expecting it to display the features of an owl—which it always did. He knew perfectly well that such objects were in fact houses and clocks, and no one could say that he *believed* in their eyes and gaping maws—but a time might well come when he *would* believe in them; one day he would really be convinced that there was a lobster trotting along behind him." [33]

Sartre's crisis might have been induced by the mescalin injections, said Dr. Lagache, but not caused by them. The other doctors to whom Castor displayed Sartre, agreed. Castor blamed "fatigue and tension," then decided that "Sartre could not resign himself to going on to 'the age of reason,' to full manhood." [34] To me, Sartre explained it thus: "Ever since lycée days, I had always lived in a collective setting, always with friends, comrades, in situations where I could be myself and a stranger simultaneously, where each of us had a voice, hence an identity, but where decisions were collective, made by the group, six, eight, ten individuals whose individual will fused into the collective will—to the point that, soon after a collective action was decided, no one quite remembered who was for and who against. In such circumstances, anxiety-ridden folk, like me, for I was always anxious, become less so, since individual decisions are no longer so individual. When I think back, it is clear that I have always been well-adapted in collective situations, at school, in the army, at the French Institute in Berlin, and later, again in the army and as a prisoner of war. I didn't realize it in 1935, but I was never such an individualist. So I guess the mescalin brought out all my renewed anxiety. Here I was back from Berlin with no more escapes. I was a professor among other professors I despised. True, I now had a life-long relationship with Castor, which was much more precious to me than my past, rather vague relationships with ten or so comrades. But it wasn't the same thing. Now the only collectivity I could experience was with my students, which is probably why I hung out with them so much. But I could no longer count on a life without the terrible weight of existence staring me in the face."[35] In other words, Sartre had become Roquentin: he had nausea. The lobsters and crabs which followed him wanted to pull him back, away from teachers and parents, away from politicians and *salauds,* away from choices and responsibilities, away indeed from the age of reason.

Castor soon began to resent Sartre's depression—and his lobsters. She could tolerate only so much moroseness and self-pity. And she became increasingly jealous of Olga, who was cherishing her newfound role of nurse, and of Audry who was also going through a horrendous depression herself. Every time they met, Sartre and Audry asked each other "about our respective madnesses. Until one day when Castor suddenly stopped on the sidewalk, slammed down her foot and shouted: 'I've had enough. I see no one but nuts. I'm the only one who isn't mad. I too want to be crazy!' We all laughed: from then on, I was half cured," said Audry.[36]

But not Sartre. "I've been thinking about what we discussed the other day," Sartre told me on 7 May 1971, two weeks after we had analyzed his crisis, "and I think we can conclude that my lobsters represented both fear of the future and loss of the past. When I was twenty, I had fantasies of great adventures, influenced of course by Pardaillan and Ponson du Terail, and those fantasies, I knew now, would never come true. So it was my collective past and my heroic future, as envisaged in the past, which I missed. But I think I should also insist that I was very much aware of the dreadful future which we all faced. Not only my fate—teaching, writing, teaching, writing—which was bleak enough, but all our collective fates—fascism. Just because I never went on demonstrations is not proof that I was apolitical. I was well aware that the *salauds* were in power, everywhere, and that we risked being engulfed in a vicious fascism here in France."[37]

All his adult life, Sartre insisted that a man is what he does, not what he imagines himself to be. There is no *vie intérieure,* Castor kept repeating. There is only existing, lamented Roquentin. Everything we do, we choose to do it, said Sartre; everything we don't do, we choose not to. By these rules and precepts, then, Sartre did nothing to stop fascism. "I didn't have a single politicized student," he explained, "neither did

Castor. There had been no tradition of discussing politics in class. Even Audry, who was so militant outside class, remained 'objective' in class, which meant of course using the Brunschvicg text and talking about the State the way Kant had approached it."[38] Why? It seems Sartre never asked himself the question. France's Croix de Feu fascists were gaining strength, its police becoming more brutal, its intellectuals more politicized. Barbusse, Gide, Malraux, Guéhenno, and Audry, Nizan, Fernando (who, with Stépha and me, was back living in Paris) and other friends of Sartre's, but not Sartre himself, joined the Association of Revolutionary Writers and Artists, to oppose fascism in France—but were kept "civilized" by its Communist leader, Vaillant-Couturier. As a result, Georges Bataille and a group of surrealist poets launched more ultraleft organizations and rarely hesitated to descend into the streets to confront right-wing processions.

Nor were these mobilizations aimed at imagined phantoms. In January 1935, the Sarre region voted to be incorporated into Nazi Germany. In October, Mussolini invaded Ethiopia. In November, Spain arrested its Socialist leaders and charged them with sedition, while in Limoges, in the center of France, Croix de Feu militants seized the streets, killing left-wing militants who tried to stop them. In March 1936, Hitler denounced the Treaty of Locarno and occupied the Rhur. It seemed as if nothing could stop the right. But thanks, in part, to the massive propaganda effort launched by left-wing intellectuals, the right did not win everywhere—yet. In Spanish elections of March 1936, the left, united in a Popular Front, crushed all other forces (winning 263 seats to 135 for the right-wing bloc and 63 for the center). In France, two months later, a similar Popular Front also won the elections, with the Communist party increasing its parliamentary representation from nine to 73 deputies. Yet, to it all, Sartre remained at best a voyeur. Wrote Castor: "For the July 14 celebrations, Sartre and I went along to the Bastille, where five hundred thousand people marched past, flourishing tricolor flags, singing, and shouting . . . Up to a certain point we shared this enthusiasm, but we had no inclination to march in procession, or sing and shout with the rest. . . . We remained spectators."[39]

"Were you that elitist that you could not join the masses?" I asked Sartre. "My view was that each of us had to do his task," he replied, not realizing he was defining himself as one of his *salauds*. "I was for the Popular Front, absolutely. But my job was to write. I remember celebrating with Fernando and Stépha, in fact, long into the night, the Front's victory. And Castor and I were there, cheering, waving, when the marchers came by. We knew very well that only the left could stop fascism. We were very happy that it had won." "But tell me," I prodded, "did you vote?" "No," Sartre admitted.[40] Nor did he write a single essay, story, or tract either in favor of the left or in opposition to the right. No wonder that Nizan, Sartre's boyhood chum, denounced him as a traitor.

Nizan was just thirty when he returned from almost a year-long visit to Soviet Russia. His first novel, *Antoine Bloyé*, had been hailed by critics, and he had been well coached in party politics by two confirmed Communist writers: Louis Aragon, the editor-in-chief of *Ce Soir* and hence his boss, so haughty and cynical that he let slip in print once that "there are days when I wished I had an eraser with which to wipe out the filthy presence of humanity";[41] and Georges Politzer, the philosopher with whom Nizan stayed friends until he quit the party in 1939. Castor described Politzer in her memoirs: "There was a striking contrast between his dogmatism and the charming changeability of his face; though I relished his conversation, I liked even more his gestures, his voice, his freckles, and that flaming red hair, which Sartre borrowed for his Antoine Roquentin."[42] Like the Surrealist Warlord André Breton, who once, before he too turned away from communism, longed to see Cossacks watering their horses in the fountain of La Place de la Concorde, Politzer, a true internationalist and genuine defender of unpopular causes, loved to imagine tough Russian sailors stumping out their cigarettes on the French tapestries of the Kremlin. In his first book, *Critique des fondements de la psychologie* (1928), Politzer had demolished Bergson as a "parade," discarded all traditional psychology for its bourgeois ideology, approved of Freud's empirical descriptions but dismissed his generalizations, and concluded, forerunning Sartre, that the future must be a "concrete psychology" which studies the intentionality of choices in an objective world.[43] Politzer who died from Gestapo torture without talking during the war, had encouraged Nizan to publish *Aden-Arabie* and *The Watchdogs;* in 1934 he pushed him to go to Russia "to see the future."

He saw it, alright, and it certainly worked, Nizan said, but not for him. Reported Castor: "He told us of vast banquets where the vodka flowed in rivers, and rhapsodized over Georgian wines; the *wagon-lits* were so comfortable, hotel rooms absolutely magnificent. His casual tone somehow contrived to suggest that this luxury reflected vast general Russian prosperity. He described a village down in the South, near the Turkish frontier: it was brimful of local color, it seemed, complete with veiled women, markets, and Oriental bazaars. His artful tricks delighted us. The friendly, almost confidential key in which his conversation was pitched excluded any suggestion of propaganda, and certainly he wasn't telling lies." But something was wrong nevertheless. "He had asked himself whether the Socialist creed might not somehow help him to exorcise it [his fear of death], and felt quite optimistic as to the prospects; but his lengthy interrogation of young Russian Communists concerning this topic had elicited a unanimous reply—in the face of death, comradeship and solidarity were no help at all, and they were all scared of death themselves. Officially—as, for instance, when he was reporting on his trip abroad at some meeting—Nizan interpreted facts in an optimistic way. To the extent that progress was made in solving technical problems, he explained, love and death would regain their former importance in the USSR: a new humanism was being born. But in private conversation with us he spoke very differently. It had been a great blow to him to discover that, in Russia as in France, the individual was alone when he died, and knew it."[44]

But Nizan understood that his fear of death was a bourgeois complex. Most people in this world worry about day-to-day survival, feeding and clothing their families, guaranteeing them some minimum of health care, educating their children. Those were the needs that fascism disregarded, that the *salauds* kept eliminating, that the right wing considered an unjustified luxury. Therefore, Nizan kept his private concerns private, and deemed Sartre a traitor for writing publicly about his. Nizan's attack was in his second novel, *Le cheval de troie (The Trojan Horse)* published in 1935, in which a main character, Lange, an anarchist provincial (Bouville?) schoolmaster who had graduated from l'Ecole Normale, was obviously patterned after Sartre. Everyone knew it, even if Nizan tactfully denied it.

Lange, wrote Nizan, "had achieved such a degree of solitary self-involvement and fixed relationships that he could no longer walk among men, could only see them from afar. . . . He had but one hobby: to play himself, for himself. This act sometimes fooled women. He would say: fakers are those who best defend themselves against themselves." Caught in the midst of a struggle between the right and the left in which his own students were committed up to their necks (which they willingly risked), Lange ignored their needs, wandered the streets of his Mudville, "alone with his city: it was his fate to be alone in cities, to wander among its cobblestones which were as paralyzed as he was, which communicated among themselves no more than he did with others. When he thought about the books he could write, he imagined a book which would describe only the encounters of a man with a city, where all other men would be nothing more than decor. The book would deal with a man alone, truly alone, as solitary as a desert islet."

Knowing that Sartre, since graduating ENS, had lived only in hotels, Nizan wrote that his Lange "could sleep only if he felt surrounded by people shuffling about, breathing, dreaming. In a hotel there's at least a night watchman, a bell boy, one can ring, cry out, one does not risk dying alone, except of course if one suffers a hemorrhage or a seizure, but then one doesn't notice death." Nor could Lange, who, like Sartre, pretended to be on the side of the proletariat, "stand the speeches of workers, of functionaries" who never emitted "a single solid argument." Also like Sartre, he wanted to stay on the sidelines, away from the rabble he supposedly supported. When he got caught inside a working-men's demonstration, he "did not sing, did not applaud . . . a strange body among them, like a stone, impenetrable, proud of being a stone, hard, distinct, separate: pride saves itself as best it can." And, of course, he certainly would never "sing the *International* to try to enter into the skin of others, he made himself look foolish—one can be a Pascalian* only to a point, he said—and besides he didn't know the words."[45]

When the chips were down, and Lange (which means *angel* in French) had to choose, Nizan had him betray his students and join the fascists. This was not fair. Sartre may have been obsessed with his meals, his chestnut tree, his lobsters, and his lovers, but he remained loyal to his students, and never once contemplated switching sides. True, when Olga had a fling with Zuorro, he exploded into such a vio-lent, childish tantrum that it abated only when Olga guaranteed him that no other man could ever matter more than he. But Sartre then pushed Le Petit Bost to take Zuorro's place, and when Bost and Olga eventually got married Sartre and Castor were their jubilant witnesses. By then, Bost himself was at least waist-deep into politics. He cam-paigned for the Popular Front, went to all its demonstrations, often even joined picket lines at the entrances to factories whose owners would not honor the Front's reform program (which included, for the first time in the capitalist world, paid vacations.) "That summer" of 1936, wrote Castor, "the beaches and countryside had their first wave

---

*Blaise Pascal (1623–1662), a French philosopher who is famous for his wager ap-proach to the future (in his case, on the existence of God: since there is no proof either way, he said, why not bet that He exists; if He does, one wins; if He doesn't, one will never know). Here Nizan is referring to bourgeois intellectuals who, in the Thirties, bet that the proletarian revolution would win.

of vacations-with-pay visitors. Two weeks is not very long; but all the same, the workers of Saint-Ouen or Aubervilliers did get a change of air from their factories and suburbs."* Sartre and Castor viewed such activity as useless: "Our habit of abstention was largely due to our powerlessness, and we did not a priori object to participating in events. The proof of this is that when the strikes came and they went through the streets taking up collections for the strikers, we gave all we could."[46]

Even as late as 1960, when *The Prime of Life* was published, Simone de Beauvoir could not understand how stupidly paternalistic that statement of "proof" had been, equivalent to the anti-Semite's defense: "But some of my best friends are Jews." It does explain, however, why Nizan felt that Sartre would some day betray. Sartre never did. But in 1936, he just could not understand that no painting, no *Nausea* was worth the death of a child. He could not even understand, then, that no special status of the intellectual could ever survive fascism. No matter what intellectuals thought of themselves when *les salauds* gave them such status, they would never be more than watchdogs.

Sartre was in Paris at the beginning of the summer of 1936. So were the Gerassis: We were living in a small, duplex apartment-cum-studio on rue Delambre, just off Montparnasse. Stépha kept us alive by giving facial massages, house to house. Fernando did some translations, painted—and babysat me. In the late afternoon of July 18, he had taken me to La Rotonde, then a wide-open popular café catering to artists, anarchists, and agitators (today, refurbished, to tourists, tax accountants, and taxidermists). Tying me to his table with a long leash, which allowed me to wander from table to table to beg croissants from acquiescing pigeons, Fernando was discussing Mondrian's objectivism with Sandy (Alexander) Calder, when Sartre suddenly walked in, flushed and excited. He announced that Franco's Moroccan army had landed on the Spanish coast. The Civil War had begun. Five years old, I had just stolen a croissant when Fernando grabbed me by both shoulders and held me so tightly I almost cried. I thought he was going to hit me, but instead he kissed me on both cheeks. "I have to go to Spain right now," he said in a staccato flurry, "Sartre will explain to your mother. But you have to be strong now, because you will be the man in the house." Then, wiping my tears awkwardly, he kissed me again, stood up, and trotted off to war without a further word to anyone. A year

---

*The two weeks soon became four, a right not yet won by workers in the United States of America, richest of the capitalist states, fifty years later.

later, Fernando, who had never even fired a hunting rifle before, became a general, one of the main defenders of Madrid. But that evening,
meanwhile, Sartre was completely befuddled. He just could not understand. He took me home and tried the best he could to explain to
Stépha. She understood alright, but became hysterical.

"He was wearing silk socks," she said, "silk socks, silk socks, silk
socks . . ."

The Spanish Civil War, wrote Simone de Beauvoir, was the "drama that for the next two and a half years was to dominate our lives."[1] But that summer of 1936, while Fernando was learning to shoot a rifle, and Colette Audry was whipping up support for the defenders of Barcelona, and Le Petit Bost was shouting his head off for France's Popular Front government to help the Spanish Republic, Sartre and Castor went off to enjoy the sights of fascist Italy. After being delighted by Rome's "food, its noise, its public squares, its old brickwork and pipes,"[2] they investigated the alleys and arcades, the dives and dumps, the bars and brothels of Naples, where Sartre cheerfully felt himself falling "into an enormous carnivorous existence."[3] While Mussolini dispatched his crack divisions to help General Franco massacre Spain's new, hard-won democracy, Sartre felt "meaningfully" uprooted by the low-life of Naples, and wrote about it.

To Olga, Sartre wrote probably one of the longest letters ever written, some fifteen thousand words about Naples's grand vias and tiny streets, flamboyant plazas and ugly buildings, delightful mosaics and disturbing frescoes—without one word of politics.[4] Then, while Castor went off to admire the Amalfi coast, he barhopped with sailors and pimps and wrote a story about "prosciutto, mortadella, and all different kinds of sausages"[5] and the "specialized" whorehouse he visited, where two women showed him the "positions of Pompeii," before trying to entice him to join them.[6] (A story he never published because, he admitted, "it was no good."[7])

A few weeks after Sartre returned from Italy, he went to see Stépha. She showed him a letter she had just received from Fernando. It said, "I lied to you. I told you I was a painter. A painter does not kill. But I do. The man you married was a fraud. Forget him."[8] When I asked him about it, Sartre remembered only that she was very depressed.[9] In *The Age of Reason,* begun in the winter of 1938–39 and published after the war, Sartre translated that depression thus:

"And Gomez [Fernando]?" asked Mathieu [Sartre].
"Just the same as usual. He's at Barcelona," said Sarah [Stépha].
"Have you had any news of him?"
"Last week. A full account of his exploits," Sarah replied ironically . . .

"You know he's a colonel now?"

"Colonel." Mathieu thought of the man of yesterday, and his heart contracted. Gomez had actually gone . . . bareheaded and without an overcoat, as though he were going to buy cigarettes at the Dome. He had not returned. The room had remained exactly as he had left it: an unfinished canvas, a half-cut copperplate on the table, among phials of acid. . . . He thought, "He was a beast to Sarah all the same . . ."

She did not want to talk about Gomez. She had forgiven him everything, his treacheries, escapades, and cruelty. But not that. Not his departure for Spain: he had gone away to kill men; he had killed men by now.[10]

Was it important for Sartre to create a contrapuntal theme to Gomez's commitment? In reality, Stépha was just as committed as Fernando in 1936; she very much wanted to "be useful" in Spain but was held back from going there by me, since I was only five years old. Early in 1937, before Sartre started writing *The Age of Reason,* she found a boarding school that was both highly recommended and sympathetic to the Spanish Republic; once I was happily stashed there, Stépha gave her professional make-up kits to the street-walkers of Jules Chaplin street, and joined Ehrenburg's propaganda bureau, first in Madrid, then in Barcelona.[11] Sartre tried to stop her. "It's an empty gesture, an absurd gesture," he said, according to Stépha, "You can't be with Fernando, you can't fight. And the Republic is going to lose anyway."

"The whole war is an empty gesture since it is lost," Stépha remembered answering, more or less. "So what? Fernando is not fighting because he thinks we're going to win. He's fighting because he's antifascist and antifascism means fighting fascism."[12]

Did Sartre really think that fighting fascism *anywhere* was an empty gesture? In *The Reprieve,* he reported this exchange between himself (Mathieu) and Fernando (Gomez):

"We have lost the war," said Gomez.

Mathieu knew it, but had thought that Gomez didn't know it yet. . . . Gomez was seated there, the moonlight on his right, and on his left a lady with a half-smile on her face; he was on his way back to Spain, and he knew that the Republicans had lost the war.

"You can't be sure," said Mathieu. "No one can be sure."

"Yes, they can," said Gomez. "*We* are sure."

He did not seem cast down; he was merely stating a fact. He looked at Mathieu with the calm expression of a man whose task is finished. He said: "All my soldiers are sure the war is lost."

"And they're fighting anyhow?" said Mathieu.

"What do you expect them to do?"

Mathieu shrugged his shoulders. "Obviously . . ."

Mathieu looked at Gomez with curiosity. "And you regret nothing?" he asked.

"Nothing at all."

"Not even painting?"

"Not even painting."

. . . and Gomez thought: "I'm strong, I love life and I risk it, I expect death tomorrow, or some time soon, and I'm not afraid, I love luxury, and I'm going back to squalor and starvation, I know what I want. I know why I am fighting, I give orders and am obeyed, I've sacrificed everything—painting, and success, and I am perfectly content." He thought of Mathieu and said to himself: "I wouldn't be in his skin."[13]

If Sartre was only Mathieu in 1940–41 when he wrote *The Reprieve,* then of course he was only a Cartesian intellectual searching for meaning. But obviously Sartre was also Gomez, insofar as he *chose* to write about him, *chose* to put in his fictional mouth the same words Fernando proclaimed in real life. True, in 1937–38, Sartre *was Mathieu.* "He was French," Sartre said about himself through Mathieu. "It would have served no useful purpose to disavow his solidarity with other Frenchmen. I decided on nonintervention in Spain, I sent no arms, I closed the frontier to the volunteers. He must defend himself with all the rest or suffer condemnation with them, together with the maître d'hotel and the dyspeptic gentleman drinking Vichy water."[14]

But by 1940, he was also riddled with guilt. Why else would he condemn Mathieu—and through him all noninterventionist Frenchmen? Sartre had changed his mind about Fernando by then. "I didn't like him for three reasons: first, because he had a habit of judging people, and always judging them badly if he liked them; second, I felt he was too intolerant of others and too tolerant of himself, and only much later did I discover that he was ferociously critical of himself, but in private; and third, I was irritated by the way he walked around as if he had the truth, the absolute truth. He could be very funny and a lot of fun, and I enjoyed being with him most of the time, *mais alors,* when he got on his high horse . . ."[15] How true. When I argued with him about anything, he was perfectly capable of saying, "How dare you talk when I am on top of the mountain and I can see you, at the bottom, taking the wrong path." Yet, when Fernando came to France on leave, Sartre went out of his way to see him: "At that moment Gomez was the only friend he did want to see."[16] And Fernando was terribly insulting: "All Frenchmen are swine," Gomez kept repeating;[17] *"Salauds de Francais!"* (French scum!), he snarled, and seemed to include Sartre and me in his rancorous attack," Castor reported.[18] "Then why pursue such a gross, insensitive false friend?" I asked Cantor. "Fernando," she explained, "was our conscience."[19]

"You have to understand my situation in France in 1936," Sartre said in 1971.

I supported the Spanish Republic, totally, absolutely. I thought of myself as an antifascist through and through. But I had never suffered. I had always been certain of my future. Commitment for me, like for any bourgeois intellectual who has not been faced with misery, poverty, torture, or death, was purely cerebral. I was on the left, yes, because rightists, conservatives, liberals end up destroying every last vestige of human morality. I knew that even then. Either they consciously, openly think only of themselves, how to get richer or have more power, and are perfectly willing to exploit anyone and everyone to have their way, or they pretend to themselves that there are always two sides of every question so as not to choose. The former are enemies, the latter are scums who end up helping the former win. I was not a liberal. Mathieu didn't think there were two sides to every question. He hesitated, he floundered about trying to commit himself but on the left, not on the right or in the center. But, like me, he analyzed every issue to pieces. What could I do in 1936? Fight in Spain, with my eyes? Join the Communist Party? There were too many nasty factors involved to do that. March? Yes, but I hated marches. I was convinced that they accomplished nothing. I had that reaction that all people have who don't understand what's going on, who don't understand that thought never made the world turn, only action did. Besides, I looked upon Spain as somewhat isolated, or special, a drama, a tragedy, but not quite part of us all, I mean, that somehow we in France, in Europe, and therefore somehow in Spain too, we'd all come out of it.[20]

Whatever Sartre's rationale in 1971, his behavior in 1936–37 was that of a typical apolitical liberal intellectual. Now teaching at a lycée in Laon, 150 kilometers northeast of Paris (while Castor was in the Paris quarter of Passy, at the Lycée Molière), Sartre made his headquarters the Dôme café at the crossing of Montparnasse and Raspail boulevards. He attended plays (Shakespeare's *Julius Caesar,* Jean-Louis Barrault's adaptation of Cervantes' *Numanicia*), read novels (Bernanos's *Diary of a Country Priest,* Queneau's *Les Derniers Jours*), and dined his women: Castor of course; Olga; her sister Wanda; Camille (who had adapted *Julius Caesar,* which Dullin directed). He wrote. And he was published.

In August 1936, *L'Imagination* appeared. In July 1937, the pres-

tigious *Nouvelle Revue Française* (*NRF*), put out by Gallimard, published his short story *The Wall*. In August, *Recherches Philosophiques*
brought out *The Transcendence of the Ego*. Sartre was well on his way.
And he knew that so was *Nausea*. On its first round, *Melancholia,* as
Sartre had titled it, had been rejected by Gallimard editors. Sartre had
been incredibly depressed, but then, recovering his self-worth, he had
refused to accept defeat and, using his contacts (Nizan, Pierre Bost,
Dullin, Malraux) to circumvent the unfavorable readers, got his manuscript to Gaston Gallimard, the head of the publishing firm. Gaston read
it, liked it, changed its title to *Nausea,* and ordered his henchmen to clean
it up. That, said editor Brice Parain, meant deleting some fifty pages of
Roquentin's past, details of life in Le Havre, a rape scene fantasy, and
Roquentin's first meeting with Anny. Also out were such Roquentin
sentences as, "I am not a chief, a responsible man, or any other type of
asshole," and, "I spit, I shit on bourgeois virtues." Roquentin's prick
became a finger, eliminating his erection, and "a pair of small gray balls"
was turned into "a pair of small gray erasers." [21] Sartre was too pleased
to be published to object too strenuously.

The Wall, set in warring Spain and provoked, said Sartre, because "I
was imagining the death of Bost," [22] who had tried to enlist in the Republican army, was the story of three anarchists awaiting execution in a
fascist jail. After two are shot, the third, Pablo, the protagonist, decides
to trick his captors, invents a hiding place for his leader, which turns out
to be precisely where the leader was hidden. It was "a spontaneous
emotional reaction to the Spanish Civil War," Sartre said, but added
that it was really more of an exposition of the "absurdity of these
deaths." In this particular story, Sartre was also saying that one should
never play by the rules of the prosecutors or inquisitors—or, more generally, of the dominant class. But his statement that Pablo was not "de-
voted enough to a cause for his death not to seem absurd to him," [23]
implied the reverse corollary—that death is not absurd if the victim is
totally committed to his acts and his cause.

That, in effect, was Sartre's purpose in writing *Les chemins de la
liberté (The Roads to Freedom)*. Meant to be a four-volume saga (only
three were completed) of various characters trying to preserve their
freedom by refusing to become involved, it showed them bounced
about by history and others like corks in a Pacific tempest, learning,
often too late, that all of us are involved in the fate of the world, that we
are responsible for our failures and for making our freedom—our existence—meaningful. But as Sartre clearly revealed in the first two *Roads*

volumes, *The Age of Reason* and *The Reprieve*, it was a tough lesson even for Sartre. Endowing Mathieu with most of his own 1936 liabilities and few of his charms—or his great sense of humor—Sartre emptied his hero's life of all authentic content by making him an absolute rationalist. Mathieu dissected every possible action into so many possibilities that, like the hero of Flaubert's *Sentimental Education*, his life floated away without offering a glimmer of self-satisfaction. As a result, Mathieu could "recognize no allegiance except to myself," though he realized that without "responsibility for my own existence, it would seem utterly absurd to go on existing."[24] Mathieu's commitment was only to himself, never to the outside: "Here I am, lounging in a chair, committed to my present life right up to the ears and believing in nothing. And yet I also wanted to set out for a Spain of mine."[25] But he couldn't, of course, because his will was rational. "I must be self-impelled, and able to say: 'I am because I will; I am my own beginning.' Empty, pompous words, the commonplace of the intellectual. . . . He ought to have made his decision at twenty-five. Like Brunet [in this case, Paul Nizan, though Nizan also became the model for another character in volume 3]. Yes, but at that age one doesn't decide with proper motivation. One is liable to be fooled. . . . He thought of going to Russia, of dropping his studies, of learning a manual trade. But what had restrained him each time on the brink of such a violent break was that he had no *reasons* for acting thus. Without reasons, such acts would have been mere impulses. And so he continued to wait . . ."[26]

And wait Sartre/Mathieu did, letting his friends fight his battles, his mistress dispose of his child, his family salvage his home—and pay his debts. "I should myself have thought," said Mathieu's reactionary brother Jacques, who was patterned after Sartre's stepfather, Mancy, "that freedom consisted in frankly confronting situations into which one has deliberately entered, and accepting all one's responsibilities. But that, no doubt, is not your view; you condemn capitalist society, and yet you are an official in that society; you display an abstract sympathy with Communists, but you take care not to commit yourself, you have never voted. You despise the bourgeois class, and yet you are a bourgeois, son and brother of a bourgeois, and you live like a bourgeois."[27] While from the other side, his Communist friend Brunet lamented that "you live in a void, you have cut your bourgeois connections, you have no tie with the proletariat, you're adrift, you're an abstraction, a man who is not there. It can't be an amusing sort of life. . . . Do you suppose you can live your whole life in parentheses?"[28] And he himself, after breaking with his mistress *"for nothing,"* wept as volume 1 ended, that "all I do, I do *for nothing.* It might be said I am robbed of the consequences of my acts; everything happens as though I could always play my strokes again. I don't know what I would give to do something irrevocable." The characteristic of all bourgeois intellectuals is that everything they do is very revocable, for reason dominates impulse so much that it can always erase action. Said Mathieu—and so feared Sartre in 1936–37—"I have attained the age of reason." [29]

Around him, in France, indeed in all of Europe and most of the world, Reason had convinced most leaders and politicians to let fascism prevail. In France that meant to let the Spanish Popular Front government sink. On the fascist side, Franco received from the Axis powers all the guns and planes, tanks and troops he needed. On the other, France's "Socialist" Popular Front Prime Minister Léon Blum refused to honor his country's treaties and obligations, closed the Spanish-French border, prohibited all arms sales to the legally constituted and recognized Republican government, and on 1 August 1936 proposed a formal "nonintervention" pact among Germany, Italy, England and France. Hitler and Mussolini accepted eight days later—and increased their aid to Franco's *falangistas*. Blum knew it, of course; every newspaper in the world proclaimed it. Even the conservative *Le Temps* reported Italy's shipments and the heavy air raids on Madrid carried out by Axis bombers. [30] Nevertheless, Blum stuck to his phony neutrality and on 1 January 1937, promulgated a law forbidding all recruitment or aid for International Brigades. Supported by most radicals and Socialists, that betrayal by Léon Blum and his party should have forever after stopped any intelligent Frenchman from joining or voting for the French Socialist Party.*

Praising Blum's "courage [and] moral integrity," Raymond Aron supported that betrayal. Even after the German Kondor legion air force carried out its infamous saturation bombing of Guernica on 26 April 1937; even retroactively after the facts became well known—that Franco could never have won without German tanks and planes, Italian troops,

---

*So endemic to that party has been that betrayal (as had been the German Socialists' prowar stance in 1918, the U.S. Socialists' heralding of Vietnamese dictator Diem, the British and Italian Socialists' support of U.S. nuclear bases on their territory) that any impartial observer should have known that Socialist Premier Guy Mollet would wage a colonial war in Algeria, that Socialist President François Mitterrand would stall first eight then ten more years on his promise of self-determination given to the Kanack natives of France's colony of New Caledonia and that, having sworn to stop nuclear testing, he would, in fact, increase them in the Pacific with a racist disregard for local opposition.

British bankers' credits, Texaco's oil, and Dupont's bombs—Aron still maintained that it was not the democrats' duty to help Spanish democracy. In 1983, he gave this ludicrous explanation: "Franco's long reign responded to a tragic necessity."[31] Would Aron have accepted an Eichmann defense that insisted "The Nazi murders of six million Jews responded to a tragic necessity?"

But that so-called philosopher, who is so adored in France today, also felt that fascism was never a real danger in France in 1936–37.[32] Yet no sooner had all extreme right-wing bands been officially proscribed in July 1936 than Colonel de la Rocque, one of the founders of Croix de Feu fascism, launched the French Social Party (PSF), which quickly gained eight hundred thousand members, more than the Socialist or Communist parties. To his right, the French Popular Party (PPF), organized by a rancorous ex-Communist named Jacques Doriot, was even stronger (but not bigger, since it claimed only one hundred thousand adherents) and certainly much richer. In 1937, Doriot's goons received some ten million francs from big banks (Vernes, Lazard, Rothschild, BNCI) and big industry (Japy, Comptoir Sidérurgique) and the backing of France's top right-wing intellectuals (including Drieu de la Rochelle and Ramon Fernandez). And there were still more fascists in France: Alsatian autonomists, financed by Hitler; Corsican and Niçois separatists, bankrolled by Mussolini; and a whole pack of secret terrorist organizations known as *La Cagoule* (the hooded ones).

Backed by a formidable array of right-wing newspapers, these fascist parties and groups constantly attacked democracy in the streets, inflicting casualties among passers-by as well as left-wingers. In May 1937, these confrontations climaxed at Clichy, a Paris working-class neighborhood, where Blum's police defended PSF and other demonstrating fascists by firing on the antifascists, killing five and wounding five hundred. Meanwhile, the *cagoulards* kept assassinating such left-wing heroes as the Roselli brothers, exiles from Mussolini who had organized the antifascist Garibaldi Battalion which, at Guadalajara, near Madrid, defeated Mussolini's crack forces, which had better arms and greater numbers. *Cagoulards* also blew up the headquarters of France's manufacturers' association, hoping to spark an antigovernment coup by right-wing officers; in this case, Blum's Interior Minister, Marx Dormoy, exposed the conspiracy and had some of its leaders arrested, for which he was later assassinated by the "non-dangerous"—as Aron had called them—*cagoulards*.[33]

In the face of all this fascist agitation, the Popular Front government remained unbelievably docile, until it was too late. Reacting at last in early 1938, Blum asked his parliament for special powers to clean up the streets and rebuild the economy. Right-wing deputies responded by openly shouting, "Better Hitler than Blum!" and the tough left just didn't trust Blum anymore. The Popular Front was dead. Instead, on 13 April, the vast majority of deputies voted for a government which included not a single Socialist. Its new chief, Radical Edouard Daladier, who was perfectly willing to betray more people and more countries than even Blum (and get rid of the forty-hour week and ignore promises made to Czechoslovakia), would quickly proceed to sell out France altogether.

In *The Reprieve* (which he originally entitled *September* since the whole novel dealt with the days leading up to that sellout at Munich), Sartre describes the anger that Aron claimed to have had. "There's no doubt," Aron almost yelled at me in 1973, "I'll repeat it until I die, I'm positive, I saw him [Sartre] right after Munich, he was relieved by Munich. He said 'We do not have the right to dispose of the life of others.' His reaction was moral, not political. He considered those who signed the Munich accords *des salauds,* scum, but he was relieved. He was in favor of those accords," which let Hitler crush Czechoslovakia.[34]

Colette Audry who had rushed off to Barcelona to help her anarcho-syndicalist-Trotskyist comrades in the summer of 1936, saw Sartre and Castor continuously during the academic years leading up to Munich. "Sartre didn't understand politics very well, in 1936," she told me.

He couldn't understand why, since I was a communist and a revolutionary, I was not a member of the Communist Party. In fact, he was so blunderingly naive about it that friends of mine kept asking me why I even bothered talking to him. (I remember answering one of them that 'I was preparing the man of the future.') But these political simplicities on his part dealt with tactics. On fundamentals, we agreed. When I returned from Cataluña and described to him the situation there, he was certainly in favor of intervention by the democracies, on the side of the Republic. And then, at the time of Munich, he shocked me. He was ready to go to war then and there. It was I who was pro-Munich; once Spain became lost, I too was lost, I gave up, so I wanted peace. He told me that unless we fought, we would have Hitler here, in France. I sort of said something like, "So what, French fascists or German fascists, what's the difference?" He answered that a writer cannot survive under fascism of any kind. I said, "Well, we can go into exile." "No," he said, "a writer must remain in contact with his reality, his national reality." Now you may say that's infantile petty bourgeois patriotism, and it is, but it shows that Sartre was certainly not *un Munichois* (a Munichizer).[35]

Sartre himself put it this way in 1971: "You know, in 1937–38, it was beginning to become extremely difficult to not see and not hear. There was no way I could hide the fact that the world in which I had to live was totally different from the one in which I wanted to live. The fascists were gaining the upper hand. I was never convinced that war was inevitable *until* Munich; when everyone else thought peace was at hand, I was sure war would come, one day or the other. That's when I really became political, passively of course. What I mean is that I started reading newspapers and magazines from cover to cover, convinced we needed the war to crush Nazism once and for all. You say, Mathieu, whose life I was then describing, was not committed. True, but he regretted it, and in *The Reprieve* I put all sorts of other digs against French pacifism, usually in the mouth of your father as a matter of fact, and once in fact in your own mouth."[36]

The passages Sartre referred to are the following:

Gomez [on leave] turned and went back into the room. Pablo [me at five years old] had put on his helmet, he was holding his rifle by the barrel and brandishing it like a club. He staggered up and down the hotel bedroom dealing violent blows all around him. Sarah [Stépha] watched him with dead 'eyes.

"It's a positive massacre," said Gomez.

"I'm going to kill them all," replied Pablo, continuing his onslaughts.

"All whom?" . . .

"All the fascists," said Pablo . . .

"Oh, Gomez," said Sarah, "look—how could you?"

Gomez had just bought Pablo a soldier's outfit.

"He must learn to fight," said Gomez, stroking the boy's head. "Otherwise he'll become a mouse, like the French."

Sarah looked up at him, and he saw that he had deeply wounded her. "I don't understand," she said, "why people should be called mice because they don't want to fight."

"There are moments when one ought to want to fight," said Gomez. . . .

Pablo twirled his rifle, and shouted: "Just wait, you dirty Frenchman, you mousy Frenchman."

"You see?" said Sarah.

"Pablo," said Gomez sharply, "you mustn't abuse the French. The French aren't fascists."

"The French are mice," shouted Pablo.[37]

Later, after Hitler seized Czechoslovakia, and war in Europe seemed imminent, Mathieu met Gomez again and said:

"People are beginning to understand."

"They understand nothing," said Gomez. "A Spaniard may understand, a Czech too, and perhaps even a German, because they're in it. The French aren't; they understand nothing; they're just afraid." [38]

Then the Munich accords were signed. At the front, defending Madrid, Gomez understood immediately that those accords meant the end of free Spain.

Gomez clenched his teeth on the stem of his pipe. He listened to the guns and thought of the quiet nights at Juan-les-Pins, and the jazz band on the seashore: Mathieu would spend many more evenings of that kind. "The bastards," he muttered.

But Daladier, returning from Munich, had no illusions.

A vast clamor greeted him, the crowd surged through the cordon of police and swept the barriers away. . . . "Hurrah for France! Hurrah for England! Hurrah for peace!" They were carrying flags and flowers. Daladier stood on the top step and looked at them dumbfounded. Then he turned,

and in the very last line of the novel,

said between his teeth: "*Les cons!* [the shmucks!]." [39]

No *Munichois* would have written such lines. But Sartre wrote them much later, when France had already lost. Castor, too, was bellicose—in retrospect. Said she in 1960: "We loathed the idea of war as much as anyone else, but we could not stomach the thought that with a few dozen machine guns and a few thousand rifles the Republicans could have finished Franco off—and that these supplies had been refused them. Blum's caution sickened us, and we were far from regarding it as a contribution to peace. . . . Our hearts bled when Fernando * talked to

---

* Castor confused Fernando's various missions to Paris to buy arms with his leaves, but correctly reported that "during some skirmish or other, it appeared, he had found himself, together with a few comrades, on open ground and exposed to enemy fire; so he had very cleverly led them off behind a low wall, where they took shelter. He had been warmly congratulated for displaying such initiative, and was quickly promoted, first to captain, then to colonel. He ended up as a full-blown general. Yet while entertaining us with the saga of his rapid military advancement, he also made it clear what a desperate shortage of trained men, discipline, and organization there was in this Popular Army; and the socio-political confusion was greater still. Communists, Radicals, and Anarcho-Syndicalists were very far from serving identical interests." (*Prime of Life*, p. 231) Fernando eventually became Chief of Operations at the battle of Guadalajara, commanded the 15th Brigade

us of conditions in Madrid: the gutted houses on the Alcalá, shell holes all over the roads around the Puerta del Sol, a heap of rubble where the University students' quarter had once stood. . . . But at Járama and Guadalajara the Popular Army held up the offensive that Franco had launched against Madrid. Despite this, the *dinamiteros* failed in their attempt to recapture Oviedo, and in the south Malaga fell. The reason for these setbacks was always the same: lack of arms. The farce of 'nonintervention' struck us daily as more criminal."[40]

Castor continued to bemoan the fate of Spain. But she wrote about herself (*She Came to Stay*), spent the summer of 1937 touring Greece and its islands, and "refused to admit that war was even possible, let alone imminent." After Seyss-Inquart's coup in Vienna, inviting Hitler to fuse (*Anschluss*) Austria into Germany (13 March 1938), she wrote, "I was still trying to delude myself, and refusing to face the facts. But the future had begun to open up under my very feet, and produced in me a sick feeling akin to anguish."[41] But even with that anguish, she was able to read Pepy's *Diary* and Swift's *Journal to Stella* (as well as Malraux's *Man's Hope* "with an excitement that far outstripped any purely literary emotion"[42]); to attend rehearsals of *Plutus*, freely adapted by Camille from Aristophanes and starring Dullin, and Marcel Achard's *Le Corsaire*, staged by Jouvet; to see *Carnival in Flanders, Outward Bound, My Man Godfrey* and *Mr. Deeds Goes to Town*; and, especially, to scrutinize the works of Dali, Man Ray, Max Ernst, Duchamp, and other surrealists at the exhibition which opened in January, 1938. That summer, Sartre and Castor trekked all over Morocco, including a walking tour in the Atlas Mountains, "tramping along lonely paths over those lush red ranges, sleeping in rest huts below the Berber villages."[43]

On 21 April 1938, Hitler had told his Wehrmacht to get set to invade Czechoslovakia. By the end of May, Sudeten Germans were ready to force an *Anschluss* with Germany of their own, and the Czechs were mobilizing. On 15 September, England's Prime Minister, Neville Chamberlain, met Hitler at Berchtesgaden. Two weeks later Czechoslovakia was abandoned by France and England as the Munich accords were signed with Germany and Hitler. Right-wingers and idiots, pacifists and ignorants screamed their delight—"Peace in our time!" So did Castor: "Czechoslovakia was perfectly justified in her indignation against the betrayal of her interests by Britain and France; but anything, even the

---

(which included the Internationals) because he spoke seven languages, and ended the war as the last commander of Barcelona.

cruelest injustice was better than war. Sartre disagreed. 'We can't go on appeasing Hitler indefinitely,' he told me. But even though his rational mind inclined him to accept the prospect of war, he still rebelled at the thought of seeing it actually break out. Our next few days were grim ones: we went to the movies a lot and read every edition of the daily papers. Sartre was making a fiercely valiant effort to reconcile his political ideas with his private inclinations, while I was fundamentally all at sea. Then the storm abruptly passed over without having broken, and the Munich Pact was signed; I was delighted, and felt not the faintest pang of conscience at my reaction. I felt I had escaped death, now and forever. There was even an element of triumph in my relief. Decidedly, I thought, I was born lucky: no misfortune would ever touch me."[44]

Sartre's thought was quite the opposite. "On that day of Munich," he told me, "I suddenly realized that I live in a society which is totally unstable and uncontrollable. A worldwide cataclysm is about to unfold, and I can't do a thing about it. I see myself anew: no longer free, on the contrary, totally determined by events. Instead of being a guy who quietly does his duty of becoming a great writer, I am a poor shmuck (*un pauvre con*) in a world ready to explode. What I say or do has absolutely no importance. So, since I am a thing, not a being, since I can't do anything about my fate or the world's, since I am totally impotent, I write."[45] In other words, since he couldn't do anything to effect change in the world, he cared not about it, only about himself.

Already in November 1936, Sartre had refused to join his fellow egghead colleagues (including Gide, Romain Rolland, Joliot-Curie, Politzer) in their "Declaration by Republican Intellectuals on the Events in Spain," in which they denounced neutrality as "an illusion" and demanded immediate renewal of trade with the Spanish Government. And he ignored appeals by his friend Nizan, who had rushed off to Spain as a war correspondent for both Communist dailies, *L'Humanité* and *Ce Soir*. Nevertheless, the tone of Sartre's concern changed. While not political, the first four of the five short stories eventually published jointly under the title *The Wall* in 1939, condemned the illusion that we can cut ourselves off from history and live, ostrich-like, in our self-created closed shop. The first, "Erostratus," written in 1936, was the story of a lonely, alienated man who wanted to matter, to be relevant, but finds no way except crime. Who recalls the name of the architect who built the temple of Diana at Ephesus, one of the wonders of the world? A lot of people remember who burned it down—Herostratus. Desperate to escape anonymity "in the heart of the mob," Sartre's modern Erostratus decides to kill five people at random and thus achieve immortality—"a striking rejection of the human condition"—and does manage to kill one. But his newly acquired relationship to his victim, to his pursuers, and his obsession with his own fate, makes him reenter the present.[46]

In "The Wall," written in 1937, Pablo tries to control, even if only as a gag, the terms of his own death. Naturally, he fails: only the decisions and actions involved in living have value. In "The Room," written in 1937 and first published in *Mesures* in January 1938, Sartre explained, "Eve tries to join Pierre in the unreal, closed world of madness," which makes Eve's father "resent her living outside the limits of human nature. . . . We don't have the right to refuse ourselves to the world; no matter what, we live in society."[47] "Intimacy," first published in August 1938 by *NRF,* debunks the psychological theory that we can lie to ourselves; we can only believe that we can, but we retain responsibility for our choices. The fifth story, "The Childhood of a Leader," finished in July 1938, was the most political, and the most devastating. It was also remarkably autobiographical. Lucien, the child, was Sartre; the adolescent, Nizan. Brought up in a very bourgeois home run by a factory owner who much resembled Sartre's stepfather Mancy, Lucien is groomed to take over the factory one day, to be a leader. He is told, as Mancy had told Poulou (Sartre), that the way to get workers to like you is to "know them all by name," and the way to get them to obey you is to maintain "the differences." Like Anne-Marie, Lucien's mother, whom the boy does not love any more, is kind, weak, and obedient to her husband; his father is polite and caring at home, paternalistic but firm at the factory. "What are they trying to give us, with their class struggle," he scoffs at one point, "as though the interests of the bosses and the workers were just the opposite. Take my case, Lucien, I'm a little boss, what they call a small fry. Well, I make a living for one hundred workers and their families. If I do well, they're the first ones to profit. But if I have to close the plant, there they are in the street. *I don't have a right,*" he almost shouts at his son, "to do bad business. And that's what I call the solidarity of classes."[48]

But like Mancy, who complained that workers' wives bought silk stockings, the adult bourgeois around Lucien lament precisely this breakdown in class differences when they see it in practice. Says one to Lucien's mother: "My maid tells me she saw that little Ansiaume girl in the cook-shop. She's the daughter of one of your husband's best workers, the one we took care of when she lost her mother. She married a fitter from Beaupertuis. Well, she ordered a twenty-franc chicken. And so arrogant! Nothing's good enough for them: they want to have everything we have." Lucien, too, feels that "arrogance": on Sunday walks with his father, "the workers barely touched their caps on seeing them and there were even some who crossed over so as not to salute them. One day Lucien met Bouligaud's son, who did not even seem to recognize him. Lucien was a little excited about it: here was a chance to prove himself a boss. He threw an eagle eye on Jules Bouligaud and went toward him, his hands behind his back. But Bouligaud did not seem intimidated: he turned vacant eyes to Lucien and passed by him, whistling. 'He didn't recognize me,' Lucien told himself. But he was deeply disappointed."[49]

The similarity between Lucien and Poulou ends when Lucien enters a mainstream lycée and meets Bergère, a homosexual surrealist poet. Quickly submerged into a life of good poetry, lousy drugs, and, eventually, offbeat sex, Lucien learns to respect strengths as interpreted by haughty blankness. Like the early Nizan, he becomes a presumptuous right-winger who considers any woman who sleeps with him a whore. A Jew-hater, he joins the fascistic Camelots du Roi and, like Nizan, dreams of marrying a virgin, having children, and possessing both as property. He now longs for his father to die so he can take over the factory and sees himself as "an enormous bouquet of responsibilities and rights. He had believed that he existed by chance for a long time, but it was due to a lack of sufficient thought. His place in the sun was marked in Férolles [site of his factory] long before his birth. They were *waiting* for him long before his father's marriage: if he had come into the world it was to occupy that place: 'I exist,' he thought, 'because I have a right to exist.'"[50]

In tracing the upbringing of this typical French fascist—thousands of such bourgeois collaborated with the Nazis in World War II, making France the most betrayed occupied country in history—Sartre was attacking his pet enemy, the ruling class, an attack he kept up all his life. Said he in 1946, for example: "Every member of the ruling class is a man by divine right. Born in a circle of leaders, he is convinced from birth that he is born to rule. . . . There is a certain social function waiting for him in the future, a role that he will step into when he is old enough, and that is, so to speak, the metaphysical reality of his individuality."[51] In addition, Sartre was also defining freedom, in this story. Lucien, like all leaders in modern society, is not free, said Sartre. He and they are conformists who spend their lives trying to make others conform. They do not tolerate the freedom of others, which is threatening to them. Freedom, said Sartre, is to dare to think for oneself, to be a rebel while never forgetting that we are born by chance (contingency) with no endowed rights (necessity). Of all the protagonists of these stories, Sartre said, Lucien for a while "is the closest to feeling he exists, but he doesn't want to; he evades himself and takes refuge in thinking of his rights; for rights do not exist, they ought to. In vain. All these efforts to escape are blocked by a wall; to flee Existence is still to exist. Existence is a plenum man cannot leave." [52]

In that plenum in 1937, Sartre still felt uncertain: sure of himself as a writer, looking forward to the launching of *Nausea,* he nevertheless remained politically uncomfortable and philosophically superfluous. Life was still nauseating, and Sartre was often nasty as a result. During the summer in Greece, for example, he was fiesty, testy—and often a bully. After a very choppy boat ride to Delos in which Castor was painfully sick, "he remained quite unmoved by my spasms of retching, which he ascribed to deliberate malice on my part," she wrote. In Stavrós a few days later, he lost his temper when, through the fault of neither Castor, Bost, who had accompanied them, nor himself, "we strayed a little from the path we should have taken." Later, in Mistra, Castor longed to climb Mt. Taygetus, but Sartre refused. "We had one of our few memorable spats," she reported. "Could we forego the wonderful spectacle of watching the sun rise over Taygetus? We could and we did." Next Castor wanted to see the Meteora. "Sartre, whom curiosities of nature left completely cold," absolutely refused. "Alone in my cabin," Castor admitted, "I shed tears of pure rage." [53]

But that fall Sartre was transferred to the Lycée Pasteur in Neuilly, which meant that they could now both live in Paris, and tensions seemed to abate. Choosing the Royal Bretagne, a comfortable hotel near the Montparnasse cemetery, they took rooms above each other, "thus we had all the advantages of a shared life, without any of its inconveniences." [54] And they got to work—she on her novel, he on a treatise on phenomenological psychology entitled *The Psyche,* of which however he published only an extract, *The Emotions: Outline of a Theory,* in 1939. Characterizing emotions as a magical way of seeing the world when rational means fail to give it order for particular ends, Sartre explained that "emotional consciousness is, at first, consciousness *of* the world." Emotion is "a certain way of apprehending the world," of "transforming" it. Emotions "assume man and the world and can only take on their true meaning if one has first elucidated these two notions."

Emotion "is a mode of existence of consciousness, one of the ways in which it *understands* . . . its 'being-in-the-world.'"[55]

In her biography of Sartre, Cohen-Solal claimed that he enjoyed teaching at Pasteur that year and next, and that he had a stimulating, often political, relationship with his students.[56] She quoted one student who purportedly asked him, "How do you accept, sir, to spend so much time with us when you have work to do?" Sartre is supposed to have answered: "One can always learn, even from imbeciles," certainly a quip he could have made twenty years later.[57] But to me, Sartre said that, unlike his teaching days in Le Havre, his days at Pasteur did not hold much time for his students: "They had no consciousness about anything. My courses were clearly left-leaning. They seemed interested, but understood nothing. They did not discuss things among themselves, or if they did, it was passively; they never argued. The classes were very calm. I injected a sort of confrontational atmosphere by trying to foment discussion, letting them smoke, and so on, but they did nothing. I was fine with them but that's all, nothing worth mentioning. There surely were some on the left, some on the right, but if there were political confrontations, and Action Française students were very active outside the school, there were none inside."[58] According to Cohen-Solal, these two academic years (1937–39) at the Lycée Pasteur, were years of happiness, and the classes were not "banal." She certainly found numerous former Sartre students to agree with her.[59] But although Sartre had always liked to develop tight friendships with his students, at Neuilly he did not. Nor did Sartre seem to have much influence on their careers. Indeed, judging by the fact that one of his best students, Jean Kanapa, turned out to be a most disgusting hatchetman on the Central Committee of the extremely Stalinist French Communist Party, it can be deduced that Sartre's tough anti-Stalinist stance was not that popular.

But his works, during this period, certainly were. *Nausea* was hailed by most critics and was nominated for the prestigious Goncourt prize. Such top critics as Maurice Blanchot, Jean Cassou, A.-M. Petitjean, Edmond Jaloux, Nizan, Albert Camus (in *Alger républicain*) all seemed to agree with their colleague, Armand Robin who wrote, in *Esprit,* that "*Nausea* is undoubtedly one of the most distinctive works of our time."[60] Sartre's short stories and articles were also creating a buzz. By praising *Sartoris,* he helped establish Faulkner's reputation in France, and Dos Passos he almost single-handedly turned into an American master. In November 1938, he also reviewed Nizan's *The Conspiracy* in which public and private lives were so intermingled that the question of the author's ideological purpose could not be avoided. Sartre raised the issue but still lauded the book, whose hero, Bernard Rosenthal, a rich bourgeois living on rue Mozart, resembled Aron. "Can a communist write a novel?" asked Sartre. "I am not convinced: he does not have the right to make himself the accomplice of his characters. But it is enough, to find this book strong and beautiful, for us to come across on each page that obsessive evocation of our unhappy and guilty age; it is enough if it is a true and hard witness to the hour when 'youths' gather round to congratulate themselves, when a young man believes he has *rights* because he is young, like the taxpayer because he pays his taxes or the father because he has children."[61]

Sartre's success affected Castor: "That was the first time the idea of public success, with all its attendant temptation, actually entered my mind. One would make new acquaintances, I thought vaguely, learn new ideas: it would be a sort of self-renewal. Hitherto I had relied upon no one but myself to ensure my happiness, and asked nothing of tomorrow but that it repeat today. Now, suddenly, I wanted something to happen to me from the outside, as it were, something new and different." But only Sartre would have that success for awhile: Castor's novel was turned down with clear enough reasons for her to start again. But she "was not discouraged. Next time, I felt sure, I would make a better job of it."[62] Sartre, meanwhile, was ecstatic. He got fan mail, and answered it; invitations to write more articles, and did: on Nabokov, whom he scolded; on Elsa Triolet, whom he encouraged; and on Jean Giraudoux, considered untouchable, whom he fervently but unmaliciously attacked. But Sartre's most famous literary criticism of that period was his total dismemberment of François Mauriac's *The End of the Night*. Showing that every narrative technique involves an ethic and a metaphysic, Sartre exposed Mauriac as a religious propagandist whose novelistic tricks are meant to fool his readers, not into believing his characters, but into believing. "God is not an artist," Sartre ended his review, "neither is Mr. Mauriac."[63]

Years later, Sartre tempered his harshness. Said he in 1960: "I think I'd be more flexible now, considering the essential characteristic of the novel to be to intrigue or interest, and I'd be a lot less finicky about his techniques of doing so. That's because I have come to realize that all techniques—including those of the American novel—are tricks. We always manage to say what we think to the reader—the author is always present. The American novel's trickery is more subtle, but it's still there. Having said this, I must also say that I don't think that making oneself too visible is the best technique for writing a good novel. If I had to write *Roads to Freedom* over again, I'd try to present each character without comment, without revealing my feelings." Years later still (1969), Mauriac explained why he had not written more novels: "I was wounded, if you like, by Sartre's attack. One of my novels . . . had been torn apart by Sartre, who was not only a very young author but the glory of his generation."[64]

That glory was blasted by traditionalists and conservatives, yet Sartre's book of short stories, *The Wall,* became the book-of-the-month for March 1939—as well as a critical success.* *Emotions,* which came out a few months later, strengthened Sartre's reputation as a philosopher, which was increased still more by *L'Imaginaire*—awkwardly translated as *Psychology of the Imagination*—when that appeared in 1940. A sequel to *L'Imagination* of 1936, *L'Imaginaire* stressed the difference between perception and imagining. Perception was passive, he said, imagination active; the latter included the creative freedom, hence responsibility, to consider what is not present; that is, to stand back from the world and frame images. Little by little, Sartre was excluding all automatic reflexes from our cognitive processes, thus laying the foundation for an ontology which allowed man no escape from himself.

To a great extent, however, Sartre was still trying to escape, if not himself, his unpleasant world. Not that he was rebellious. He had lunch with Anne-Marie and his despised stepfather every Sunday. He continued to meet his friend Guille, who had scampered much too much to the right for Sartre's liking (until Guille, thinking Sartre disapproved of his marriage to a cousin, stopped seeing him). And he continued to console Zuorro, whose escapades Sartre now found boring. With his publishers, Sartre remained respectful and restrained. One letter to editor Brice-Parain went like this:

My dear Parain:

Would you kindly drop me a note telling me what evening at 5:30 I could pick you up at your office to offer you a drink. I'd like to ask you something.[1] With friendly regards . . .

JP Sartre

1) not money

---

* In a rave review in *Alger républicain* (12 March 1939), Albert Camus said, "Sartre seems fascinated by impotence, in its full as well as psychological sense, which forces him to deal with characters who are pushed to their limits and who keep tumbling over an absurdity which they cannot go beyond. It is against their own life that they clash, and, if I may say, do so out of an excess of freedom." Without knowing it Camus struck a sensitive cord: Sartre's sexuality has since often aroused curiosity because of his fascination with homosexuality, his obsession with visual scenes, his reveling in seduction and foreplay, his disinterest in actual copulation.

In another letter, Sartre, who would later turn down all honors and prizes—including the Nobel—informed Gallimard, who had recommended him for the Populist Prize and asked him to write the required candidate's letter, that he had done so.[65]

Sartre's form of escape was the same as anyone's—ignoring unpleasant realities or becoming so involved in daily activity as to shut out the rest of the world. Reading his letters makes that quite clear. He wrote about sex, money, his novels and stories, food, and even the weather. On 14 July 1938, he complained that his tailors had the nerve to "demand what I owe them (925 francs). But I believe that I will simply not pay them." In another July letter to Castor, Sartre talked at length of "la petite Bourdin," a virgin who was in love with him. In still another, he told of meeting Paul and Rirette Nizan: "Nizan brought me *The Conspiracy,* dedicated thus: 'To J.-P. Sartre, especially page 92, his friend P. Nizan.' I ran to page 92 and I found indeed: 'the commander Sartre, who was a perfect imbecile . . .'" After dining together, Sartre said that they went to see a "very Nizan" film about the Spanish Civil War, *Blockade,* which was written by Dalton Trumbo and starred Henry Fonda, a film "tending to be pacifist, boring as the rain, favoring the Republicans but, in the final analysis, in which all the Republicans were spies." Added Sartre, "Nizan kept repeating in a monotonous voice: 'We're just like in 1914, we'll be at war within three months.' Otherwise, they were boring as hell . . ."[66]

But the world kept closing in on Sartre. During the Munich talks, Fernando, in Paris, made Sartre uncomfortable: "Naturally, he wants a war right away, like José, and fumes against the cowardice of our government. La Baba [Stépha] observed me with a critical eye: I was no longer Sartre but a French petit bourgeois intellectual who had no political interest and whom one suddenly places in front of reality." After the Munich accords were signed, Sartre wrote with amazing perspicacity: "If Czechoslovakia accepts to be eaten, Yugoslavia, Romania, Hungary will sooner or later be under German hegemony. Russia will have to break its alliance with France . . . a real victory for fascism not only internationally but also in various nations. . . . But here it looks like we have a reprieve for a few years. At this moment I cannot ask for more." But then he saw Fernando off to Spain again. "He leaves in despair. . . . We parted with true emotion, less because of our real friendship, than because we realized that we did not know where or how we would see each other again and because we felt a sort of complete indetermination about the future." And he added a few weeks later: "No

more escapes. In my next novel, I will try to show the possibility of a
moral life without escape."[67]

Indeed, it was increasingly difficult to escape. Even Castor, who, she
admitted, "had gone on trying to live exclusively in the present, to grasp
each flying minute," failed. She, like Sartre, read that the Nazis had organized a reign of terror in Bohemia and Austria, that concentration
camps existed "where millions of Jews and anti-Fascists were interned,"
that Canton had been burned to the ground and Hankow had been occupied. Fernando "told us about the bombardments and the famine:
nothing to eat except for the odd handful of dried peas, not even any
tobacco to appease one's hunger, not even a fag-end to be picked up in
the streets. The children were haggard and emaciated, with swollen
bellies. In January, after being devastated by liquid-air bombs, the city
[Barcelona] fell. An ever-increasing number of gaunt and ragged refugees streamed toward the frontier. Madried was still holding out, but
already England had given recognition of the Franco government, and
France was sending out Pétain as Ambassador to Burgos. After a pro-
longed final struggle Madrid, too, fell, and the whole of the French Left
mourned its loss, for which they felt in some sense responsible. Blum
admitted that in 1936, promptly dispatched shipments of arms could
have saved the Republic, and that nonintervention had been an idiotic
policy: why, then, had public opinion failed to make him change it? I
was coming to realize that my political inertia did not guarantee me a
certificate of innocence; nowadays when Fernando muttered about
'bastard Frenchmen' I felt personally involved."[68]

Nevertheless, Castor and Sartre "tried hard to believe that there
would be no war." After all Hitler's foreign Minister, Joachim Ribben-
trop, had signed a nonaggression pact with France on 6 December
1938,* and Soviet Russia had proposed a military alliance with France
and England. While it was true that Hitler had marched into Prague
(16 March 1939) and Italian fascists had seized Albania (7 April) and
were stirring trouble from Tunisia to Ethiopia and even in Corsica,
which Italy had long claimed, Castor still believed that "in the last resort we wouldn't go to war over Djibouti."[69] She and Sartre hung out
at the Café Flore, on St. Germain, and Sartre studied Heidegger. But
when a friend reported to her that throughout Austrian towns Nazis
had herded Jews out of bed and into the main squares to brand them

---

*Interestingly, those who like to condemn Russia for signing a similar pact with Ger-
many never even mention this French pact.

with red-hot irons, that all synagogues had been burned, and Jewish shops ransacked, and, breaking down, had wept, "How can anyone still work and play and carry on life as usual when things like *that* are being done?," Castor "felt ashamed of my egocentricity."[70]

Anti-Semites to the core, the French and British government negotiators who arrived in Leningrad at the beginning of August 1939 hated communism more than fascism. They did not conceal their hope that Hitler would continue east instead of west and invade Russia. Arrogant and pompous, they made the Russians feel exactly what they thought. Result: on 18 August, while the tripartite talks were still going on, Stalin began secret negotiations with Germany. On 21 August, the tripartite talks were suspended. On 23 August, the Russo-German pact was signed. World War II, inevitable ever since France betrayed Spain in 1936, was now nearer than ever.

Staunchly anti-Nazi for so long, French Communists were stunned. At first they tried to be both pro-Russian and anti-German. In the 25 August issue of *Ce Soir,* which was seized, along with *L'Humanité,* by the French government, Aragon editorialized: "Ever since this newspaper existed, our policy has been anti-Hitler. We intend, viewing Hitler as France's enemy No. 1, to continue such a policy." The General Confederation of Workers broke with the Communist Party. No less than eighteen of the Communist deputies and senators quit the party. The CP-dominated Union of French intellectuals condemned Stalin's attitude on 29 August. And on 2 September, Communist deputies voted in favor of the war credits requested by Premier Daladier. Among them were Maurice Thorez and Jacques Duclos, heads of the party.[71] But in *L'Humanité,* neither they nor any other top CP official commented on the pact. It took the party several weeks to get its instructions from Moscow. When it got them, France was at war, a war of imperialists, now said the CP. It had been forced to change its policy of "national defense" to one of "revolutionary defeatism," as historian Jacques Fauvet put it.[72]

No Communist was more crushed by the pact than Paul Nizan. Ferociously anti-Nazi, Nizan had campaigned against France's noninterventionism since the beginning of the Spanish Civil War. He had denounced the Munich accords in *Ce Soir* on the grounds that "it is not merely a question of recording the loss of Czech friendship, but of grasping that the whole system of French security has just collapsed. A diplomatic disaster has occurred."[73] At the beginning of August, Nizan and family bumped into Sartre and Castor in Marseilles on their way to

Corsica to vacation with Laurent Casanova, member of the party's Central Committee and chief of the party's intellectual affairs. "He had a drink with us," Castor wrote, "and declared, confidentially yet triumphantly, that the Tripartite Agreement was in the process of ratification. Normally the most reserved of men, he now spoke in a voice of positively feverish jubilation. 'Germany will be on her knees!' he asserted. His views on the situation were very different from those that appeared in *Ce Soir;* he obviously was privy to secrets in high places, and his optimism gave us a great feeling of reassurance."[74]

In a letter to a new lover dated that day, Sartre did not mention Nizan's new hopes, though he did find his old friend "at ease." Sartre quipped about Nizan and family "rapidly guzzling down a *bouillabaise*" for lunch, then sailing off to Ajaccio.[75] So either Castor remembered the event incorrectly, or Sartre did not wish to retransmit the news; either Casanova was not privy to Stalin's negotiations, or he lied to Nizan. In any case, Nizan was appalled not by the pact but by his French CP superiors who "confuse faithfulness with dumb acquiescence to the hierarchy's views."[76] He complained that they had lacked the necessary political cynicism, "the political power to lie," to put on a show of disassociation from Stalin's strategy of self-protection, which was perfectly comprehensible.[77] While secretly approving of Stalin's reluctance to trust the West—Russia had seen too many betrayals for that—the French CP, according to Nizan, should never have flinched in its anti-Hitler policy—even if that meant, callously, denouncing Russia. But when the party publicly praised the pact, Nizan, who had been one of the first to be called up, quit the party. From the front, he sent this open announcement to *L'Oeuvre,* the only non-Communist daily which had protested the seizure of *L'Humanité:* "Paul Nizan, ex-student at the École Normale Supérieure, *agrégé,* in charge of the foreign affairs section of the newspaper *Ce Soir,* has just sent to M. Jacques Duclos, vice-president of the National Assembly, the following letter: 'I am sending you my resignation from the French Communist Party. My present situation as a soldier of the French Army prevents me from adding anything further to these few lines.'"[78] Assigned to the British Fourteenth Army Field workshop as an interpreter and liaison agent, he was shot through the head at the battle of Audruicq, near Dunkerque, on 23 May 1940.

By then the French Communist Party had already turned Nizan into a traitor. In March, no less than Maurice Thorez himself, the party's Secretary General, had dubbed him a "police informer" and "bourgeois collaborationist." [79] Nor did the slander stop with his death. In February 1941, a clandestine CP pamphlet, warning its members against provocateurs, referred to Nizan as a policeman. Other CP articles and leaflets followed suit. Aragon, who had worked so closely with him, grossly and recognizably patterned the journalist and repugnant spy Patrice Orfilat on Nizan in his trashy novel, *Les Communistes*. But by far the most outrageous smear was dished out by Nizan's once-close friend, Henri Lefebvre, who in his 1946 book, *L'Existentialisme*, meant to demolish Sartre, said that he always suspected Nizan to have been what he indeed turned out to be, a liar, an informer, "obsessed with betraying." [80] (Reacted the writer René Etiemble: "My dear Lefebvre, prove to me that from the time you used to have dealings with him as an existentialist, Nizan stank of treachery. If you can't, leave him in peace! For the sake of your beliefs, I must hope that you can't find any proof, for, if you had sensed for years that Nizan was the police spy he's supposed to be, what were you doing in his company? And if the Party for years was proud of an informer, who are we to blame except the Party's blindness, or its complicity?") [80]

In 1959, Lefebvre was himself out of the Communist Party. He tried to explain his years of accepting "mystification, moral blackmail and ideological swindling" in a book called *La somme et le reste (The Total and the Rest)*. In it he admitted that his *L'Existentialisme* was "not a good book. Not because it's insincere, but because I wrote it out of defiance." [82] But it included not one word of recantation, of apology to his dead friend, that tormented Communist who was always willing to subordinate his fear and complexes to fight for the common man, that formidable journalist who was always ready to set pen aside and pick up the gun to defend the world against fascism and injustice. No, in two long volumes of some self-criticism and lots of self-justification, Henri Lefebvre, who is still respected today by friend and foe as one of France's great intellectuals, did not even try to rehabilitate the man with whom he once agreed on all fundamental issues. That the French Communist Party never forgave Paul Nizan for being right two decades too soon should have been enough, right there, to stop any intellectual from joining that party. That it didn't, that such intellectuals still speak reverently of such *salauds* as Henri Lefebvre, explains why so many French intellectuals have so often betrayed their ideals—and their friends.

But Paul Nizan *was* rehabilitated—thanks to Jean-Paul Sartre. In open letters, petitions, and such brilliant articles as the preface to *Aden-Arabie*, Sartre did more than anyone to bring Nizan's work back into public view and defend his integrity and moral worth. It has been said that "Paul Nizan haunted Sartre from the day he entered the classroom in Henri IV until the last years of Sartre's life."[83] Perhaps. It was also said that "compared to Nizan, Sartre could have considered himself a failure, the one who could not commit himself to anything, either love, or politics, or even, before 1938, to literature,"[84] which would imply that his dogged determination to rehabilitate Nizan was motivated by guilt—in effect, "he deserves fame more than I do." To me, Sartre simply said, "Nizan was a very difficult man, really hard to get along with. But he was genuinely committed to that morass of humanity most of us like to avoid. He was a great writer. And for me, when all is said and done, he was the only friend I ever had as an adolescent and young man."[85]

In 1939, Sartre did not share Nizan's conviction that war was about to explode. Castor wrote later that they were sure "war was imminent," as soon as the Russo-German pact was signed. "Stalin was leaving Hitler free to attack Europe: there was no hope whatsoever of peace now. . . . Though we had plenty of reservations about goings-on inside the U.S.S.R., we nevertheless had believed hitherto that the Soviet Government served the cause of world revolution. This treaty proved, in the most brutal way, that Colette Audry and the Trotskyites and every left-wing opposition group were right after all: that Russia had become an imperialist power like any other, obstinately pursuing her own selfish interests. Stalin didn't give a damn for the proletariat of Europe."[86]

Castor notwithstanding, Sartre did not think war was at hand: "I don't believe it," he wrote a young paramour on 30 August 1939. "People are very calm and without too much worries. Of course there's always the possibility of *la connerie* [total idiocy]." Then he explained how Brunet, who was somewhat patterned after Nizan, "disgusted by the Russo-German pact, would quit the communist party" in the fourth volume of the *Roads*.* Nor did fear of war affect his appetite: Sartre told her he had enjoyed a meal of "hors-d'oeuvre, trout, *cassoulet, fois gras,* cheese and fruit, with wine from the region." Next day, 31 August, Sartre wrote her again, insisting that "it is impossible that Hitler thinks of starting a war with the state of mind of the German people

---

*In interview no. 11, Sartre told me that Brunet was much too aggressive to be the model for Nizan. The fact remains that Nizan was the only good friend Sartre had who was a Communist. Sartre's letter, incidentally, was written before Nizan did in fact quit the party.

being what it is. . . . It's a bluff. We might go as far as general mobilization, but . . . mobilization is not war."[87]

Three days later, Sartre was mobilized. It *was* war. During the night
of 2–3 September, he wrote her for the last time: "So, has triumphed
la connerie."[88]

9   The Soldier

Jean-Paul Sartre went off to war on Saturday, 2 September 1939, in a "Kafkaesque" train ride which took ten hours to get to Nancy, some 160 miles east of Paris. But "I felt fine," he said. "My legs wanted to stretch and my gut drink, but *me,* I could never be better." Three days later he was settling in as a meteorologist for an artillery unit 40 miles behind the silent front. His task: to calculate the "complicated" velocities of the "ballistic wind." What he actually did, however, was "to wait, to go for walks along the pleasant countryside, to pick berries (because, by force of circumstance, I am becoming a bit of a country bumpkin). A strange solidarity is developing among us, due neither to esteem nor sympathy but to our situation." Indeed, a week later, he told Castor: "I must confess something to you: if I can sustain the separation lightly, the waiting, the life I lead here, it is because war *interests me.* I feel like a stranger in a country I am going to explore little by little."[1]

But more than explore, Sartre of course wrote. "My novel is going full blast," he told Castor just ten days after being drafted, referring to *The Age of Reason.* "If we continue a bit in tranquility, I'll be finished in *four months.* In the final analysis, I work here more than in Paris. After four months, if the war continues, I'll start the second volume."[2] He had tentatively entitled it *September,* but it would be published under the name *The Reprieve.*

The war did last, and Sartre did get his tranquility. From 3 September 1939 until he returned to Paris at the end of March 1941, he wrote almost a million and a half words, the equivalent of seven or eight hefty volumes. He did finish *The Age of Reason* in four months, though he kept going back to it to change or correct passages. He filled fourteen notebooks with his tight, tiny script, often extremely difficult to decipher (of which only five have survived; they have been published in one volume). Nor did his habits change after the front was overrun by the Germans and Sartre was captured and interned in stalag 12D near Tier. He drafted a few hundred pages of his major philosophical work, *Being and Nothingness.* He wrote, directed and played in *Bariona,* a passion play put on at Christmas 1940 for his fellow prisoners at the camp where he was interned. And he dispatched enough letters—one a day to Castor, five per week to Wanda, three to two former lovers, one to his mother, plus occasional epistles to his students, Ecole Normale buddies, editors and publishers—to fill five or six more books, though only two have been published.

In these two volumes some passages have been deleted and some names have been changed (Wanda, for example, is called Tania). Castor made some of these changes herself to protect Sartre's former lovers, she claimed, but also because, still jealous at seventy, she did not want her readers to know how often Sartre wrote to other women and who they were. The other changes, however, were made by Arlette Elkaïm, Sartre's adopted daughter, who calls herself Elkaïm-Sartre since his death and who wasn't even born when most of the letters which she has now altered were written. This violation is made possible in France by an absurd law called *Le droit moral* (the moral right) according to which the legal heir can arbitrarily contradict or nullify all the contracts and agreements signed by his or her benefactor, after the latter dies. In Interview no. 13 (11 June 1971), Sartre told me that he had legally adopted Elkaïm because: (1) he needed someone to keep distributing his royalties to the five women, all former lovers, whom he kept (including Elkaïm herself), long after Castor too would be dead; and (2) it was a perfect, courteous way of ending his sexual relationship with Elkaïm without hurting her pride. But Sartre certainly expected Castor to decide which of his unpublished works to publish posthumously and not Elkaïm (or me, for that matter, though he gave me or asked Castor to give me copies of many of them). Thus, Elkaïm decided to "present" Sartre's *Ethics* (which he never wanted published at all) and his *War Diaries* (which were written long before she was born).

Since all civil contacts between Elkaïm and Castor and other members of "the family" were destroyed, mostly by Elkaïm's former mentor, the fanatic onetime Maoist leader turned rabbinical and Talmudic scholar Benny Levy (aka Pierre Victor or Pierre Bloch), who keeps trying to prove that Sartre was really a Jewish philosopher all along, I cannot ask Elkaïm to approve for publication in France my interviews with Sartre. At some future date, however, they will be published in the United States, where my contract with Sartre is legally binding.

In any case, the beginning of World War II was certainly Sartre's most productive period and may well have been one of his happiest. But it was disastrous for most of his friends: Nizan, killed at the front; Politzer, tortured and murdered; Jean Cavaillès, philosopher, resistance leader, shot; student Yvonne Picard, dead in a concentration camp; Bourla, one of Sartre's favorite students, deported, never to return; Alfred Péron, a boyhood friend, seized by the Gestapo, dead. Bost, wounded at the front, survived. So did Fernando, denounced by an informer in the rear. That kind of thing happened all the time in wartime France. A storeowner, envious of a competitor's business, told the police he saw him distributing leaflets, and he was gone. A spurned woman ratted on her rival: she disappeared. Reported Castor, "We were told one morning that Sonia [a neighbor] had just been arrested; she had apparently been made the victim of another woman's jealousy—someone, at any rate, had certainly denounced her. . . . The blonde Czech girl who lived with Jausion vanished; and a few days afterward, when Bella was asleep in her boyfriend's arms, the Gestapo came knocking on their door at dawn and took her away, too. Another girl, a friend of theirs, was living with a well-connected young man who wanted to marry her; she was denounced by her intended father-in-law."[3]

The informer who denounced my father, Fernando, was Nicolas de Staël, the famous Russian-born (1914) painter who made his living in Montparnasse as a paid police provocateur and eventually (1955) committed suicide at Antibes. He had asked Fernando how one could get to Spain. "Walk!" Fernando had answered haughtily. That afternoon Fernando had been charged with "propaganda designed to prevent foreigners enlisting in the Legion." But Stépha pleaded with the mistress of a socialist deputy to intervene, and he did; Fernando was freed on condition he command a frontline regiment, as a French colonel. When the French government fled and the Germans reached the outskirts of Paris, he gave his Jewish recruits safe-conduct passes to Switzerland, led the rest to Paris and dismissed them, picked up Stépha, then me at the boarding school, and dashed to Biaritz where the Germans caught up with us. Leaving us behind with Dominican diplomatic passports, he crossed Spain via the underground railroad, then told us to join him in Lisbon. And that's where we would have stayed had Franco agents not tried to machine-gun him in broad daylight in front of our hotel (they missed). Four days later, my father, mother, and I were on our way to the United States, arriving in New York 3 September 1941—exactly one year after World War II had started.[4]

This is not quite the way Sartre told it in his novel, however. In *Iron in the Soul,* the third volume of *The Roads to Freedom,* written after the war, Gomez is alone in New York, having left Sarah and Pablo behind to face the exodus by themselves. Lonely, miserable, and guilt-ridden, Gomez is both pleased that Paris has fallen—"a righteous punishment"—and incredibly sad, drinking "to the liberation of France" with an old stranger in an Eastside saloon. Discarding Mondrian because he "doesn't pose any questions . . . any embarrassing questions," Gomez realizes that his artistic eyes have gone blind. An American acquaintance says: "We Americans like painting to appeal to happy people or to people who are trying to be happy."

"I'm not happy," answers Gomez, "and I would be a bastard if I tried to be, what with all my friends either in prison or shot."

"Look," the American comes back at him, "I know all about your personal troubles. Fascism, the defeat of the Allies, Spain, your wife, your kid—sure! But it's a good thing to rise above all that occasionally."

"Not for one single, solitary moment!" Gomez fires back as even Sartre would have in 1941.

"Not for a single moment!"[5]

In France, meanwhile, the silent war had gotten very loud. Earlier when Russia attacked Finland, the French bourgeois deputies had felt free first to impeach their Communist colleagues, then to jail them. Now it was their turn. In March 1940, German troops swept through Denmark and defeated the Anglo-French-Norwegian forces defending Norway. In May 1940, German Panzer divisions poured through Holland, Belgium, and Luxembourg. On 4 June, the debacle of Dunkerque ended. On 6 June, the French lines evaporated. On 14 June, as Hitler had promised six months earlier, German troops entered Paris. Two days later, Marshal Philippe Pétain, ordained as the new chief of a defeated France, immediately sought armistice with Germany. He got it on the 21st, signed it on the 22d, and ordered all hostilities stopped as of the 22d. On 9 July, the National Assembly of the French Republic, now seated in Vichy, voted 468 to 80, to give Pétain the right to enact a new constitution. Among those who opted for a French fascist state were no less than 88 socialists (29 opposed it). Edouard Herriot, who would be heralded as one of France's great patriots after liberation and be elected president of the national assembly, couldn't even vote no. He merely abstained.

Marshal Pétain's armistice on 21 June 1940 was Jean-Paul Sartre's thirty-fifth birthday. It was also the day he became a German prisoner. But that didn't change much in his life. He still wrote letters, still made entries in his journal, still worried about Nothingness and still devised novelistic plots. As a soldier, he was shuttled about to Brumath, Morsbronn, Bouxwiller, and other towns of Lorraine and Alsace, behind the supposedly impregnable Maginot Line. As a prisoner, first in the barracks of the mobile police of Baccarat, a Lorraine center between Strasbourg and Nancy, then in Stalag 12D above the German town of Trier

(Treves), near the Luxembourg border, Private Second Class Sartre was a witness to the betrayal of his countrymen and to their subsequent hopelessness—and so reported in his novel *Iron in the Soul,* the third volume of his *Roads to Freedom*. He witnessed the people of Alsace evacuated to Dordogne, the native land of his father, and heard from cousins and escapees how the "pure" French called the Alsatian French filthy *boche* (Heinie) and *sale métèque* (dirty foreigner). He felt the class structure first hand, his officers eating, drinking, sleeping, and traveling first class, while ordinary soldiers slept on floors and ate cabbages or rutabaga. Most importantly, he saw how those officers filled trucks, cars, and vans with their belongings plus whatever foodstuffs and cases of wine they could requisition and fled, leaving their troops to deal with the oncoming German armies as best they could.

"Who would have believed it! Who would have believed it! . . .

The general passed by. Mathieu had never before seen him at such close quarters. The general, a stout, imposing-looking man, with a deeply lined face, leaned heavily on the colonel's arm. The orderlies followed, bearing the officers' kits; a whispering, laughing party of subalterns brought up the rear . . .

"Perhaps the chauffeurs will refuse to start."

Mathieu shrugged his shoulders. Already the engines were humming, like the pleasant echo of grasshoppers very far away. A moment later the cars started and the sound of the engines was lost. Pinette folded his arms. "Officers! By God, I begin to believe France is really done for."

Mathieu turned: masses of shadow were moving away from the walls as soldiers crept silently out from alleyways, carriage entrances, and barns. Real soldiers, of a second-line formation, ill-kempt, ill-fed, slipping past the shadowed whiteness of the house-fronts; of a sudden, the street was full of them. So sad were their faces that Mathieu felt a lump in his throat . . .

"Now we're on our own!" Grimaud observed. "Alone at last."

No one laughed. Somebody, in a low, anxious voice, asked: "What happens now?"

There was no answer; they did not give one damn what was going to happen to them. . . . The soldiers looked anxiously at one another. They did not want to separate, but there seemed no point in sticking together. Suddenly a voice, a voice edged with bitterness, cried: "They never liked us anyhow!"

Its owner was expressing a general thought. Everyone started talking.

"That's right—you said it—they never liked us, never, never! For them the enemy wasn't Heinie, it was but us. We fought this war together, and now they've gone and left us high and dry. . . .

Tongues were loosened, talk had become a necessity. No one likes us, no one: the civilians blame us for not defending them, our wives have no pride in us, our officers have left us in the lurch, the villagers hate us, the Heinies are coming up through the darkness. More accurately they should have said: we are the scapegoats, the conquered, the cowards, the vermin, the offscourings of the earth; we have lost the war, we are ugly, we are guilty, and no one, not one solitary being in the whole world has any use for us. Mathieu dared not voice this sentiment, but Latex, behind him, spoke it calmly and unemotionally: "We're pariahs."

There was a sputter of voices; everywhere the word was repeated, harshly, pitilessly: "Pariahs!"[6]

The next day, the Germans arrived. For no apparent reason, Pinette, Chasseriau, Clapot, Dandieu, and the others decided to fight. Outnumbered and outgunned, they died, one by one. "It was all true, every bit of it," Sartre told me in Interview no. 13.

"I saw it with my own eyes, the officers fleeing, the sad, lost faces of the men, the incredibly courageous and stupid last gestures of those poor abandoned souls. Only the church tower where Mathieu, finally a man of action, irrational and free, fires at the Germans, is made up, although I saw Germans firing at such a church tower in the next village the night before. That's one of the reasons that the French hated *Iron in the Soul*. It said the truth and they knew it. *The Reprieve* was bad enough: it showed that their government was run by traitors, people who would rather kneel to Hitler than give workers paid vacations. But then *Iron in the Soul* showed that all of France's upper class was the same, that the whole bourgeoisie were traitors to the ordinary Frenchmen on whom they depended, off of whom they thrived. That, no one wanted to hear, and the book was a flop."[7]

It also flopped because the Communists hated it. In the numerous arguments between the characters Schneider, who had quit the party because of the Nazi-Soviet pact, and Brunet, who was still the dogmatic Stalinist, it was always the former who won. Seeing their fellow prisoners totally depressed, Schneider at one point yells at Brunet:

"You're all in cahoots, Pétain with Hitler, Hitler with Stalin, the whole lot of you are busy explaining that these poor devils are doubly guilty—guilty of having made war, guilty of having lost it. You're running around, taking from them all the reasons they thought made it necessary for them to fight. That poor guy thought he was embarked upon a crusade for Justice and the Rights of Man; now you want to persuade him that he was just cheated into taking part in an imperialist war. He doesn't know what he wants, he's not even sure what he's done. It's not only the army of his enemies that has triumphed, but their ideology as well. He's bogged down, he's fallen flat out of the world of men, out of history, and he's trying to build up some kind of defense mechanism, to think out the whole situation, to get it straight from the beginning. But what with? Even his tools for thinking straight are outdated, thanks to you. He's suffering from the iron that has entered into his soul and it's you who are to blame."[8]

Sartre had planned a fourth volume of *The Roads to Freedom* to be called *The Last Chance*. He worked on it, off and on, until 1952. "I just couldn't make a situation which had been crucial and absolutely valid in 1942 relevant in 1950," he told me. "Besides no one wanted to hear the truth—the truth that the French police, the *milice,* did a hell of a lot more for the Gestapo than the Gestapo asked it to do, and with much more zeal than any German. Nor did leftists want to hear the truth that in France, at least, it is absolutely impossible to talk politics to a Communist; you agree with them on an action and go along, or you don't, but you can't talk to them; they are the most closed minds ever invented. And of course Frenchmen, who are as chauvinistic as any white supremacist in America, did not want to hear the truth about their army, their officers, their rulers, their racist, anti-Semitic, exploiting bosses. Yet unless one shows all of that, one cannot understand the collapse of France in 1940 nor the extent of subsequent French collaboration. So you might say, politics killed *The Last Chance*." Besides, added Sartre, in France in 1952, "the Communists were fighting the good fight, and the anti-Communists were the same scums who had betrayed France in 1938–40. So I just couldn't keep going."[9]

The Last Chance meant the last chance to be free. The answer, said Sartre, was commitment. In the novel, Brunet would ignore his party pals, hacks, and hatchetmen, to escape from the prisoner of war camp with Schneider. When the latter is killed and smeared (like Nizan) by the party as an informer, Brunet would try again to escape, succeed, and spend the rest of his short life defending Schneider. Mathieu, too, would escape and become a resistance leader. While he would fight with the Communists, the novel remained staunchly critical of the Party. Only an extremely moving section, published under the title "Drôle d'amitié" ("A Weird Friendship"), about the Schneider-Brunet relationship, survived completely. In it, Brunet, no longer a Stalinist, explained why he (and by then Sartre) felt compelled to continue to struggle. "We are not men yet, old chap. We are miscarriages, half-portions, half-animals. All we can do is work so that those who will come after us do not resemble us."[10]

Sartre's way of struggling was still, of course, writing. In his letters, whether at the front or as a prisoner, he couldn't say very much because of censorship. He described his barrack mates, the beard he was growing (which at first made him look "hard and skeptical" but then "ridiculous"), the irritating requests he received from former students (including from Kanapa "a definition of Aristotle's physics"), and the books he read (five per week, from Dickens to Kierkegaard, *Moll Flanders* to *Candide,* the Journal of Julien Green to that of Dabit). On Malraux who had said that Sartre's generation was useless because "they never experienced war or revolution," Sartre exploded: "The shmuck. That guy gets on my nerves. We'll have to tell him off one day. Meanwhile, I hope with all my heart that he gets *deferred* because of his nervous tics [he was], so that a whole generation of young people one day refers to him as that old fuddy-duddy who never fought in '39." He wondered how Fernando reacted to the Russian invasion of Finland, which Sartre condemned, and bitched about his publisher's cutting his royalties from 10 to 7 percent on *L'Imaginaire,* which would soon come out.[11]

On 9 December 1939, Sartre told Castor he had finished his *Ethics,* a long essay to show that all moral problems are specifically human, supposing choice and will, hence totally irrelevant to animals or gods. Since "one can seize the world only through a technique, a culture, a condition," in other words only through what humans create, "man finds anew everywhere his project, only his project." Thus, "human reality is moral only insofar as it is without God"; or put another way: "without the world," in which people determine themselves by choosing their concrete projects, "there can be no values." His conclusion: "Through all his enterprises, man seeks neither to go beyond himself nor to conserve himself, but to establish himself. At the end of each of such enterprises, he finds himself as he was: gratuitous to his very bones." He always seeks to be relevant, and never is.[12]

Like any other soldier, Sartre went through crises, self-doubts and even self-tortures. He sometimes even doubted his "mission" in life and his earthly immortality, as when he wrote Castor: "I envy the courage of guys like Kafka who could coldly tell his friends: 'After my death, burn my writings.'" But mostly Sartre's crises involved his women, and he wrote a great deal about his relations to them. There was Wanda, who was as spoiled, egotistical, self-involved and tantrum-prone as her older sister Olga; "Martine," the ethereal virgin Sartre talked into bed before the war; Bianca, called Louise Védrine by Castor, her former student; various casual flings back in Paris as well as in the towns where he was stationed; and of course Castor, to whom he described everything and to whom he often appealed for help in smoothing over problems with the others. On 19 February 1940 for example, he asked Castor to calm Wanda after she had discovered Sartre's "intimate life" elsewhere by reading one of his notebooks. On the 23d, he was all upset that Martine and Wanda had compared notes, both of them lying, and hoped Castor would salvage his relationship to Wanda. Next day, he sent Castor a copy of his letter to Martine which said, in part, "I never loved you, I found you physically pleasant though somewhat vulgar, but I have a certain sadism which your vulgarity appealed to. I never expected—from the very first day—that there would be between us anything more than a brief adventure." To save his relationship with Wanda, he wrote her on 24 February: "You know very well that I will walk on the stomach of anyone (even Castor despite my 'mysticism' [perfect rapport]) to be well with you," but admitted to Castor: "Who wants the ends wants the means, though I was not proud of writing that one."[13]

Castor was often shocked, occasionally horrified, so Sartre had to explain.

You yourself, my little Castor, for whom I have always had respect, I often bothered, especially at the beginning, and you found me a bit obscene. Not a stud, to be sure. That I know I never was. But simply obscene. It seems to me that there's something wrong in me, and you know, I have felt it vaguely for a long time, in our physical relations in Paris during my leave, you could have remarked that I had changed. Maybe the power of our physical relations is waning a bit, but I find it is gaining in purity. In any case, with M. Bourdin [Martine] whom I did not respect like you, or I did not manipulate like T. [Wanda], I was awful. . . . We're going to have to change all that. . . . Conclusion: I have never been able to deal correctly with my sexual life nor my sentimental life; I feel myself profoundly and sincerely a *salaud*. A scum of little weight to boot, a sort of university sadist and Don Juan functionary to puke. I must change all that. I must stop (1) my little conniving affairs: Lucile, Bourdin, etc.; (2) big affairs lightly taken. I shall keep T. if it's salvaged because I care for that. . . . Tell me what you think.[14]

Castor didn't think well at all. She accused him of being "sexist," "chauvinistic" and "disgusting."[15] Yet for all his promises, Sartre changed very little. He continued to seek flighty relationships, and continued to lie to all his lovers except Castor. She asked why towards the end of his life. Intercourse was never "very important for me, not as important as caresses," he answered. "Said in other terms, I was more a masturbator of women than a coiter. . . . Essential and caring relationships for me implied kissing, caressing, wandering my lips over the body. But the sexual act—it existed, I did it, even often—but with a certain indifference." Nor did Sartre really enjoy seeing a woman naked. "When she's dressed, it's not that she's more real but more social, more approachable." Concluded Castor: "You were always cold sexually." [16]

But not artistically. Before his captivity, in addition to the letters and novel, he filled his notebooks. Most of the time he wrote about himself, his efforts to understand what made him tick. He liked Jules Romains's sentence: "Men are like bees. Their product is worth more than they." He complained to himself that "I took myself seriously," whereas in fact "I make like a buffoon, that's what I'm guilty of. At the bottom is my moral pedantry." But that attitude pleased him; it allowed him "to play a role. Because I am social and playful." He lamented the lack of combat "for, finally, if there's no war, what the fuck am I doing here?" Was he really obsessed with his message, he asked himself, for "compared with Gauguin, Van Gogh, and Rimbaud I have a clear inferiority complex because they knew how to lose themselves. Gauguin by his exile, Van Gogh by his madness, and Rimbaud, more than all others, because he knew how to renounce even writing. More and more I think that, to attain authenticity, something has to crack. That's the lesson Gide finally derived from Dostoyevski and which I must communicate in the second volume of my novel." [17]

One of his mates asked Sartre: "Like you, I noticed that they all say they miss their children more than their wives. Why?" Sartre answered: "To conceal the fact that their conjugal lives failed. With the declaration of war, they could draw a line on their past life and add it up. . . . What am I worth? Well, their relationships with their wives appear to them to have been a total flop. So they look away from it, hide it by thinking of their children. The child is nothing yet, there's no total to add up. He's the future. Their future as well as his own. . . . It's a way of saying: my life is not yet closed, the total is missing, there's still a reprieve. The child is the reprieve of a dead life." Was such a negativism a Sartrean quirk? "When all uglinesses will disappear," he wrote, "consciousness will also disappear, the act will be automatic. That's why when someone praises me I always have the impression they're talking about somebody else. There is no act without a secret weakness. The others see the style, I see the weakness." But he saw a lot of strength around him, not from officers but from ordinary soldiers who had everything to lose. "What I have learned and jot down here without further development, is that it is much easier to lead a clean and authentic life in wartime than during peace."

"Authenticity comes in a bloc: one is authentic or inauthentic," Sartre wrote. "But that doesn't mean that once you got it you keep it. I've already said that the present has no hold on the future, nor the past on the present . . . At best one can say that it is less hard to conserve authenticity than to acquire it. But, in fact, can one talk of 'conserving'? Every moment is new, every situation is new. One must constantly invent a new authenticity." And while he struggled with his inauthenticity, he saw his Castor almost as his superego (though he never believed in one). "Castor is authentic without effort," he said, "I would say by nature if authenticity could ever pull its origins out of nature."[18]

Reviewing his life, Sartre remembered how lonely and isolated he had been as a child, how hurt he had been because of his ugliness. "What changed profoundly after my arrival in Paris was that I found comrades and a friend. Friendship was crucial. It's something which appeared in my life with my sixteenth year and with Nizan and which, under various forms, never left it. I have had three 'intimate friends' and each corresponded to a specific period of my life: Nizan-Guille-Castor (because Castor was *also* my friend and is still). What friendship brought me, much more than affection (whatever that may have been), was a federated world where we put in common, my friend and I, all our values, all our thoughts and all our tastes. And that world was constantly renovated by incessant invention. At the same time each of us strengthened the other and the result was a *couple* of considerable power."[19]

Sartre kept that friendship with Castor all his life—but with no one else. Nizan, who stayed close "until his marriage and even a bit beyond," died in the war. Guille "had a much more bourgeois way of living than I." Aron, Maheu, Camus, Merleau-Ponty, and many others had been friends with whom Sartre broke harshly. "Why?" asked Castor in 1974. "When something is dead, that's it," answered Sartre. But Castor pressed and Sartre said, "I can't stand revelations." Insisted Castor, "You've never been bothered by women who reveal secrets." Sartre agreed. "In fact, on the contrary, I solicited them." Reacted Castor, "To reject with disgust men who confide in you while accepting women who do, that's a certain form of machismo."[20] But that did not explain Sartre's break with Camus or Merleau, who were not confessors. Nor did it take into account the master-disciple relationship he had with Bost and other younger men. The fact is Sartre never did offer a satisfactory explanation why he could never maintain male friends. To me Castor said, "Sartre never really liked any man, Genet, Queneau, Leiris, etc., no one. He saw them out of commitment to a situation, politics, the theatre (Dullin) or whatever. Giacometti, yes, for a while, but then he got cancer. Nizan, Guille, friends of youth. Bost, yes, but he was his student . . ."[21]

My own feeling is that Sartre just never wanted to argue. Except for Castor, the women in his life adored him without understanding what he thought or wrote—and didn't care. The men of his generation did, but they didn't always agree with him. They may have respected him, admired him, even loved him. But they did not idolize him. Sartre, as he admitted himself, never overcame his liabilities. He was small, wall-eyed, ugly. To conquer the inferiority complex which these conditions generated, he felt almost bound to constantly seduce attractive women, and surround himself with younger men who venerated him. But at the same time he was aware of his bad faith. He needed the truth, and he got it from Castor. As his letters to her clearly demonstrate, he constantly appealed to her sound judgments, not only in matters of the heart, but on his writing as well. For example, Sartre worked long and hard at perfecting a prologue for *The Age of Reason;* Castor said it stunk and he threw it out.[22] To me he said, "Castor made me rewrite hundreds of pages in my life, whole plays. She was the only critic who mattered."[23] To her he said, "I had a privileged reader, who was you; when you said okay, it was okay; I published the book and didn't give a damn about critics. You were a great help; you gave me the confidence in myself which I would never have gained alone."[24] Indeed, it is because of such candid revelations, which fill his letters and notebooks, that Arthur Danto, reviewing his *War Diaries,* could say that Sartre "got a lot out of the enterprise. He learned something about himself, framed a deep philosophical theory, went on to become an engaged consciousness and to lead one of the exemplary lives, perhaps even to achieve authenticity."[25]

Sartre led an exemplary life as a prisoner of war. One month after being captured, he started *Being and Nothingness.* Two weeks later, he had polished off 76 pages of this highly complicated treatise. Typically, he asked Castor to send him books (including *L'Imaginaire,* which was out but which he had not yet seen) and food. But he told her if she had to choose, to send the books. Once in Germany, he made himself interpreter at the infirmary, then joined the "artist" prisoners who "have a real little theatre where they put on shows for 1500 prisoners every other Sunday. . . . I live with them in a big room furnished with guitars, banjos, flutes, trumpets stuck on the wall, with a piano on which some Belgians play [jazz] all day . . . I write for them plays that no one puts on." But he loved it and them, "the nicest folk I've met since the war began."[26]

He also liked a bunch of priests to whom he gave lectures on Heidegger, and they certainly liked him. One of them, Father Marius Perrin, was motivated to write a book about Sartre at the camp partly because he read in the *Times Literary Supplement* that Sartre owed his release from camp to "the good offices" of the fascist writer Drieu de la Rochelle (who had replaced antifascist Jean Paulhan as editor of Gallimard's review, *NRF*). Since Perrin himself had falsified Sartre's military passbook so he could escape, he obviously knew better. In that book he described Sartre's first camp lecture: "He had no notes at all. He spoke simply, but as if he were used to speaking. . . . He did not search for words, but his words were carefully chosen. . . . The line of his discourse was crystal clear! But it was the man, above all else, who interested me." That man, Perrin found, was "genial and generous, . . . dedicated to the impossible pursuit of an authentic freedom"; a man who forces you "to go to the very depth of yourself," who is polite, considerate but "not at all tender toward those he doesn't like."[27]

With these priests, Sartre sang Gregorian chants. "He had a gorgeous voice," Henri Leroy, another cleric who had been captured about the same time as Sartre, told me. (By French law, priests have no special sinecures in the army; drafted like anyone else, they can end up with rifle in hand in the infantry, like anyone else). "He was amazing. He could write anywhere, in the midst of rehearsals, in chow line, in the latrines, which were public. And he would do anything that might help his fellow prisoners. They were sad, downcast, despairing, riddled with guilt and dishonor. Sartre suggested that we put on a passion play for Christmas. We knew he was an atheist and that he would use the play as a vehicle to give the men back a bit of dignity and spur them on to hope, to want to see the Axis defeated, not necessarily to bring them closer to God. It was a tough undertaking, but when we all agreed, he went at it with such enthusiasm that we caught it too. He would write a scene, then direct us in it, changing it, adapting it to our personalities, pushing us to accentuate our commitment, then write the next scene and start all over again. For the lead he chose a Jesuit priest named Feller. I had a role in it. So did he."[28]

Almost at once, Perrin wrote in his journal, Sartre was going full tilt. "He must have jotted down the main themes of the play which he has called *Bariona* [overnight] since he's already casting the principle parts.

I think he wants . . . to match physical types to the play's personalities. Leroy, Bénard [a journalist from Le Havre] and especially Feller are already cast and he has the intention to play in it too. Nor is he forgetting his artist colleagues."[29] And Sartre himself wrote to Castor: "Imagine what it can be like for an author to know his public and then write for that public. I've written a Christmas play which, apparently, so moves the actors that one of them feels like crying while playing. I will take the role of one of the three Kings [Balthazar]. I write the play in the morning and we rehearse it in the afternoon. Thirty characters. I've met two or three who really interest me and have made contact with a new theatrical form of art for which one can do much. I read Heidegger and I have never felt so free."[30]

"My radicalization process had begun," Sartre insisted during our Interview no. 13, "I knew I had to escape from the camp. But I decided to wait, to put on *Bariona* first, to help my fellow prisoners take hope. I did that by refusing to let Bariona commit suicide. On the contrary, he became convinced that even though Rome, meaning Germany, would probably win, which is what we all thought in December 1940, he should nevertheless continue fighting as hope comes in the doing, never in the waiting. It was a tough message to throw at prisoners who couldn't do very much even if they wanted to. But it worked. Believers and atheists sat silently and took it all in, indeed so united in spirit were they that I decided that a successful theater night is like a religious experience, and knew then that I would continue writing plays."[31]

"It was a tremendous success," said Leroy. "No one even snickered when this awkward professor from Montpellier turned up dressed as the Virgin. There were three showings, each to 1500 prisoners, and believe me they loved it. When Bariona, about to die, shouted at the end 'I hold my fate in my hands' and to his men 'You're going to fulfill your destiny. You're going to die like fighters just the way you dreamed of dying' I could feel 1500 chests swell a bit, 1500 chins rise a notch."[32] Added Father Perrin in his diary: "And now, like Bariona, I must face the tempest head on and charge, take my fate into my hands."[33] With Sartre, Perrin decided to escape.

Sartre too learned from the experience. "I found in the Stalag a form of collective existence I hadn't had since l'Ecole Normale, and in the final analysis I was happy," he said in 1971.[34] Four years later he added, "Every man is political. But I did not discover that for myself until the war."[35]

By faking documents and pretending to be a semiblind civilian, Sartre got himself out of Stalag 12D in mid-March 1941. It took him another fifteen days of hassles before he arrived in Paris. Castor was jubilant, then shocked. "He had not come back to Paris to enjoy the sweets of freedom, he told me, but to *act*." Castor demurred. "We were so isolated, so powerless!" she said. What could they possibly do? Break down that isolation, said Sartre, unite, "organize a resistance movement." [36]

To most Parisian bourgeois, German occupation was not so bad. The metros ran well, the theatres were successful, the cafés full. True, the coffee was ersatz, and the liquor slightly raw-gut, the swastika flew over the Tuileries, the Chamber of Deputies, and the Luxembourg Palace, and almost the whole Avenue Kléber was turned into German offices and billets. The Eiffel tower was adorned with a gigantic V accompanied by an equally huge poster claiming *"Deutschland siegt auf allen Fronten"* (Germany wins on all fronts).

Still, the bourgeois ate well enough, thanks mostly to countryside connections and the black market. And many fun-loving Parisians had a ball: Sacha Guitry with the German ambassador, Otto Abetz; Tino Rossi sang at the Opera; Maurice Chevalier and Edith Piaf toured prisoner camps, sponsored by their jailers of course, while the great actresses Danielle Darrieux and Viviane Romance forgot all about the prisoners when they jaunted about in Germany. The writers Drieu de la Rochelle and Robert Brasillach went off to applaud Goebbels in Nuremberg, and the master artists Derain, Vlaminck, and Maillol crossed the Rhine to receive honors due their works from their conquerors. There were lots of films around and Paris cinemas were full, even though American pictures were banned, as was jazz, because, to quote a collaborationist newspaper, of its "judeo-negro" flavor.[1]

Fuel was a problem in occupied Paris. Taxis were rare, if not nonexistent. Buses ran on gasogene, and apartments were cold—one reason why the leisure class hung out in warmer cafés. But Parisians insisted that their city was still the intellectual capitol of the world and flocked to its "events" as if God himself was taking attendance. These events included the opening nights of such hit plays as Henri de Montherlant's *La reine morte,* Paul Claudel's *Soulier de satin,* Camus's *Le malentendu* and, of course, Sartre's *Les mouches (The Flies)* and *Huis clos (No Exit).* While every Frenchman complained of a lack of food and fuel, which was true for the poor and the unconnected, film-makers had no trouble finding materials to produce no less than 220 features and 400 shorts in three years, establishing the reputation of Bresson, Clouzot, especially with his *Le corbeau (The Raven),* Delannoy (with *L'Eternel retour,* written by Jean Cocteau), and the powerful team of Marcel Carné (director) and Jacques Prévert (writer), whose *Les visiteurs du soir,* though first-rate, is the best of the "acquiescing" Occupation films. Though, of course, not all film-makers profited from the occupiers' generosity. Some who fled to Hollywood included Ophuls, René Clair, Duvivier, and the actors Michèle Morgan, Jean-Pierre Aumont, Dalio, and Jean Gabin (who joined the Free French forces).[2]

Censorship, of course, was rigid. By the end of June 1941, no less than 2000 titles by 850 authors were banned, and all publishers, except Emile-Paul, who had brought out *Le grand Meaulnes,* approved. René Philippon, head of France's publishers' association, said, "These dispositions [the taboo lists], which do not create a serious problem for publishing in France, it seems to me, allow French thought to grow, as well as feed its civilizing mission to bring peoples together." Gallimard, Sartre's publisher, was not the worst of the lot. He did name Drieu de la Rochelle as head of his prestigious review, *NRF,* and did publish the translations of German Nazi authors. But he found excuses not to publish Lucien Rebatet's *Les Décombres,* a trashy exultation of the Nazi hero (also turned down by Grasset but published by Denoel). Some writers refused to publish under such conditions, and joined the Resistance: Jean Guéhenno and Rená Char, for example. Others who went underground included Jean Bruller, a cofounder of the clandestine Editions de Minuit; he wrote Resistance novels under the pseudonym Vercors. But most writers, though far from being pro-Nazi, nevertheless went on with their craft as if there were no war and no Germans: Georges Simenon, Jean Paulhan, Aragon. Said Sartre's friend, philosopher Politzer in 1941, "Today in France, legal literature means literature of treason."[3]

After the war, Sartre tried to explain: "For four years, our future was stolen," he told the English who had felt that the French didn't seem so badly off. "All our acts were provisional, their meaning limited to the day in which they were committed." True there was a Resistance. But it affected history very little, "it had symbolic value; and that's why so many resistants despaired: always symbols. A symbolic rebellion in a symbolic city—except the tortures were real." What was terrible, he added, "was not to suffer and to die, but to suffer, to die in vain. . . . During this period, France—with the exception of the Resistance—did not always show herself valiant. But first, one must understand that active Resistance had to be by necessity limited to a minority. And then, it seems to me that this minority, which offered itself deliberately and without hope to martyrdom, amply suffices to buy back our weaknesses."[4] (It certainly did not.) And to Americans who might have concluded that the whole of France's bourgeoisie collaborated, Sartre said, "Collaboration is a fact of disintegration, and is in every case an individual decision, not a class position. . . . It would be unjust to call the bourgeoisie a 'class' of collaborators. But one can and one must judge that class by the fact that just about every collaborator came out of its ranks."[5]

To Frenchmen, Sartre was much more upbeat:

Never have we been as free as during the German occupation. We had lost all our rights, beginning with the one of speaking; we were insulted everyday and we had to shut up; we were deported en masse, as workers, Jews, political prisoners; everywhere on walls, in newspapers, on the screen we found that bland and repulsive face which our oppressors wanted us to have of ourselves: because of all that we were free. Since the Nazi venom snuck even into our thoughts, every correct thought was a conquest; since an all-powerful police tried to keep us silent, every word became precious like a declaration of principle; since we were watched, every gesture had the weight of commitment. . . . The choice that each one of us made was authentic since it was made in the presence of death, since it could always be expressed in the form 'Rather death than . . .' And I'm not talking here of that elite who were the true Resistants, but of all the French who, at any hour of day or night, during four years, said *no*. The very cruelty of the enemy pushed us to the extremity of the human condition by forcing us to ask the questions which we can ignore in peacetime: all of us— and what French person was not in such a situation?—who knew some interesting detail on the Resistance asked with anguish: "If they torture me, can I hold out?" So the question of freedom itself was posed and we were at the edge of knowing the most profound thing anyone can know about himself. For the secret of a man is not his Oedipus or inferiority complex, but the very limit of his freedom, his power to resist pain and death.[6]

Using *Lettres Françaises,* organ of writers in the Resistance, Sartre ended his tribute to the clandestine army thus: "for those who carried messages whose content they ignored as well as for those who decided all combats, the same fate: prison, deportation, death. There is no army in the world where we can find similar equality of risks for the soldier as for the generalissimo. And that's why the Resistance was a true democracy: for the soldier as for the chief, same danger, same responsibility, same absolute liberty in discipline. Thus, in shadow and in blood, the strongest of all Republics constituted itself."[7]

No sooner had Sartre returned to Paris at the end of March 1941 than he tried to join that Republic. Every functionary, every teacher, in

those days, had to sign a loyalty oath.* Simone de Beauvoir was made
to sign such an "oath that I was neither a Freemason nor a Jew. I found
putting my name to this most repugnant, but no one refused to do so;
the majority of my colleagues, like myself, had no possible alternative."[8]
In April 1941, Sartre refused. His explanation in October 1971 (Interview no. 15) follows: "Castor and I argued about it. She said that my
dogmatism was stupid, didn't serve anything, that I should sign so I
could have a job and money to do what I wanted to do, which was to
set up a Resistance group—I had told her as soon as I had returned
from camp. Anyway, she was right of course, but I refused to sign. I
was too full of the camp, of my decision not to compromise. But that
wasn't a political decision, it was moral. Fortunately, the inspector-
general of education was a secret Resistant, and he gave me my job back
at the Lycée Pasteur anyway."[9]

Next, Sartre decided to bring together those he knew well enough to
trust to form "the group." First there was the immediate "family"—
Bost, Olga, Wanda, Pouillon, Castor. Then he called Merleau-Ponty, a
fellow phenomenologist after all, and they contacted a few students
from l'Ecole Normale and the Sorbonne: Jean-Toussaint Desanti and
his wife Dominique; a mathematician named Raymond Marrot; a phy-
sician, Georges Chazelas, and his student brother Jean; three politicized
philosophy students, François Cuzin, Simone Debout, and Yvonne Pi-
cart; and finally two of his Pasteur students, Raoul Levy and Jean
Kanapa.

"We called our group 'Socialisme et Liberté' [Socialism and Lib-
erty]" Sartre told me, "because it had two purposes: to fight for our
freedom now and to do so in the hope of establishing a new collective
society in which we would all be free because no one would have the
power to exploit anyone else. And then we had to fight precisely because the Americans were coming. We had to make it hard and bloody
for the Germans to leave so that we showed we could take over from
them and not, after the Germans left, be ruled by another kind of
American *gauleiter*. Of course we were all petit bourgeois intellectuals
and didn't know what to do except write. We did that, of course, in all
sorts of leaflets, and I even wrote a Constitution for our new, postwar
society, a Socialist Constitution. But we wanted to do more."[10]

---

*Seemingly a perennial but always avidly-sought symbol for dictators, reactionaries,
mafiosos, and all other totalitarians who distrust people who think for themselves. U.S.
institutions, including all colleges and universities, private and public, demanded such
loyalty oaths during the McCarthy era, and many still do.

But they didn't. Castor said that Desanti proposed "with cheerful ferocity" that the group attack collaborators, but "none of us felt qualified to manufacture bombs or hurl grenades." So instead they decided to compile information and distribute it in leaflets and pamphlets—exactly what most other intellectual resistants were doing. Sartre contacted some of them, including his boyhood chum, Alfred Péron, an English teacher turned British agent, and Jean Cavaillès, a philosopher who had set up the Second Column group; too deeply involved to accommodate Sartre's bourgeois amateurs, both were eventually executed by the Germans. Sartre's group, as well as most others, met in cafés and were "guilty of extraordinary lack of caution," said Castor. "Bost walked through the streets carrying a duplicating machine, and Pouillon went around with his briefcase stuffed full of pamphlets." [11]

"Resistance from the Café Flore," Raymond Aron quipped disparagingly when I interviewed him. [12] He, of course, had risked much as he sat in London during the war, working for General de Gaulle, eating well, and never once worrying about being tortured by the Gestapo, a fate that struck many of the Flore resistants. In fact, the Flore was not much different from Aron's office—except that the coffee was made of bark or root, and there was that chance of Gestapo intrusion. "Our hotel rooms were not heated," said Sartre, "so I always worked in cafes. During the war, Castor and I worked on the first floor [second floor to Americans] of the Flore, she at one end, I at the other, so we wouldn't be tempted to talk. We wrote from 9:00 to 1:00, went to Castor's room to eat whatever she had scrounged up the night before, or whatever our friends, who ate with us, brought along, then back to the Flore to write some more, from 4:00 to 8:00 or 9:00." [13] They interrupted only for Socialism and Liberty business.

By summer vacation time in 1941, Sartre was fed up with how little that business was. He decided to try to make contact with more serious resistants. The Communists, of course, would not help him. Germany had only recently (22 June) launched its invasion of Russia and most French Communists were still trying to curtail their scoffing at the "war of imperialists." True, the Party had stopped its requests for permission to bring out *L'Humanité* legally, and was in fact frantically setting up resistance units throughout France. But it considered such groups as the one formed by Sartre to be amateurish and unreliable, and tried to spread the rumor that Sartre had been freed from prisoner of war camp in order to spy for the Germans. So Sartre and Castor decided to sneak into France's unoccupied zone—relatively easy to do via some farmer's field—to look up other writers whom Sartre felt would help. They spent the whole summer biking from Roanne to Marseilles, Arles to Grenoble, Lyon to Narbonne, Aix to Bourg. On the way, Sartre decided to get officially demobilized, which could only be done where the French were still technically in charge, hence in the "Free Zone."

"When I presented my military notebook to the appropriate French officer," Sartre remembered, "he complained that it had been 'doctored.' 'If not,' I told him, 'I would still be in the camp.' 'That's not the question,' he shouted, 'a military passbook is sacred. This one is disgusting. You should not have touched it!' Again, I said, 'And what, stay in the camp?' He never answered, but kept repeating that one should never make a mark on a military passbook. He finally did give me my discharge paper, but he continued to believe that it was better to stay in a German prisoner camp than to turn a comma on a French military record."[14]

Such French bureaucrats were far from the worst. As Gilles Perrault reported in *Lire* in June 1987, "By the end of 1943, for every Abwehr or Gestapo agent stationed in Paris [there were] forty to fifty French agents. It was they who struck the hardest blows to the Resistance. . . . No profession, no state body was spared. After Liberation, the policemen in charge of the investigation [of the collaboration] found that the rottenness went so high and so far that they were ordered to close all files on the arguable grounds that the morale of the nation, already well shaken, would not survive the shock of such far-reaching revelations. . . . 'A generalized cancer,' said Commissioner Clos, in charge of the investigation."[15]

Even then, before the real facts were known, it certainly seemed as if most French police and government officials joyfully and zealously tracked down Jews, infiltrated resistance groups, made fortunes accepting bribes for travel documents or selling whatever they requisitioned on the black market. That was why André Gide, whom Sartre saw in Grasse, was so discouraged. Though never a collaborationist, he had written in his journal "Collaboration with Germany appears to me acceptable, desirable even, were I sure that it would be honest. I even go as far as believing that we would be better off as German subjects, with its painful humiliations, yet still less destructive for us than the discipline Vichy proposes to impose on us today."[16]

To Sartre, Gide seemed simply beaten. While they talked at his hotel, he "kept a very suspicious eye on our fellow customers, and changed his table three times." He offered no help, but wished Sartre better luck with Malraux.

Which Sartre got indeed: an exquisite "Chicken Maryland" lunch at Malraux' sumptuous villa near Saint-Jean-Cap-Ferrat, on the Cap d'Ail of the French Riviera. But otherwise, not much more. Malraux was courteous but said that there wasn't much to do except to wait for "Russian tanks and American planes to win the war." [17] In Marseilles, Sartre told me, "I went to see Daniel Mayer who, with Blum in jail, was deemed head of the French Socialist Party. He couldn't care less about resistance. All he did was repeat that it was Blum's birthday and we should send him a card, it would please him so. Colette Audry, in Grenoble, couldn't help either, nor could the other contacts we went to see. I had been very naive. No one even seemed interested in my Constitution, which was a complete one, with articles on the structures of the state, the economy, minorities, etc. There were a few copies around, but I lost them, or everyone else who had a copy lost it. We came back to Paris disappointed. Before long 'Socialism and Liberty' was dead." [18]

In her memoirs, Castor has summarized that defeat. "We found ourselves reduced to a condition of total impotence. When Sartre started 'Socialism and Liberty,' he hoped this group would attach itself to a much larger central body; but our trip had produced no important results, and our return to Paris proved no less disappointing. Already the various movements that had sprung up right at the beginning were disbanded or in the process of breaking up. Like ours, they had come into being through individual initiative, and consisted mainly of middle-class intellectuals without any experience of underground action—or indeed of action in any form. . . . The Communists, on the other hand, were well organized, well disciplined, and possessed an excellent administrative machine, with the result that from the moment they decided to intervene they obtained spectacular results." [19]

No wonder that the younger folk in the group were attracted to the Communist Party. Ignoring its political flip-flops, its smears and lies and frame-up (they, of all people, knew that Sartre had never been a traitor, as the CP claimed until the end of 1942), they flocked to it: Georges Chazelas joined in 1942, the Desanti couple in 1943, Raoul Levy and Jean Kanapa after the war. And then, to justify their own lack of independent thought, they smeared Sartre, and still do. In 1982 Chazelas said that Sartre, forty years earlier, "did not know how to think." In 1983, Levy referred to Sartre as a "buffoon." The Desantis mocked the "lack of competence" Sartre never claimed he had, which was why he so desperately tried to link up with those who knew how to fight.[20] As for Kanapa, who led a successful career up the Party ladder, he remained Sartre's official denouncer all his life; but after a 1954 Sartre counterattack ("It takes more than one swallow to make a spring, and more than one Kanapa to dishonor a party"), written while Sartre was allied to the CP, the weekly left-wing *L'Observateur* declared that Sartre had successfully "executed" Kanapa, and the latter was never taken seriously again.[21]

Sartre's failure of resistance was inevitable. As Pouillon said, "he was neither an organizer nor a capo, neither a politician nor an orderly."[22] Leroy put it this way: "Sartre was incredibly courageous. Given a machine gun and told, 'Go there and fire,' he would have done exactly that even if he felt that with his eyes he could not hit anything. But on one condition. He had to feel that his action was morally justified."[23] Stuck midway between Gaullists, who were simply more arrogant and more paternalistic than France's prewar *salauds,* and the French Communists, whose stated aim of defending the little man Sartre supported but whose means were often to sacrifice that man for the greater glory of party leaders in France and Russia, Sartre remained a loner. He kept failing, but he kept trying. He was "never a resistant who wrote," he told me; he was "a writer who resisted," and tried harder each time.[24]

There were still Communist leaders in those days who were both intelligent and idealistic. One of them was Claude Morgan (whose real name was Lecomte, a former engineer who, in 1942, had become editor of the underground literary magazine, *Les Lettres Françaises.* Morgan and the other party intellectuals who ran it opened the review to all anti-Nazi writers, and gained a wide distribution (20,000 during the occupation, 200,000 six months after liberation, but 40,000 by 1947 once Morgan was out). During the winter 1942–43, Morgan asked Sartre to write for *Les Lettres Françaises* and join the Communist-sponsored Comité National des Ecrivains (CNE, the National Committee of Writers). "But," said Sartre, "your people call me a traitor." Responded Morgan, "Not my people, idiots. I'll fix that."

Sitting in the spacious kitchen of his vast estate—38 hectares he purchased from the sale of the two Impressionist paintings he had inherited from his father, Georges Lecomte, an academician—ex-communist Morgan told me in 1973: "I did fix it. Those rumors stopped. Sartre was a tremendous guy. He never looked for what could divide, only for what united us all. He was ready to do anything for the Resistance. He was the kind of guy that, once he decided something, he would go all the way. He faithfully attended all the meetings. He wrote for us a fantastic piece on Drieu de la Rochelle, showing how Drieu's self-hatred led him into collaborating, and then three more articles which ran in subsequent issues. Most people really liked and everybody respected Sartre—except our chiefs, people like Aragon who kept telling me not to trust him; 'Use him but don't trust him,' he kept saying." * [25]

Meanwhile, in the fall of 1941 Sartre had been transferred to the Lycée Condorcet, in the heart of Paris, and had started writing seriously. Early in 1943, Gallimard published his major philosophical work, *L'Etre et le néant (Being and Nothingness)*. An amazing volume, it was almost totally ignored until after the war, when Sartre became somewhat of a cult figure. Still, as one critic remembered later, "the work was massive, hirsute, overflowing, irresistable in its strength, filled with exquisite subtleties, encyclopedic, superbly technical, and characterized throughout by an insight of diamantine simplicity. The anti-philosophical riffraff was already starting to raise a hue and cry in the papers. There could be no doubt about it: a new system had been born." [26] But the hue and cry was miniscule. The book didn't sell at all, except perhaps to flour merchants, for, as Raymond Queneau teasingly quipped, "This Sartre, really, he's right on. To publish, in 1943, a book which weighs exactly a kilo. . . . All the grocers who sell flour or potatoes by weight will be obliged to have a volume in their stores." [27]

Being and Nothingness was not the least bit political. Though its primary concern was to reveal man's fundamental alienation in a world where nothing had a real reason for being the way it is—or even for existing—that alienation was described phenomenologically, without any attempt to trace its historical or social causes. "When I wrote *Being and Nothingness*," Sartre said earlier in our interview series, "I was still considering politics like Camus did, that is, one gets involved in politics from time to time when things go badly, but the rest of the time one thinks of death—Camus did, not me—of the meaning of life or of love." [28] Or, as he added in another of our conversations, "You could say that *Being and Nothingness* was both the end of my bourgeois, individualistic, all - acts - are - equivalent - as - long - as - you - accept - full - responsibility-for-them upbringing and the beginning of something

---

* Added Morgan: "Aragon trusted no one. He was always manipulating to be in the limelight. After the war, when our circulation zoomed, he had me transferred to some peace magazine so he could take over *Les Lettres Françaises* and get the credit." Under his tutelage, it collapsed.

new, something whose germ was certainly there, with my notions of freedom and responsibility, bad faith and inauthenticity, which would eventually become a very social and moral commitment."[29]

It is true that Camus at the time did view politics as an occasional but unfortunate necessity. In both *The Stranger,* his first novel, and *The Myth of Sisyphus,* his first book-length essay, Camus described the world as absurd and man's actions as irrelevant in the order of things. In a favorable review published in the major wartime magazine *Cahiers du Sud,* Sartre congratulated Camus for showing that "our feeling of absurdity comes from our impotence to *think* with our concepts, with our words, the events of this world." Said Sartre: "The poles of the absurd include death, the irreducible pluralisms of truth and beings, the unintelligibility of reality, chance."[30] But both were rapidly changing. Said Castor, who met Camus with Sartre shortly thereafter, "Like us, Camus had moved from individualism to a committed attitude; we knew, though he never mentioned the fact, that he had important and responsible duties in the Combat movement. He relished his success and fame, and made no secret of the fact; to carry it off with a blasé air would have been something less than natural . . . What I liked most about him was his capacity for detached amusement at people and things even while he was intensely occupied with his personal activities, pleasures, and friendships."[31]

Sartre liked Camus, at first. "He was funny, extremely rude but often very funny,"[32] and eventually joined him in his Resistance group. But, said Sartre, "Camus was just fine as a sort of Algerian punk, a wise-ass, very brazen, very funny, but not pompous. Then he changed. He began to think of himself as a very serious philosopher. He attacked Merleau-Ponty without cause, had an affair with Wanda, and just generally, because of his success, decided that he was not bound by parameters, by common courtesies."[33]

"I think Sartre was a bit jealous," Castor told me, "but there's no doubt that, later, Camus changed a lot. He became an always-be-against type of moralist, too pompous."[34] According to Olga, Wanda's older sister, the coolness which set in between Sartre and Camus, and their actual break later on, was not due to political differences. "There's that myth," she told me, "that Sartre always broke with men for political reason. Not true. He broke with them because he didn't like the way they lived or loved or whom they loved or simply the manner in which they talked, to others mind you, not to himself."[35]

By the spring of 1943 it had become clear that the Allies would win the war. Rommel had been defeated at El-Alamein and Von Paulus at Stalingrad. But in France, the war was harder. Key cities were now being bombed regularly by U.S. and British planes, while the fascist French militia, aided by increasingly brutal Gestapo squads, were massacring hostages by the hundreds. In June 1943, while de Gaulle was eliminating his rivals in Algeria, and the Allies were landing in Sicily, the great French Resistance leader Jean Moulin was tortured and killed. And at the famed Sarah Bernhardt theatre, which had been renamed Théatre de la Cité because Bernhardt was Jewish, Charles Dullin launched Sartre's *Les mouches (The Flies)*, with the approval of both the German censors and the resistant CNE.

Despite this consent by Communist resisters, Sartre, many believe to this day, should have refused to let his play be staged in that particular theatre. Some even insist that he should not have submitted it to the German censor in the first place. Of course, that means that Sartre should not have written it, that painters should not have exhibited, that porters should not have cleaned offices, and so forth. Since the meaning of his play was precisely to praise and encourage the Resistance, it is true that it never did occur to Sartre that by letting it go on in that theatre he was also sending a strange message, especially to those who would not see the play but would know that it was being performed in a theatre whose namesake had been stricken from the public record because she was Jewish.

Still, for those who saw it, there could be no doubt that *The Flies* was vehemently antioccupier, hence, in the context, anti-German. Based on the Greek myth of Orestes avenging the murder of his father, Agamemnon, by Aegisthus and Clytemnestra, his mother, the play, said Sartre in front of the censors, deals with "the tragedy of freedom in opposition to the tragedy of fatality. In other words, the subject of my play could be characterized thus: 'How does a man behave in the face of an act for which he accepts fully the responsibility and consequences, when at the same time the act horrifies him?'" [36]

The German censors bought the explanation. But, said Castor, "it was impossible to mistake the play's implications; the word Liberty, dropped from Orestes' mouth, burst on us like a bomb. The German critic of the *Parizer Zeitung* saw this very clearly, and said so," but his review of the play was favorable nevertheless. [37] In *Les Lettres Françaises,* meanwhile, Michel Leiris anonymously praised the play hoping "each of us will do like [Orestes] and accomplish the jump, committing himself dangerously and of his own free will in the arid road now begun, in search of the Good which is '*their* good,' that of all men alienated from themselves by their respect of the established order," that is, the German occupation.[38] Said Sartre after liberation, "Why make the Greeks declaim . . . if it isn't to disguise the thought under a fascist regime? . . . The real drama, the one I would have liked to write, is the one of the terrorist who, by shooting Germans in the street, unleashed the execution of fifty hostages."[39]

At first glance, Sartre's message in *The Flies* was simple: those who fight the Germans fight for France; the acts may be horrendous, but by refusing to feel guilty, the Resistance fighter frees himself and all Frenchmen. But there was another message, nice and pat so that all the Parisian bourgeois might feel safe: the Resistance will not become the government after the war. Orestes kills Aegisthus and Clytemnestra (the Germans) but then leaves Argos (France) with the furies (the blood of all the dead hostages) flocking behind him, letting the nice citizens of Argos (old or new bourgeois leaders, the *salauds*) take over—exactly what did happen after 1946. "*Les mouches* was not a revolutionary play," Sartre told me in 1971. "But neither were the Communists. They were tough, courageous, valiant fighters and martyrs, but also hacks for the Russian politburo. They did not want power. Oh yes, they had excuses: America would intervene, de Gaulle and Leclerc had all the tanks, and so on. But the fact is, no Communist Party in a country whose borders did not touch Russia (or a satellite), ever wanted to seize power, because Moscow said not to. Communists never thought they could rule without Russian tanks to back them up, in case. Our great Communist Resistance fighters—or rather their leaders—were not revolutionaries, only very brave Russian messengers. And that's what my play reflected."[40]

But he didn't know it in 1943. "I was then like Camus was in the fifties," he said in Interview no. 16, "I did not understand that war is the consequence of certain inner conflicts in bourgeois societies. Workers don't go to war, peasants don't go to war, unless they are pushed into it by their leaders, those who control the means of production, the press, communications in general, the educational system, in one word, the bourgeois. When I think of Camus claiming *years later,* that the German invasion was like the plague *—coming for no reason, leaving for no reason—*quel con,* what a shmuck! The German invasion was an

---

*The allusion is to Camus's novel *The Plague,* whose message was that the brave and the just should fight it, even though nothing they do can really help since there are no explanations why it comes or why it leaves.

invasion of *men*, and it was eventually defeated by *men*. But at the time
I was almost like that: it was our duty to our fellow citizens to fight the
Nazi plague until it left us. But mind you, I was no revolutionary. The
communists supposedly were, and yet they too thought like that—and
gave up their arms once they won." Then, he added in Interview no. 17,
"Today I understand Orestes. After he killed the King and Queen he
should have taken command. That he didn't was not just politically stupid. It was immoral."[41]

And yet Orestes certainly had the strength. Not only did he free
Argos of its usurpers of power, he handily confronted Zeus, the king of
kings, god of gods, who made one terrible blunder: he created man
free. "You are God and I am free; each of us is alone, and our anguish is
akin," Orestes tells Zeus, who wants to stop him from opening the eyes
of his countrymen:

ZEUS: Poor people! Your gift to them will be a sad one; of loneliness and
    shame. You will tear from their eyes the veils I had laid on them, and they
    will see their lives as they are, foul and futile, a barren boon.
ORESTES: Why, since it is their lot, should I deny them the despair I
    have in me?
ZEUS: What will they make of it?
ORESTES: What they choose. They're free; and human life begins on the far
    side of despair.[42]

But what most people choose to do with their freedom is hide it.
Such people Sartre condemned in his next play, *Huis clos (No Exit)*, first
performed at the Théatre du Vieux-Colombier on 27 May 1944. Three
people in hell all pretend to be different than they really were in life,
until loneliness and dependence force each to break down and reveal the
truth. Sartre explained that his much-quoted statement, "Hell is other
people," had often been misunderstood. What he meant was that "no
matter what circle of Hell we're living in, I think we're free to break out
of it. And if people don't break out of it, they still stay there freely. So
that they condemn themselves to Hell."[43] Which was another way of
saying that those who claim they cannot do anything about the German
occupation don't want to. In our search for self-knowledge and self-
identity, we use what others say and think about us; the whole lesson is
that there is no such thing as moral isolation or irresponsibility; and
since others judge us by our acts (a genuine commitment) and not by
our gestures (a comedy), we are not only defined by others, we define
ourselves by what we do.

What Sartre did during that last year of German occupation was write: various screenplays (of which two, *Typhus,* without credit, and *The Chips Are Down* would eventually be produced), various articles, including one praising Maurice Blanchot and Franz Kafka ("Aminadab") and one criticizing Georges Bataille, Emile Durkheim, and Sigmund Freud ("Un nouveau mystique"), and polished once more the first two volumes of his *The Roads to Freedom.* He worked hard in the CNE and also, since *The Flies,* in the CNT (the National Theater Committee). Through his comrade on *Les Lettres Françaises,* Michel Leiris, who had become a wealthy art patron (by marriage) as well as a Communist, Sartre became friends with Pablo Picasso, and on 19 March 1944, he starred in the painter's surrealist play, *Le Désir attrapé par la queue (Desire Caught by the Tail),* a one-shot (but well-rehearsed) reading held in Leiris's living room. Sartre played Round End, a main part, Castor The Cousin, a small one. Both of them, and Camus who sort of directed it, thought the whole thing was a great joke; the others took it seriously.

In mid-July 1944, a member of the Combat team was captured and tortured, and talked. Camus tipped off the rest of the team in time, and Sartre and Castor made a beeline first for Leiris's apartment, then for a safe house in Neuilly-sous-Clermont. On 11 August, the radio announced that the Allies were in Chartres; jumping onto their bicycles, Sartre and Castor rushed back to Paris to witness its liberation. They made it in time to join the uprising led by the French Forces of the Interior, the resistance FFI. Sartre and forty other CNT members were ordered to seize and hold the Théatre Française—with two pistols. Then, writing for Camus's *Combat,* Sartre described the end of an era in vibrant, vivid street scenes:

Day I (22 August): It begins like a festival and even today the Boulevard Saint-Germain, deserted and swept intermittently by machine-gun fire, keeps its air of tragic solemnity. . . . The street has once again become—as it did in 1789 and 1848—the theater for great collective movement and social life. . . . In the middle of the road an enormous truck lies dying, turned over on its back like a crab.

Day 2: The Senate, enormous and dark at the very end of the empty street, seems venomous with its unbearable flag which you look at in spite of yourself.

Day 3 and 4: They've just pointed out to the F.F.I. a group of Darnand's militia who are trying to fire into the street from a hotel on the rue de Buci. The F.F.I. men go into the hotel and soon come down with a dozen little yellow guys with anxious but inscrutable faces and hands up. *Japanese.* So these are the men who make up Vichy's 'real French' militia. The laughter suddenly becomes Homeric: some people have grabbed hold of a few of these assassins, taken their pants down, and energetically spanked them.

Day 5: A German truck went by, heading east. Big blond, rather handsome men, not distrusting us, were standing in the back of it. The Parisians hanging over their balconies knew they only had to make a gesture, call out, and these men would be saved from death. But they did not want to, could not do it. They let the truck roll on toward its destiny, with the obscure feeling of taking part in a tragic and mortal festival, a bull fight.

Day 7: Never in human memory have rebels been so friendly and fraternal toward the army. Never before have civilian fighters . . . and impeccable soldiers and their leaders been seen parading to the same approving cheers. . . . And Monday shops and offices will open up again: Paris will go back to work.[44]

And so it did. Eventually most Parisians forgot about those awful years. The *salauds* hurried back and occupied the same seats in the same buildings and issued the same orders as they had five years before. New wars came, and new betrayals, and Sartre spent the rest of his life denouncing them. He was never forgiven for that.

What his critics hated most about Sartre was not the many mistakes he inevitably made, but that he never compromised again. Sartre defined modern-day fascists as those who use their power, or who would use it if they had it, to silence dissent for their personal gain or glory. He saw such fascists in every party, every institution in both America and Russia, as well as in France. So he joined no party, worked for no institution, supported no establishment. He related only to the young, but remained the conscience of most of us.

The Communists called him a capitalist hyena. The capitalists dubbed him a Communist stooge. When such attacks neither stopped him from rushing for the barricades nor dissuaded the young from listening to his message, especially in the Third World, whose most eloquent defender he had become in the First, his enemies resorted to digging up the past. Ignoring the fact that none of France's so-called great ones had been active during World War II (not Breton, nor Picasso, nor Braque, nor Gide, nor Monterlant . . .), they once again condemned him for not having picked up the gun against the Nazi invaders.

The most serious attack on Sartre was launched after he was dead by Vladimir Jankelevitch, a mediocre philosopher but brave man who had fought well during the war. Bitter and unforgiving, swearing never again to listen to German music or to read German poetry, Jankelevitch spent his last four decades on earth cultivating his rancor. Then, in his own dying gasps, he charged that "Sartre's postwar commitment was a sort of sickly compensation, remorse, hunger for the danger he did not want to risk during the war. He invested everything into the after-war."[45]

Immediately, France's new generation of apolitical *salauds* applauded. So did the equivalent so-called intellectuals in America.[46] Secret reactionaries posing as democratic socialists, they must have thought that the best way to convince their readers not to become *engagé*, not to be interested in the fate of the poor and the weak was not to condemn the commitment of the greatest philosopher of action, but to go back forty years and show that he had not been very committed then.

The fact is, Sartre had never pretended to be a resistant during the war, only a writer who wanted to resist. He did his best. His eyesight, his awkwardness, his bourgeois upbringing, his Protestant ethic, his prewar philosophy stopped him. He never denied that, but learned from it. Specifically, as he told me, he learned that "every man is political, everything we do affects someone else, even when we do nothing, and that's political. But I learned all that late, gradually, and it jelled after I saw that by not really caring who would rule us after we were free again, the same gang of bastards would take other people's freedom."[47] From 1945 on, Sartre did more than any other intellectual in the world to denounce injustice and to support the wretched of the earth. And he did so taking more risks than any other intellectual, risks to his person, to his reputation, to his immortality. Thus, as Professor Danto said, he edged closer every day to becoming one of the very few men of this world to live a life authentically.

Notes

Works listed in the bibliography are cited in these notes in shortened form. Interviews with Sartre are referred to by number. Full information appears in the bibliography.

Chapter One: "L'Enfant Terrible"

1. Beauvoir, *Prime of Life*, 68.
2. Sartre, *The Ghost of Stalin*, 7–8.
3. Jean-Paul Sartre, "Elections, piège à cons," *Le Temps Modernes,* no. 318 (January 1973).
4. Jean-Paul Sartre, "Self-Portrait at Seventy," *Life/Situations* (New York: Pantheon, 1977), 7.
5. Paul Nizan, *Ce Soir,* 24 November 1938, 5.
6. Jean-Paul Sartre, "Justice and the State," *Life/Situations,* 185.
7. Ibid., 185–86.
8. "Questions sur Sartre," *Le Débat,* no. 35 (May 1985): 76–78.
9. Annie Cohen-Solal, *Sartre* (Paris: Gallimard, 1985).
10. *Liberation,* 23 October 1985.
11. Ibid.
12. Richard Bernstein, "Revisionists and Storytellers—Is It Passé to be *Engagé?*" *New York Times Book Review,* 5 January 1986.

Chapter Two: L'Adulte Terrible

1. Sartre, *Situations II,* 35–43.
2. Pierre Brisson, in *Figaro Littéraire,* 1947, cited in Jeannette Colombel, *Sartre ou le parti de vivre* (Paris: Bernard Grasset, 1981), 63.
3. *L'Humanité,* 7 April 1948; George Lukacs, *Existentialisme ou Marxisme* (Paris: Editions Nagel, 1948), 20.
4. Henre Lefebvre, "Existentialisme et Marxisme: réponse a une mise au point," *Action,* 8 June 1945.
5. *Le Figaro,* 25 April 1949; *Le Figaro Littéraire,* 7 May 1949.
6. Sartre's correspondence with the Nobel Committee in *Le Monde,* 24 October 1964; André Breton, "Le rappel de Stockholm," *La Bréche,* December 1964.
7. Gabriel Marcel, "Prise de position," *Nouvelles Littéraires,* 29 October 1964.
8. *Paris-Match,* 1 October 1960.
9. A. J. Ayer, "Jean-Paul Sartre," *Horizon,* July 1945.
10. A. J. Ayer, *Language, Truth, and Logic* (London: Penguin, 1949), 98.
11. Iris Murdoch, *Sartre: Romantic Rationalist* (New Haven: Yale University Press, 1953), 91–103; Mary Warnock, *The Philosophy of Sartre* (London: Hutchinson University Library, 1965), 11, 72–73.

12. Warnock, *The Philosophy*, 11; Denis O'Brien in *Commonweal*, 4 July 1980.

13. Denis Hollier, *Politique de la prose: Jean-Paul Sartre et l'an quarante* (Paris: Gallimard, 1982), 260.

14. Alexandre Leupin, "A New Sartre," *Yale French Studies*, no. 68 (1985): 234.

15. Germaine Brée, *Camus and Sartre* (New York: Delta Books, 1972), 72, 71.

16. Beauvoir, *Force of Circumstance*, 260.

17. Brée, *Camus and Sartre*, 33, 114, 152–53, 232.

18. Robert Dennon Cumming, *The Philosophy of Jean-Paul Sartre* (New York: Modern Library, 1966), 5.

19. Jack Newfield, *Robert Kennedy: A Memoir* (New York: 1969), 58.

20. David Caute, *New Statesman*, 9 May 1980.

21. Ibid., 23 May 1980.

22. *New York Times*, 14 June 1980.

23. Ibid.

24. Olivier Rolin, "Un immense dépôt," *Le Débat*, no. 35 (May 1985), 74.

25. Clement Rosset, "Questions sur Sartre," ibid., 78.

26. John Weightman, "Summing Up Sartre," *New York Review of Books*, 13 August 1987.

27. Bernstein, "Revisionists and Storytellers" (see chapter 1, note 12).

28. *Time*, 22 June 1983.

29. Bernstein, "Revisionists and Storytellers."

30. *London Sunday Times*, 20 April 1980.

31. István Mészáros, *The Work of Sartre* (New Jersey: Humanities Press, 1979), vol. 1, *Search for Freedom*, 7.

32. Cited in Stephen Spender, "Notes on the International Congress, Summer 1937," *New Writing* (Autumn 1937).

33. Hazel E. Barnes, *Sartre and Flaubert* (Chicago: University of Chicago Press, 1981), 389.

34. Sartre, *The Words*, 159.

35. Françoise Sagan, *Avec mon meilleur souvenir* (Paris: Gallimard, 1984), 183–85.

Chapter Three: The Faker

1. Sartre, *The Words*, 9.

2. Ibid., 9–10.

3. Ibid., 11.

4. Interview no. 3.

5. Sartre, *The Words*, 12.

6. Interview no. 4.

7. Sartre, *The Words*, 12.

8. Ibid., 11.

9. Ibid., 12–13.

10. Ibid., 12.

11. Ibid., 13–14.

12. Albert Schweitzer, *Souvenirs de mon enfance* (Paris: Albin Michel, 1984), written in 1924; first published commercially in 1951. Schweitzer does mention cousin-once-removed Sartre in his later autobiographical *Ma vie, ma pensée* (Paris: Albin Michel, 1960).

13. Sartre, *The Words*, 7–8.

14. Ibid., 10.

15. Interview no. 1.

16. Ibid.

17. Sartre, *The Words*, 32.

18. Ibid., 25.

19. Interview no. 1.

20. Sartre, *The Words*, 13.

21. Ibid., 21n.

22. See A. James Arnold and Jean-Pierre Piriou, "Les Mots de Jean-Paul Sartre: Genèse et critique d'une autobiographie," *Archives des Lettres Modernes*, no. 144 (1973).

23. J-B. Pontalis, "Reply to Sartre," *Les Temps Modernes*, April 1969; English version in *Between Existentialism and Marxism* (New York: Pantheon, 1974), 22.

24. Sartre, *Search for a Method*, 60.

25. "The Man with the Tape Recorder," in *Between Existentialism,* note 23 above, 199–205; Interview no. 34.

26. Interview no. 1.

27. Sartre, *The Words*, 65–66.

28. Ibid., 55.

29. Interview no. 1.

30. Sartre, *The Words*, 55.

31. Interview no. 2.

32. Interview no. 1.

33. Sartre, *The Words*, 18.

34. Ibid., 19, 21.

35. Ibid., 52–54.

36. Interview no. 1.

37. Sartre, *The Words*, 54.

38. Ibid., 82, 84.

39. Interview no. 1.

40. Ibid.

41. Cohen-Solal, *Sartre,* 51; see her last one hundred pages for her attempt to turn Sartre into a conservative.

42. Interviews nos. 1, 2, 3.

43. Interview no. 2.

44. Sartre, *The Words*, 87.

45. Interview no. 1.

46. Sartre, *The Words*, 88; interview no. 1.

47. Ibid.

48. Sartre, *The Words*, 88–89.

49. Ibid., 90.

50. Interview no. 1.

51. Interviews nos. 2, 3; Sartre, *The Words*, 39: "Genius is only a loan: it must be merited by great suffering, tested by ordeals that must be accepted modestly and firmly."

52. Sartre, *The Words*, 90.

53. Ibid., 91.

54. Interview no. 2.

55. Karl Marx, *The Eighteenth Brumaire of Louis Bonaparte* (New York: International Publishers, 1963), 15.

56. Interview no. 1.

57. Ibid.

58. Sartre, *The Words*, 49.

59. Ibid., 76.

60. Interview no. 2.

61. Sartre, *The Words*, 98.

62. Interview no. 2.

63. Sartre, *The Words*, 103.

64. Ibid., 113.

65. Interview no. 2.

66. Sartre, *The Words*, 131, 133.

67. Archives, Lycée Henri IV, Year 1915–16.

68. Sartre, *The Words*, 139.

69. Archives, Lycée Henri IV, Year 1916–17.

70. Sartre, *The Words*, p. 139.

71. Interview no. 1.

72. Sartre, *The Words*, 158.

73. It is the theme of Jeanson's *Sartre par lui-même* (Paris: Editions du Seuil, 1955).

74. Interview no. 5.

75. Derived from Jeanson's *Sartre* (Paris: Desclée de Brouwer, 1966), pp. 186–88.

76. Interview no. 2.

Chapter Four: The Follower

1. Interview no. 2: "The three or four worst years of my life." Also, Sartre, *The Words*, 102.

2. Sartre, *The Words*, and Interview no. 1.

3. Interview no. 2.

4. Ibid.

5. Ibid.

6. Sartre, "Jesus the Owl," in Contat and Rybalka, *The Writings*, 2 : 12.

7. Ibid.

8. Interview no. 2.

9. Ibid.

10. Ibid.

11. Interview no. 1.

12. Ibid.

13. Sartre, "Jesus the Owl," 15.

14. Interviews nos. 3, 2.

15. Ibid.

16. Interviews nos. 2, 3, 4.

17. Conversation at La Coupole, 14 February 1971.

18. Interview no. 2.

19. Ibid.

20. Interview no. 3.

21. Interview no. 4.

22. Ibid.

23. Ibid.

24. Interviews nos. 1, 2.

25. Interview no. 1.

26. Interview no. 2.

27. Interview no. 3.

28. Ibid.

29. Michel Guillet, "Jean-Paul Sartre au lycée de la Rochelle," *Sud-Ouest Dimanche,* 25 October 1964.

30. Interview no. 4.

31. Interview no. 3.

32. Ibid.

33. Interview no. 5.

34. Interview no. 4.

35. Ibid.

36. Ibid.

37. Ibid.

38. Interview no. 5.

39. Ibid.

40. Interview no. 4.

41. Ibid.

42. Ibid.

43. Cited in Philippe Bernard, *La fin d'un monde: 1914–1929* (Paris: Editions du Seuil, 1975), 11.

44. Jean-Paul Sartre, "Paul Nizan," preface to Nizan's *Aden-Arabie* (1960); reprinted in *Situations IV,* trans. Benita Eisler (New York: 1965), 127.

45. Sartre, *The Words,* 143.

46. Sartre, "Paul Nizan," 128.

47. Ibid.

48. Interview no. 1.

49. Sartre, "Paul Nizan," 128–29.

50. Jean Gaulmier, "Quand Sartre avait dix-huit ans . . ." (When Sartre was eighteen . . .), *Le Figaro Littéraire,* 5 July 1958.

51. Interview no. 5.

52. Sartre, "Paul Nizan," 151.

53. Jean-Paul Sartre, *La semence et le scaphandre;* Unpublished manuscript in my possession; my translation. Contat and Rybalka plan to include it in the forthcoming Pléiade volume of Sartre's youthful writings.

54. Claude Bonnefoy, "Rien ne laissait prévoir que Sartre deviendrait 'Sartre,'" *Arts* (January 1961), 11–17.

55. Paul Nizan, *Aden-Arabie* (Paris: Reider, 1932); reprinted in Paris (François Maspero, 1960), 68; Sartre, "Paul Nizan," 134.

Chapter 5: The Loser

1. Cited by Cohen-Solal, *Sartre,* (pp. 94–95) and identified only as "National Archives," without drawer or file numbers, dates, or names.

2. Interview no. 9; also Interview no. 3.

3. Bonnefoy, "Rien ne laissait" (see chap. 4, n. 54).

4. Interview no. 7.

5. Interview no. 8.

6. Ibid.

7. Ibid.

8. Ibid.

9. Ibid.; Interview no. 3; Interview no. 6.

10. Interview no. 6.

11. Ibid.

12. Ibid.

13. Interview no. 8.

14. Interviews nos. 6, 7, 8.

15. *L'Oeuvre,* 22 March 1926.

16. Beauvoir, *Cérémonie,* 237.

17. Cited by Cohen-Solal, *Sartre,* 99; liberally translated by me.

18. Sartre, *Lettres au Castor,* 1 : 35.

19. Interview no. 8.

20. Interview with Raymond Aron, 25 May 1973.

21. Raymond Aron, *Mémoires* (Paris: Julliard, 1983), 35, 98.

22. Interview no. 8.

23. Ibid.

24. Beauvoir, *Prime of Life,* 58.

25. Ibid., 59.

26. Interview no. 7.

27. Interview no. 3.

28. Jean-Paul Sartre, "Empedocle," typed manuscript copy in my possession, given to me by Michel Contat.

29. Ibid.

30. See his *La révolution communautaire* (Paris: 1941).

31. Jean-Paul Sartre, *L'Image dans la vie psychologique: rôle et nature,* typed manuscript in my possession, given to me by Simone de Beauvoir.

32. Sartre, "Paul Nizan," 130 (see chap. 4, n. 44).

33. Georges Politzer, *Principes élémentaires de philosophie* (1929; reprinted, Paris: 1970), 21.

34. See, for example, Pascal Ory, *Nizan, destin d'un révolté* (Paris: 1980); and William D. Redfern, *Paul Nizan* (Princeton University Press, 1972). The most flagrantly biased biography, however, is the best known, perhaps because

it gives credit to Madame Nizan on the cover: Annie Cohen-Solal's *Paul Nizan, communiste impossible* (Paris: Bernard Grasset, 1980), relies almost exclusively on interviews with Rirette Nizan, whose impartiality Sartre and de Beauvoir questioned vehemently.

35. Interview no. 8.

36. Cited in Redfern, p. 11; Interview no. 8; interview with René Maheu; interview with Raymond Aron.

37. Interview no. 8.

38. Ibid.

39. Paul Nizan, *The Watchdogs* (1932; reprinted, Paris: 1965; New York: 1971), 43, 53–54, 57.

40. Ibid. (New York, 1971), 85.

41. Ibid. 157–58.

42. Sartre, *Lettres au Castor*, 23.

43. Nizan, *The Watchdogs*, 171n.

44. Ibid., 58–59, 61.

45. Ibid., 91, 69, 102.

46. Ibid., 92, 140.

47. Interview with Maheu.

48. Interview with Aron; see Paul Nizan, *Aden-Arabie* (see above, chapter 4, note 55.).

49. Sartre, "Paul Nizan," 134.

50. Interview no. 6.

51. Interview no 7.

52. Interview with Aron.

53. Sartre, *Lettres au Castor*, 28.

54. Jean-Paul Sartre, *Les Nouvelles Littéraires*, 2 February 1929; English version in Beauvoir, *Memoirs of a Dutiful Daughter*, 363.

55. Interview no. 8.

56. Cohen-Solal, *Sartre*, 115.

57. Interview with Aron.

58. Interview with Simone de Beauvoir.

59. Interview no. 8; conversation with Sartre at La Coupole, 18 November 1974.

60. Vincent Descombes, *Le Même et l'autre* (Paris: Edition de Minuit, 1979), 17. It is my projection in the present, not Descombes's.

61. Conversation at La Coupole, 18 November 1974.

62. *Sartre*, the film, 33–34.

63. Interview no. 9.

64. Beauvoir, *Memoirs*, 329, 331–32, 345.

65. Ibid., 355.

66. Ibid., 359.

67. Interview with Maheu.

68. Raymond Aron, *Le Nouvel Observateur*, 15–21 March 1976.

69. Interview with Aron.

70. Beauvoir, *Memoirs*, 366.

Chapter Six: The Watchdog

1. *Le Temps,* 4 January 1928; 14 October 1928; 5 January 1929; 6 April 1929.

2. *Le Temps,* October 1929; constantly during the year 1930.

3. Beauvoir, *Prime of Life,* 32.

4. Ibid., 18, 19, 20, 22.

5. Ibid., 32.

6. Ibid., 29.

7. Sartre, *Lettres au Castor,* 42.

8. In order: Interview no. 6; Contat and Rybalka, *The Writings,* 1:42, 2:37–52; Beauvoir, *Prime of Life,* 41; Interview no. 6.

9. Contat and Rybalka, *The Writings,* 1:43; Interview no. 6.

10. *Bifur,* no. 8 (June 1931): 77–96.

11. Beauvoir, *Prime of Life,* 31–32.

12. Sartre, *Lettres au Castor,* 15.

13. Beauvoir, *Prime of Life,* 32.

14. Ibid., 23–24.

15. Interview no. 8.

16. Beauvoir, *Prime of Life,* 62.

17. Interview with Simone de Beauvoir.

18. Beauvoir, *Prime of Life,* 99.

19. Interview no. 10.

20. Beauvoir, *Prime of Life,* 99.

21. Interview with Olga Kosakiewicz, Paris, 9 May 1973.

22. Interview with Simone de Beauvoir.

23. Beauvoir, *She Came to Stay* (New York: World, 1954), 238–39.

24. Beauvoir, *Prime of Life,* 24.

25. My interview with Simone de Beauvoir in *Society* magazine, January–February 1976.

26. Beauvoir, *Prime of Life,* 27.

27. Ibid.

28. Beauvoir, *Memoirs,* 259–61.

29. Ibid., 261.

30. Ibid., 293.

31. Ibid., 303.

32. Ibid.

33. Interview no. 7.

34. Ibid.

35. Sartre, *Nausea,* 26, 67.

36. Conversation with Sartre at La Palette restaurant, 16 November 1973.

37. Beauvoir, *Memoirs,* 380–82.

38. Interview no. 9.

39. Discharge certificate for Jean (sic) Sartre, no. 1991, cited by Contat and Rybalka in their "Chronologie," for Sartre's *Oeuvres Romanesques,* xlviii.

40. Interview no. 9.

41. Ibid.

42. Genevieve Idt, *Profil d'une oeuvre: La Nausée* (Paris: Hatier, 1971), 11.

43. Interview no. 9.

44. Ibid.

45. Beauvoir, *Prime of Life*, 197.

46. Interview with Jacques-Laurent Bost.

47. Cited in *Les Nouvelles Littéraires*, 17–24 April 1980, 26.

48. Interview with Jean Pouillon.

49. Interview with Troupe Matthews, then a sixty-nine-year-old health teacher of the Alexander technique.

50. Beauvoir, *Prime of Life*, 68, 72.

51. Ibid., 73.

52. Ibid.

53. Ibid.

54. Interview no. 10.

55. Beauvoir, *Prime of Life*, 65–66.

56. *Sartre*, the film, 36.

57. Beauvoir, *Prime of Life*, 76.

58. Sartre, *Lettres au Castor*, 45–51; the unedited typescript of the letter, given to me by Simone de Beauvoir, is in my possession.

59. Beauvoir, *La cérémonie des adieux*, 182.

60. Interview no. 10.

61. Beauvoir, *Prime of Life*, 95–96.

62. Ibid., 100.

63. Interview with Colette Audry.

64. Beauvoir, *Prime of Life*, 111–12.

65. Interview no. 9.

66. Beauvoir, *Prime of Life*, 112.

67. Ibid., 113.

68. Ibid., 114; Interview no. 10.

69. Jean-Paul Sartre, "On Dos Passos," *La Nouvelle Revue Française*, no. 299 (August 1938); reprinted in *Situations I*, 24–25.

70. Conversations with Fernando and Stépha Gerassi, Putney, Vermont, summer 1972.

71. Beauvoir, *Prime of Life*, 112; Interview no. 10.

72. Beauvoir, *Prime of Life*, 112.

73. Interview no. 10.

74. Beauvoir, *Prime of Life*, 126.

75. Paul Nizan, "Eté 1914," *La Nouvelle Revue Française* (January 1937), 97.

Chapter Seven: The Traitor

1. Interview no. 10.

2. "Une idée fondamentale de la philosophie de Husserl: L'Intentionalite," (January 1939); reprinted in *Situations I*, 34–35.

3. *The Transcendence of the Ego*, 85–123.

4. Interview no. 10.

5. Beauvoir, *Prime of Life*, 149.

6. Sartre, *The War Diaries*, 282, 284–85.

7. Interview no. 11. He repeated this point in Interviews nos. 4, 21, 24, 30, and 34.

8. Sartre, *War Diaries*, 281.

9. George Lichtheim, *Marxism in Modern France* (New York: Columbia University Press, 1966), 40, 43.

10. Beauvoir, *Prime of Life*, 155.

11. Ibid., 157, 155–56.

12. Sartre, *Nausea*, 96.

13. Contat and Rybalka, *The Writings*, 1:52–53.

14. Sartre, *Nausea*, 178.

15. Sartre, *The Words*, 157–58.

16. Sartre, *Nausea*, 111–12, 133, 122, 19–20, 156–57.

17. Interview no. 11; see also Beauvoir, *La Cérémonie des adieux*, 264–66.

18. *Le Monde*, 18 April 1964, translated in *Vogue*, 1 January 1965, 94–95, 159.

19. Paul Nizan, *Ce Soir*, 16 May 1938.

20. Interview no. 11.

21. Idt, *Profil* (see chap. 6, n. 42), 13.

22. Sartre, *Nausea*, 55.

23. Interview no. 11.

24. Sartre, *Nausea*, 84, 86.

25. Beauvoir, *Cérémonie*, 228–29; Sartre, *Lettres au Castor*, 7.

26. Iris Murdoch, *Sartre* (see chap. 2, n. 11), 7. She added (on p. 13), "*La Nausée* represents the naked pattern of human existence, illuminated by a degree of philosophical self-consciousness that reveals the fruitlessness which the particular determinations of our projects usually obscure."

27. *Sartre*, the film, 58–59.

28. Beauvoir, *Cérémonie*, 252–53.

29. Sartre, *Lettres au Castor*, 56.

30. Colette Audry, *La Statue* (Paris: Gallimard, 1983), 207, 209, 208, 207.

31. Sartre, *L'Imagination*, 162.

32. Mary Warnock, *The Philosophy* (see chap. 2, n. 11), 28–29.

33. Beauvoir, *Prime of Life*, 169.

34. Ibid., 170.

35. Interview no. 10.

36. Audry, *La Statue*, 212.

37. Interview no. 11.

38. Ibid.

39. Beauvoir, *Prime of Life*, 174.

40. Interview no. 11.

41. Louis Aragon, in a 1924 surrealist article cited in Maurice Nadeau, *Histoire du surrealisme* (Paris: 1945), 200.

42. Beauvoir, *Memoirs*, 220.

43. Georges Politzer, *Critique des fondements de la psychologie* (1928; reprinted, Paris: 1967).

44. Beauvoir, *Prime of Life*, 190.

45. Paul Nizan, *Le cheval de Troie* (Paris: Gallimard, 1935), 52–53, 105–6, 111, 161–63.

46. Beauvoir, *Prime of Life,* 212.

Chapter Eight: The Writer

1. Beauvoir, *Prime of Life,* 220.

2. Ibid., 213.

3. The story Sartre wrote, entitled *Depaysement,* was never published except for some excerpts under the title "Nourritures" (Foods), in *Verve,* 15 November 1938; translation in Contat and Rybalka, *The Writings,* 2:63.

4. Sartre, *Lettres au Castor,* 63–89.

5. Contat and Rybalka, *The Writings,* 2:61.

6. Sartre, *Depaysement,* typed manuscript in my possession, given to me by Simone de Beauvoir; see also the Pléiade edition of Sartre's *Oeuvres Romanesques,* 1537–58.

7. Beauvoir, *Cérémonie,* 233.

8. Conversations with Fernando and Stépha Gerassi, Putney, Vermont, summer 1972.

9. Interview no. 11.

10. Sartre, *The Age of Reason,* 49–50.

11. Conversations with Fernando and Stépha; see also Ilya Ehrenburg's chapter in *From Spanish Trenches,* ed. Marcel Acier (New York: Modern Age Books, 1937), 104–12; and Ilya Ehrenburg, *Memoirs: 1921–1941* (New York: Grosset and Dunlap, 1966), 346 and passim.

12. Conversations with Fernando and Stépha.

13. Sartre, *The Reprieve,* 212–13, 215, 224.

14. Sartre, *The Reprieve,* 206.

15. Interview no. 7.

16. Sartre, *The Reprieve,* 69.

17. Sartre, *The Age of Reason,* 144.

18. Beauvoir, *Prime of Life,* 255.

19. Interview with Simone de Beauvoir.

20. Interview no. 11; see also *Sartre,* the film, 47.

21. Michel Rybalka, "La Nausée," *Magazine Littéraire,* nos. 103–4 (September 1975): 16.

22. *Sartre,* the film, 63.

23. Jean-Paul Sartre, *Jeune Cinema,* no. 25 (October 1967): 24–28.

24. Sartre, *The Age of Reason,* 14–15.

25. Ibid., 60.

26. Ibid., 63–64.

27. Ibid., 138.

28. Ibid., 153–54.

29. Ibid., 395, 397.

30. *Le Temps,* 2, 3, 7, 12, 13, 15 August 1936.

31. Aron, *Mémoires,* 137, 142.

32. Ibid., 132–33.

33. Henri Dubief, *Le déclin de la IIIe République, 1929–1938* (Paris: Editions du Seuil, 1976), 204–13.

34. Interview with Aron.

35. Interview with Audry.

36. Interview no. 11.

37. Sartre, *The Reprieve*, 377–78.

38. Ibid., 205.

39. Ibid., 342, 345. The English edition translates those last words as "The god-damned fools!" which leaves out the sexual connotation of the French insult.

40. Beauvoir, *Prime of Life*, 222, 231.

41. Ibid., 254, 256.

42. Ibid., 257.

43. Ibid., 265.

44. Ibid., 267–68.

45. Interview no. 12.

46. Sartre, *The Wall*, 51; and his "Insert" for the first Paris edition, cited in Contat and Rybalka, *The Writings*, 1:63.

47. Sartre, "Insert" (see above, note 46); *The Wall*, 29.

48. Sartre, *The Wall*, 93, 121–22.

49. Ibid., 100–101.

50. Ibid., 143.

51. Sartre, "Matérialisme et révolution," in *Situations III*, 184.

52. Sartre, "Insert" (see above, note 46), 63.

53. Beauvoir, *Prime of Life*, 244, 246, 248–50.

54. Ibid., 251.

55. Sartre, *The Emotions*, 51–52, 11, 91.

56. Cohen-Solal, *Sartre*, 174.

57. Ibid., 175.

58. Interview no. 12.

59. Cohen-Solal, *Sartre*, 672 (notes); also my interview with Pouillon.

60. Armand Robin, *Esprit*, no. 70 (July 1938).

61. Sartre, *Situations I*, 29–30.

62. Beauvoir, *Prime of Life*, 260.

63. Sartre, *Situations I*, 57.

64. Contat and Rybalka, *The Writings*, 1:66–67.

65. Gallimard's dossier on Sartre, 1937–48, xerox copies in my possession, given to me by Robert Gallimard.

66. Sartre, *Lettres au Castor*, 183, 194, 204–5.

67. Ibid., 211, 215–16, 219.

68. Beauvoir, *Prime of Life*, 282–83.

69. Ibid., 283.

70. Ibid., 283–84.

71. See J. J. Brochier, ed., *Paul Nizan, intellectuel communiste, 1926–1940*, 2 vols. (Paris: François Maspero, 1970), 1:10–11.

72. Jacques Fauvet, *Histoire du parti communiste francais* (Paris: 1964), 2:40.

73. Paul Nizan, *Ce Soir*, 4 October 1938.

74. Beauvoir, *Prime of Life*, 298.

75. Sartre, *Letters au Castor*, 246.

76. Letter to his wife, 20 December 1939, in Redfern, *Paul Nizan*, (see chapter 5, note 34), 192.

77. Redfern, *Paul Nizan*, 193.

78. Ibid., 191.

79. In "Les traitres au Pilori," *Die Welt*, 21 March 1940 (Stockholm).

80. Henri Lefebvre, *L'Existentialisme* (Paris: Le Sagittaire, 1946), 17.

81. René Etiemble, *Hygiène des lettres*, vol. 1 (Paris: 1952), in Redfern, *Paul Nizan*, 200.

82. Henri Lefebvre, *La somme et le reste*, 2 vols. (Paris: La Nef, 1959), 1:421, 511.

83. Patrick McCarthy, "Sartre, Nizan and the Dilemmas of Political Commitment," *Yale French Studies*, no. 68 (1985): 191.

84. Genevieve Idt, "Les chemins de la liberté: les tobogans du romanesque," *Obliques*, special nos. 18–19 (1979): 83–84.

85. Interview no. 13.

86. Beauvoir, *Prime of Life*, 301, 299–300.

87. Sartre, *Lettres au Castor*, 268–69, 271.

88. Ibid., 272.

Chapter Nine: The Soldier

1. Sartre, *Lettres au Castor*, 273, 280–81, 283, 289.

2. Ibid., 291.

3. Beauvoir, *Prime of Life*, 423.

4. Ibid., 315–16, 322; conversations with Fernando and Stépha Gerassi, summer 1972.

5. Sartre, *Iron in the Soul*, 38, 40, 28–29.

6. Ibid., 122–25.

7. Interview no. 13.

8. Sartre, *Iron in the Soul*, 372–73; also Interview no. 14.

9. Interview no. 11.

10. Sartre, "Drôle d'amitié," *Les Temps Modernes* (November and December 1949); reprinted in *Oeuvres Romanesques*, 1523.

11. Sartre, *Lettres au Castor*, 319, 326, 415, 351–52, 497, 482.

12. Ibid., 469–72.

13. Sartre, *Lettres au Castor*, 2:181, 79, 88, 90, 94.

14. Ibid., 93–94.

15. Beauvoir, *Cérémonie*, 360–61; Sartre, *Lettres au Castor*, 2:105.

16. Beauvoir, *Cérémonie*, 385, 387, 385.

17. Sartre, *Les carnets*, 15, 29–30, 31, 35, 43.

18. Ibid., 73, 161, 242, 267, 407.

19. Ibid., 328.

20. Beauvoir, *Cérémonie*, 352, 360–61.

21. Interview with Simone de Beauvoir.

22. Sartre, *Lettres au Castor*, 2:159.

23. Interview no. 11.

24. Beauvoir, *Cérémonie*, 218.

25. Arthur Danto, "Thoughts of a Bourgeois Draftee," *New York Times Book Review,* 31 March 1985.

26. Sartre, *Lettres au Castor,* 2 : 285, 294, 288, 299.

27. Marius Perrin, *Avec Sartre au stalag 12D* (Paris: Jean-Pierre Delarge, 1980), 17, 166, 41.

28. Interview with Henri Leroy.

29. Perrin, *Avec Sartre,* 66.

30. Sartre, *Lettres au Castor,* 2 : 301.

31. Interview no. 13.

32. Interview with Leroy.

33. Perrin, *Avec Sartre,* 104.

34. Interview no. 13.

35. Sartre, "Self-Portrait at Seventy," *Life/Situations* (New York: Pantheon, 1977), 44–45.

36. Beauvoir, *Prime of Life,* 381.

Chapter Ten: The Resistant

1. See the following: H. Amouroux, *La vie des français sous l'occupation,* 2 vols., full of details (Paris: 1971); P. Ory, *Les collaborateurs, 1940–45,* very useful (Paris: 1977); also G. Walter, *La vie à Paris sous l'occupation* (Paris: 1960); André Halimi, *Chantons sous l'occupation* (Paris: 1976).

2. André Bazin, ed., *Le cinéma de l'occupation et de la résistance* (Paris: 1975).

3. Pierre Assouline, "Les trahisons ordinaires des écrivains français," *L'Histoire,* no. 80 (1985), 73, 75, 78–79.

4. Sartre, "Paris sous l'occupation," in *Situations III,* 28–31, 42.

5. Sartre, "Qu'est-ce qu'un collaborateur?" in *Situations III,* 46, 49–50.

6. Sartre, "La république du silence," in *Situations III,* 11–13.

7. Ibid., 13–14.

8. Beauvoir, *Prime of Life,* 369.

9. Interview no. 15.

10. Ibid.

11. Beauvoir, *Prime of Life,* 383.

12. Interview with Aron.

13. Interview no. 15.

14. Ibid.

15. Gilles Perrault, "Paris sous l'occupation," *Lire,* no. 141 (June 1987), 54.

16. André Gide, *Journal, 1939–42* (Paris: Gallimard, 1946), 123.

17. Beauvoir, *Prime of Life,* 393.

18. Interviews nos. 14, 15.

19. Beauvoir, *Prime of Life,* 396.

20. The comments from Chazelas, Lévy, and the Desantis are in Cohen-Solal, *Sartre,* 242, 235, 242.

21. Sartre, "Operation 'Kanapa,'" *Les Temps Modernes* (March 1954): 1723–28; also in *Situations VII.*

22. Interview with Pouillon.

23. Interview with Henri Leroy.

24. Interview no. 15.

25. Interview with Claude Morgan.

26. Michel Tournier, in *Les Nouvelles Littéraires,* 29 October 1964, cited in Contat and Rybalka, *The Writings,* 83.

27. Raymond Queneau, cited by Patrick Lorriot in *Nouvel Observateur,* 21–27 April 1980.

28. Interview no. 13.

29. Interview no. 16.

30. Sartre, "Explication de *L'Etranger,*" *Cahiers du Sud* (April and May 1943), in *Situations I,* 111, 100.

31. Beauvoir, *Prime of Life,* 444.

32. Beauvoir, *Cérémonie,* 341.

33. Interview no. 16.

34. Interview with Simone de Beauvoir.

35. Interview with Olga Kosakiewicz.

36. Interview with Sartre by Yvon Novy, *Comoedia,* 24 April 1943 (a pro-Nazi publication that pretended to be apolitical).

37. Beauvoir, *Prime of Life,* 427.

38. Michel Leiris, "Oreste et la cité," *Les Lettres Françaises,* clandestine, no. 12 (1943).

39. Sartre, *Carrefour,* 9 September 1944.

40. Interview no. 16.

41. Interviews nos. 16 and 17.

42. Sartre, *The Flies,* in *No Exit,* 122–23.

43. Sartre, in Contat and Rybalka, *The Writings,* 99.

44. Sartre, *Combat,* 28–31 August and 1, 2, and 4 September 1944.

45. Vladimir Jankelevitch, *Libération,* 10 June 1985; *Le Monde,* 11 June 1985.

46. See, for example, *The Village Voice,* 17 December 1985.

47. Interview no. 17.

Bibliography

There are numerous, well-annotated bibliographies of the works of Jean-Paul Sartre, among which I found the most useful to be that of Michel Contat and Michel Rybalka, *The Writings of Jean-Paul Sartre,* in two volumes (Evanston, Ill.: Northwestern University Press, 1974). An updated edition is due soon.

Works by Jean-Paul Sartre

The following are the primary sources I used for this volume, listed in the order in which they were published in France, but given in the editions from which I quoted.

L'Imagination. Paris: Presses Universitaires de France, 1936.

The Transcendence of the Ego. Trans. Forrest Williams and Robert Kirkpatrick. New York: Noonday, 1957. Originally published in *Recherches Philosophiques VI* (1936–37).

Nausea. New York: New Directions, 1964.

The Wall. New York: New Directions, 1948.

The Emotions: Outline of a Theory. New York: Philosophical Library, 1948. References in notes are to *The Emotions*.

L'Imaginaire. Paris: Gallimard, 1940.

L'Etre et le néant. Paris: Gallimard, 1943; also the U.S. edition: *Being and Nothingness*. New York: Philosophical Library, 1956.

No Exit and Three Other Plays. New York: Vintage, 1949. References in the notes are to *No Exit*.

The Age of Reason. New York: Vintage, 1973.

The Reprieve. New York: Bantam, 1960.

Situations I. Paris: Gallimard, 1947.

The Ghost of Stalin. New York: George Braziller, 1968.

Situations II. Paris: Gallimard, 1948.

Iron in the Soul. New York: Vintage, 1973.

Situations III. Paris: Gallimard, 1949.

Search for a Method. New York: Vintage, 1963.

The Words. New York: Fawcett Premier Book, 1964.

Situations IV. Paris: Gallimard, 1964.

Situations V. Paris: Gallimard, 1964.

Situations VI. Paris: Gallimard, 1964.

Situations VII. Paris: Gallimard, 1965.

Situations VIII. Paris: Gallimard, 1972.

Situations IX. Paris: Gallimard, 1972.

Situations X. Paris: Gallimard, 1976.

Sartre, full text from film produced by Alexandre Astruc and Michel Contat, with Simone de Beauvoir, Jacques-Laurent Bost, André Gortz, and Jean Pouillon. Paris: Gallimard, 1977. References in notes are to *Sartre,* the film.

Oeuvres Romanesques. Paris: Gallimard (Bibliothèque de la Pléiade), 1981.

Les carnets de la drôle de guerre. Paris: Gallimard, 1983; references in notes are to *Les carnets;* also the U.S. edition: *The War Diaries.* New York: Pantheon, 1984.

Lettres au Castor et à quelques autres. 2 vols. Paris: Gallimard, 1983; references in notes are to *Lettres au Castor* and are to vol. I unless identified as from vol. 2.

Other Primary Sources

Aron, Raymond. *Mémoires.* Paris: Julliard, 1983.

Audry, Colette. *La Statue.* Paris: Gallimard, 1983.

Beauvoir, Simone de. *Memoirs of a Dutiful Daughter.* New York: World, 1959; references in notes are to *Memoirs.*

———. *The Prime of Life.* New York: World, 1962.

———. *Force of Circumstance.* New York: Harper Colophon, 1977.

———. *La cérémonie des adieux.* Paris: Gallimard, 1981; references in the notes are to *Cérémonie.*

Sagan, Françoise. *Avec mon meilleur souvenir.* Paris: Gallimard, 1984.

Pre-1945 Newspapers and Magazines Published in Paris

Bifur

Ce Soir

L'Oeuvre

La Revue sans Titre

Le Temps

Verve

Interviews with Sartre

1. 2 November 1970.
2. 20 November 1970.
3. 4 December 1970.
4. 18 December 1970.
5. 29 January 1971.
6. 12 February 1971.
7. 26 February 1971.
8. 12 March 1971.
9. 26 March 1971.
10. 23 April 1971.
11. 7 May 1971.
12. 14 May 1971.
13. 11 June 1971.
14. 15 October 1971.
15. 29 October 1971.
16. 12 November 1971.
17. 26 November 1971.
21. 21 January 1972.
24. 21 April 1972.

30. 27 October 1972.
34. 28 June 1973.

Other Interviews

Aron, Raymond. Paris, 25 May 1973.
Audry, Colette. Paris, 14 March 1973.
Beauvoir, Simone de. Paris, 30 January 1973.
———. Printed in *Society* (January–February 1976).
Bost, Jacques-Laurent. Paris, 14 May 1973.
Kosakiewicz, Olga. Paris, 9 May 1973.
Kosakiewicz, Wanda. Paris, 23 March 1973.
Leroy, Henri. Paris, 26 June 1973.
Maheu, Rene. Paris, 22 May 1973.
Matthews, Troupe. New York, 5 February 1985.
Morgan, Claude (Lecomte). Marailly en Villette, 6 June 1973.
Pouillon, Jean. Paris, 16 March 1973.

Index